ACBL Bridge Series

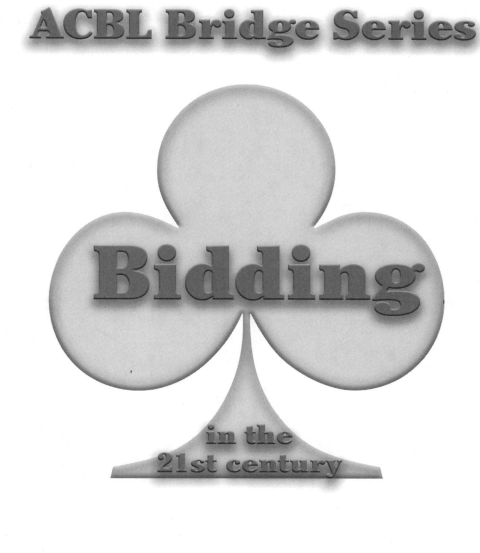

Bidding

in the 21st century

ISBN 978-0-939460-93-9

Updated ACBL Bridge Series

Bidding in the 21st Century is the first in a series of texts developed by the American Contract Bridge League. This series is designed to introduce a new player to the game of duplicate bridge.

These materials were written in 1986 by Audrey Grant. In 2006, the ACBL enlisted Betty Starzec, a TAP (Teacher Accreditation Program) Teacher-Trainer and ABTA (American Bridge Teachers Association) Master Teacher, to update the series to more accurately convey the latest duplicate bridge ideas and philosophy. The update complements the *Learn to Play Bridge* computer programs written for the ACBL by Fred Gitelman which were used as the basis for this update. Download this program free at www.acbl.org.

There are five textbooks and teacher manuals with coordinating E-Z Deal decks of cards:

Volume One —
> *Bidding in the 21st Century – The Club Series*

Volume Two —
> *Play of the Hand in the 21st Century – The Diamond Series*

Volume Three —
> *Defense in the 21st Century – The Heart Series*

Volume Four —
> *Commonly Used Conventions in the 21st Century –*
> *The Spade Series*

Volume Five —
> *More Commonly Used Conventions in the 21st Century –*
> *The Notrump Series*

Trained teachers across North America offer bridge courses using these materials. Information on teachers in your area is available on the ACBL web site **www.acbl.org** through the Find a Teacher link.

Coordinated decks of E-Z Deal Cards, which allow the reader to deal out the exercise hands at the end of each chapter, are available for each bridge text.

These materials can be purchased through Baron Barclay Bridge Supplies 1-800-274-2221.

The American Contract Bridge League

The American Contract Bridge League (ACBL) is dedicated to the playing, teaching and promotion of contract bridge.

The membership of 160,000 includes a wide range of players — from the thousands who are just learning the joy of bridge to the most proficient players in North America.

ACBL offers a variety of services, including:

- **Tournament play.** Thousands of tournaments: North American Bridge Championships (three a year), as well as tournaments at the regional, sectional, local and club levels — are sanctioned annually.

- **A magazine.** The Bridge Bulletin, a monthly publication, offers articles for all levels of players on tournaments, card play, the Laws, personalities, special activities and much more.

- **A ranking plan.** Each time a member does well in any ACBL event, whether at the club level or at a North American Bridge Championship, that member receives a masterpoint award. Players achieve rankings and prestige as a result of their cumulative masterpoint holdings.

- **A teaching program.** ACBL has trained more than 5,000 people through the Teacher Accreditation Program (TAP) to teach beginning bridge lessons. You can find a teacher in your area at ACBL's web site — **www.acbl.org**, Find a Teacher.

- **A newcomer program.** ACBL offers special games and programs for players new to bridge and new to duplicate. The Intermediate-Newcomer (IN) Programs at the three North American Bridge Championships are very popular and are offered as examples of what ACBL hopes regionals and sectionals will offer to their local newcomers.

- **Access to 3,200 bridge clubs.** ACBL offers sanctioned bridge play at clubs across the United States, Canada, Mexico, Bermuda, on cruise ships and even at a few foreign-based bridge clubs. You can locate a club in your area at ACBL's web site — **www.acbl.org**, Find a Club.

- **A charity program.** Since 1964, the ACBL Charity Foundation has made substantial contributions to a wide range of charitable organizations, now with $100,000 in annual allocations.

- **A cooperative advertising program.** ACBL assists teachers, clubs, units and districts by subsidizing costs incurred for advertising programs designed to recruit students and promote bridge lessons and games.

- **A Junior program for players age 25 and under.** ACBL offers a funded teaching program, a funded school bridge lesson series program, student membership, a youth web site (www.youth4bridge.org) and special events.

- **Membership benefits.** Credit-card programs, special hotel rates at tournaments, airline discounts for NABCs, an 800 line for member services, discounted entry fees at most tournament play, recognition for levels of achievement, discounted Hertz car rental and supplemental insurance products, including a prescription discount card, are offered.

ACBL has been the center of North American bridge activity since it was founded in 1937. You can enjoy the fun, friendship and competition of bridge with an ACBL membership available online at www.acbl.org.

Be an ACBL member

Join the

www.acbl.org

TABLE OF CONTENTS

CHAPTER 1 — GETTING STARTED

Introductory Concepts.. 2

The Language of Bidding 8

Scoring.. 12

Guidelines for Play... 14

Summary 17

Exercises... 18

Sample Deals 24

CHAPTER 2 — OBJECTIVES

Hand Valuation 30

The Golden Rules... 32

The Roles of the Partners 34

Opening the Bidding.. 36

The Bidding Messages.. 39

Guidelines for Play... 40

Summary 43

The Finer Points 46

Exercises... 48

Sample Deals 56

CHAPTER 3 — RESPONSES TO 1NT OPENING BIDS

Responder's General Approach 66

Responder's Decision with 0 to 7 Total Points........................... 69

Responder's Decision with 8 or 9 Total Points 71

Responder's Decision with 10 to 15 Total Points........................ 73

Opener's Rebid after a 1NT Opening Bid.................................. 75

Guidelines for Play... 76

Summary 78

Exercises... 80

Sample Deals 84

CHAPTER 4 — RESPONSES TO OPENING BIDS OF ONE IN A SUIT

Responder's General Approach 94

Responder's Decision with 0 to 5 Total Points.............................. 96

Responder's Decision with 6 to 9 Total Points.............................. 97

Responding to a Major Suit.. 98

Responding to a Major Suit with 6 to 9 Total Points..................... 99

Responding to a Minor Suit with 6 to 9 Total Points 102

Responder's Decision with 10 or 11 Total Points 105

Responder's Decision with 12 or More Total Points.................... 106

Guidelines for Play.. 109

Summary 112

The Finer Points 113

Exercises... 116

Sample Deals 122

CHAPTER 5 — REBIDS BY OPENER

Opener's General Approach to the Second Bid 132

Opener's Rebid after Responder Makes an Invitational Bid.......... 135

Opener's Rebid after Responder Makes a Forcing Bid 145

Guidelines for Play.. 152

Summary 155

The Finer Points 158

Exercises... 160

Sample Deals 170

CHAPTER 6 — REBIDS BY RESPONDER

Responder's General Approach to the Second Bid 180

Responder's Decision with 6 to 9 Total Points.......................... 183

Responder's Decision with 10 or 11 Total Points 193

Responder's Decision with 12 or More Total Points.................... 199

Guidelines for Play.. 204

Summary 206

The Finer Points 208

Exercises... 210

Sample Deals 220

CHAPTER 7 — OVERCALLS AND BIDS BY THE ADVANCER

Bidding with Competition.. 230
The Overcall 234
Advancing after an Overcall 241
Guidelines for Play.. 248
Summary 250
The Finer Points 252
Exercises.. 254
Sample Deals 262

CHAPTER 8 — TAKEOUT DOUBLES AND RESPONSES

The Takeout Double... 272
Advancing after a Takeout Double 277
The Advancer Considers Notrump 281
Rebids by the Takeout Doubler.................................... 282
Guidelines for Play.. 284
Summary 287
The Finer Points 289
Exercises.. 292
Sample Deals 300

CHAPTER 9 — THE STAYMAN CONVENTION — BONUS CHAPTER

The Stayman Convention 310
Responding with Game-Forcing Hands 312
Responding with Invitational Hands.............................. 315
Responding with Weak Hands 318
Handling Interference 318
Summary 322
Exercises.. 324
Sample Deals 330

APPENDIX

Scoring.. 348
Strong Opening Bids.. 353
Slam Bidding 356
Preemptive Opening Bids.. 358
Balancing 360
Glossary of Terms 363

INTRODUCTION

The American Contract Bridge League's (ACBL) *Bidding in the 21st Century* student text is the first in a series of bridge books for beginning and advancing players. It is followed by four additional texts: *Play of the Hand in the 21st Century, Defense in the 21st Century, Commonly Used Conventions in the 21st Century* and *More Commonly Used Conventions in the 21st Century.* The books focus on introducing students to all aspects of the game of bridge.

The ACBL, the sanctioning body for bridge in North America, developed these books to address the needs of students and teachers. This series of books, written originally for the ACBL by Audrey Grant, a professional educator, has been used successfully by bridge teachers and students for more than 20 years.

In the late 1900s, the ACBL produced a computer program, *Learn to Play Bridge I* and subsequently *Learn to Play Bridge II,* written by bridge champion Fred Gitelman. The response to these programs has been tremendous with more than a 150,000 copies now in circulation. (LTPB can be downloaded for free by visiting the ACBL's web site, **www.acbl.org**, or Fred Gitelman's web site at **www.bridgebase.com**.)

In this current publication of the *Bidding in the 21st Century* text, Betty Starzec a Senior TAP Trainer and ABTA Master Teacher, was enlisted to update the material for the ACBL. The goal was not only to convey more accurately the latest bridge ideas and philosophy but also to allow the material to be used as a tool in conjunction with the *Learn to Play Bridge* programs.

The *ACBL Bridge Series* updated material encompasses these changes:

- 25 total points required for games of 3NT, 4♠ and 4♥.
- Opening bids still require 13 total points or more. Therefore, the opener's bidding ranges as well as responder's ranges were adjusted slightly in order to conform to the 25 total points required for game. For example, responder's ranges are 6 to 9 total points for the minimum range, 10 or 11 total points for the medium range and 12+ total points for the maximum range.
- 1NT opening bids are 15 to 17 and are based on high-card points (HCP).
- 2NT opening bids are 20 or 21 HCP.
- Overcalls are allowed with as few as 10 total points with an upper limit of 17 total points.
- Each of the first three books contain a bonus chapter. The bonus chapter for the *Bidding Series* is *Stayman.*
- Strong 2♣ bids are used along with weak two-bids.

The goal of this update is to enable the reader to learn basic bridge or to review and improve bridge techniques in a logical and progressive fashion. More importantly, the reader will have fun while learning the fundamental concepts of modern bridge bidding, play and defense which will be beneficial for a lifetime.

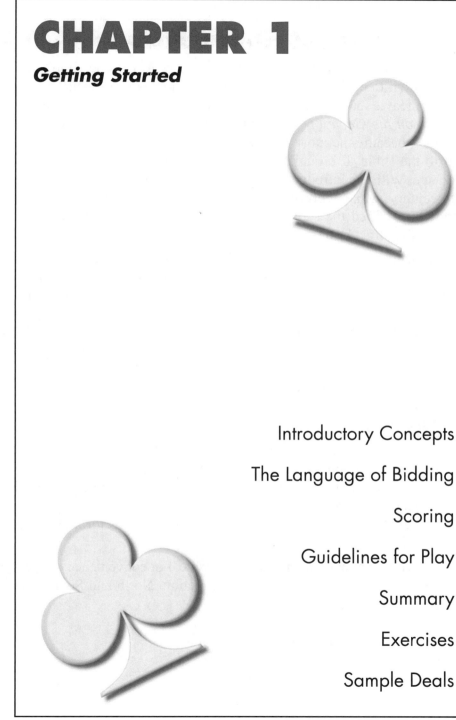

CHAPTER 1
Getting Started

Introductory Concepts

The Language of Bidding

Scoring

Guidelines for Play

Summary

Exercises

Sample Deals

INTRODUCTORY CONCEPTS

As early as the 16th century, Europeans were playing triumph, a game similar to bridge. Triumph evolved into the game of whist, which Edmond Hoyle made internationally famous through his book, *A Short Treatise on the Game of Whist,* published in 1742. A later version of this book became the most widely circulated book of the 18th century next to the Bible. It brought the phrase "according to Hoyle" into the language. With the introduction of the auction concept at the end of the 19th century, whist evolved into auction bridge. Around 1925, Harold Vanderbilt refined the scoring to bring the game into its present-day format of contract bridge.

This game, popularized by Ely Culbertson in the 1930s and by Charles Goren in the 1950s, became the world's most popular card game. Home-style or rubber bridge is played by nearly 40 million people in North America. Duplicate bridge is played principally under the auspices of the American Contract Bridge League. It is enjoyed in more than 3,200 bridge clubs and at hundreds of bridge tournaments held annually across the country. Bridge is a game for four people. All you need is a deck of cards and a scorepad, and you are set to go.

The Players

Bridge is a partnership game. Partnerships may be arranged ahead of time, as is commonly done in duplicate bridge, or players may draw for partners. To draw for partners, the cards are shuffled and fanned face down on the table. The two players drawing the higher cards form one partnership; the two players drawing the lower cards form the other partnership.

Partners sit opposite each other at the table. For convenience, players are often referred to by their compass direction. North and South play against East and West.

Your relationship with your partner is a very important part of the game. You will get much better results if you learn to work with and appreciate your partner.

The Deck and the Deal

Bridge is played with a deck of 52 cards. There are four suits: clubs (♣), diamonds (♦), hearts (♥) and spades (♠). The cards are ranked within each suit. The ace is the highest card in each suit followed by the king, the queen, the jack, the 10 ... and on down to the 2.

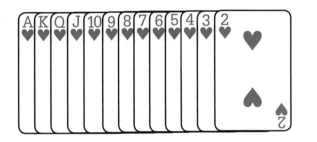

RANK OF THE CARDS

The game starts when one of the players shuffles and deals the cards. In duplicate bridge, the dealer is predetermined. In home-style bridge, it is customary to determine the dealer on the first deal by having each player draw a card from the deck and turn the drawn card face up on the table. The player who drew the highest card deals.

Suppose you are the dealer. You give out the cards one at a time face down. You start with the player on your left and continue around the table clockwise until all of the cards are gone. Each player's 13 cards constitute a hand.

The players pick up their hands and fan them so they can see their cards. Evaluation of the hand is easier if the cards are sorted into suits, alternating colors, with the cards in each suit arranged from left to right according to rank.

However, that is a matter of personal preference. A sorted hand might look like this:

SORTED
BRIDGE
HAND

When a hand is discussed in a textbook or newspaper, it is usually displayed in a symbolic fashion with letters and numbers for the cards (A – ace, K – king, Q – queen, J – jack, 10, 9, etc.). The suits are displayed one underneath another with the spades first, followed by the hearts, diamonds and clubs. The hand from above looks like this:

♠ K 10 6 3
♥ Q J 9
♦ A Q 7 2
♣ 8 5

Sometimes symbols are used for the suits as in this textbook. Sometimes alphabetic abbreviations are used (S – spades, H – hearts, D – diamonds, C – clubs). When discussing a complete deal, all four hands are shown in the following manner:

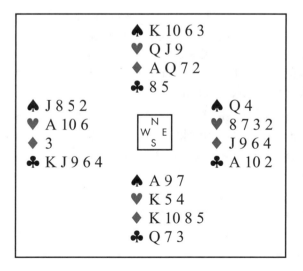

The Game's Two Stages

There are two stages in the game of bridge. First, there is *bidding*, as in an auction, to determine which partnership will undertake a *contract*. Second, there is the *play of the cards,* where one side tries to *fulfill* the agreed contract while the other side tries to *defeat* it. Before looking at how the bidding works, it is helpful to understand something about how the cards are played out.

The Trick

The play of the cards starts when one player *leads* a card by placing it on the table and turning it face up. Each player, in clockwise rotation, plays a card of the same suit and places it face up on the table. This is called *following suit.* The four cards played constitute a *trick.* The player who contributes the highest-ranking card wins the trick. This is a partnership game, so, if either you or your partner plays the highest card, your side wins the trick.

Here is an example of a trick:

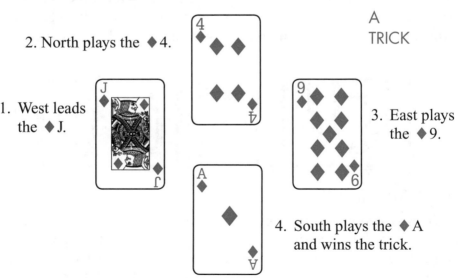

2. North plays the ♦4.

A
TRICK

1. West leads the ♦J.

3. East plays the ♦9.

4. South plays the ♦A and wins the trick.

The player who wins the trick by playing the highest-ranking card leads to the next trick. You must follow suit if you can. If you don't have any cards in the suit led, you play a card from another suit. This is called *discarding.*

For example:

A
DISCARD

2. West plays
   the ♥ K.

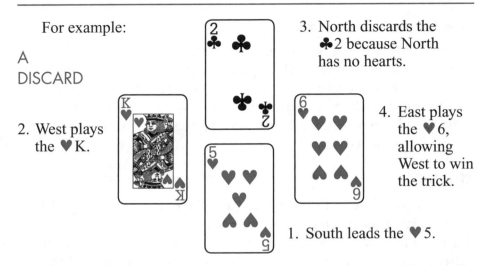

3. North discards the
   ♣2 because North
   has no hearts.

4. East plays
   the ♥ 6,
   allowing
   West to win
   the trick.

1. South leads the ♥ 5.

By the end of the deal, 13 tricks will have been played with one side having won more tricks than the other. Whenever your side wins a trick, place your card face down vertically in front of you. When your side loses a trick, place your card face down horizontally in front of you. By placing the card played to the first trick on your left and slightly offsetting each subsequent card to the right, at the end of the deal you will be left with a row of 13 cards in front of you. The row of cards will look something like this:

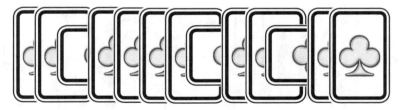

RECORDING TRICKS

This is a good way to record your winners and losers. At the end of the deal, you will have all of the cards you played in front of you. Now, you can have an instant replay. If you play other card games that have tricks, you may be accustomed to keeping track of winners by picking up all the cards in the trick, turning them over and putting them in a stack in front of you. When you are learning bridge, it helps to keep your hand and look at it again when the play is over. This is also the required method of play in duplicate bridge.

Notrump and Trump

When the contract is played without a trump suit (notrump), the highest card played to a trick wins the trick, provided it is of the same suit as the card led. On many deals, one suit is designated through the bidding as "wild" or as a *trump* suit. When there is a trump suit, a trump beats any card in another suit.

Here are some things to remember when playing with a trump suit:

- You still must follow suit if you can. You may play a trump if you have no cards left in the suit led. This is called *ruffing*.
- You do not have to ruff. If your partner plays the ♦ A and you have no diamonds, you may discard from another suit, since your partner's card will probably win the trick without your help.
- If more than one player puts a trump on a trick, the highest-ranked trump wins.
- The trump suit does not have to be led at any particular time. It is up to the discretion of each player to decide when to lead a trump.

Here is an example of a trick played with spades as the trump suit:

RUFFING
A TRICK

1. West leads the ♥ A.

2. North, having no hearts left, ruffs with the ♠ 7.

3. East follows suit with the ♥ 10.

4. South plays the ♥ 8.

THE LANGUAGE OF BIDDING

Before the play of each deal, the contract must be determined. This is done through an *auction*. Having looked at the hands they were dealt, the members of each partnership would like the right to decide whether the deal is to be played in notrump or with a particular suit as trump.

To do this, each partnership must exchange information about their hands. They do this through the special language of bidding.

Bidding

After the cards have been dealt and the players have looked at their hands, the dealer starts the auction by making the first *call*. The dealer either makes a *bid* or refrains from bidding by saying "pass." The auction proceeds clockwise around the table with each player having an opportunity to bid or *pass*. This continues until three players in succession pass following a bid, which now becomes the final contract.

A bid consists of two parts: a *level*, indicating the number of tricks the bidder proposes to take, and a *strain*, indicating which suit or notrump the contract is to be played in. An example of a bid is:

ONE SPADE **(1 ♠)**

Level   Strain

The Level

Since the partnership that wins the auction must offer to take at least a majority of the 13 tricks available, the level named is in addition to the first six tricks. The first six tricks, called the book, is assumed as a part of every bid. In other words, a bid at the one level represents 6 + 1 = 7 tricks. Similarly, a bid at the two level is an undertaking to take 6 + 2 = 8 tricks.

The highest level to which the bidding can proceed is the seven level. This implies a contract to take all 13 tricks. Thus, the level named in a bid is always a number from one to seven.

The Strain

In addition to the level, a bid states whether the contract is to be played in a trump suit or in notrump. There are only five possible strains — clubs, diamonds, hearts, spades and notrump.

The Bidding Scale

As in an open auction, each bid must be higher than the preceding bid. For this purpose, the strains are ranked with clubs as the *lowest*, then diamonds, hearts, spades and notrump as the highest. The suits are ranked in alphabetical order (♣, ♦, ♥, ♠).

The bids are put on a scale called the *Bidding Scale*. The lowest bid is 1♣, and the auction proceeds through the levels and strains to the highest bid of 7NT.

BIDDING SCALE

The bidding must always move up the Bidding Scale. If the preceding bid was 1♥, you may bid 1♠, since it is higher on the scale. However, you can't bid 1♣. If you want to bid clubs, you would have to bid at the next higher level, 2♣. Of course, if at any point you do not want to bid any higher, you may pass.

Suppose North is the dealer. Here is a typical auction:

WEST	NORTH	EAST	SOUTH
	(Dealer)		
	Pass	Pass	1 ♥
Pass	2 ♥	Pass	Pass
Pass			

Bidding is written across the page in this manner. You visualize it proceeding clockwise around the table.

The player who makes the first bid, South in the above example, is called the opening bidder. Note that the dealer is not forced to start the bidding. Also, although a player has said pass, that player may bid later.

Three passes following a bid ends the auction, and the final contract in the above example is 2 ♥. During the play, the partnership that won the auction becomes the offense and tries to take the number of tricks required to fulfill the contract. If the players on offense succeed, they make their contract. In the above example, North and South have contracted to make 2 ♥, a total of eight tricks (2 + 6 = 8) with hearts as the trump suit. The other partnership becomes the defense and tries to prevent the offense from fulfilling their contract. If they succeed, they defeat or set the contract.

Declarer and Dummy

At the end of the auction, the deal is played out. The member of the partnership who first suggested the strain of the final contract is called the declarer. The declarer will play both of the partnership hands and try to fulfill the contract. Declarer's partner, who will not take part in the play of the cards, is appropriately called the dummy.

Here is how the play works:

The player to the left of the declarer makes the opening lead by placing a card on the table. The card is first placed face down and soon after placed face up. If you are declarer's partner, the dummy, you are next to play. You place all of your cards face up on the table in front of you and arrange them in four columns, one for each suit. If there is a trump suit, you place it on your right (declarer's left).

The table might look like this:

THE
DUMMY

OPENING LEAD

The declarer now decides which card is to be played from dummy and names the card dummy is to play. For example, if you were declarer, you might say, "Play the queen of diamonds please, partner." Your right-hand opponent (RHO) then plays a card to the first trick, and you play a card from your hand. This completes the first trick. The play continues in this fashion with the lead to each subsequent trick coming from the hand, including dummy, that won the previous trick. *(Declarer may physically play the cards from dummy's hand if necessary.)*

SCORING

At the end of the deal, points are awarded based on the final contract and whether or not it was fulfilled. Points can be earned in three ways:

- Trick score for fulfilling a contract.
- Bonus for fulfilling a special contract.
- Penalty for defeating the opponents' contract.

Trick Score

For each of the tricks bid and made (in excess of book), the partnership is awarded points based on the strain of the contract.

- 20 points per trick in clubs or diamonds (minor suits).
- 30 points per trick in hearts or spades (major suits).
- 40 points for the first trick in notrump, 30 points for each subsequent trick.

For example, the trick score for making a contract of 2 ♠ is 60 (30 + 30). The trick score for making a contract of 3NT is 100 (40 + 30 + 30).

Bonuses

A bonus is awarded if the partnership bids and makes a contract worth 100 or more points. This is called a game bonus. This can be earned by bidding to one of the following contracts:

- 5 ♣ or 5 ♦ (20 + 20 + 20 + 20 + 20 = 100).
- 4 ♥ or 4 ♠ (30 + 30 + 30 + 30 = 120).
- 3NT (40 + 30 + 30 = 100).

Because of the possible bonus involved, a lot of the bidding centers around trying to reach one of these game contracts. Bonus points are discussed in the Appendix, and getting to game contracts will be discussed in the next chapter.

A contract worth a trick score of fewer than 100 points is called a partscore. For example, a contract of 3 ♠ is a partscore, since it is worth only 90 points (30 + 30 + 30). In duplicate bridge, a small bonus is awarded for bidding and making a partscore contract.

Note that you do not score the game bonus if you do not bid to a game contract, even if you take enough tricks. For example, if the contract is 3 ♠ and you take 10 tricks, the extra trick is worth the trick score (30 points) but does not entitle you to the game bonus. You must have bid 4 ♠ in order to score the game bonus.

You receive an additional bonus if you bid and make a contract at the six level (12 tricks). This is called a small slam. An even larger bonus is awarded for bidding and making a contract at the seven level (all 13 tricks). This is called a grand slam.

The size of the bonuses is explained in the Appendix. For now, it is sufficient to know that there are certain key contracts on the Bidding Scale that are worth a bonus in the scoring.

Penalties

If you don't make your contract, the opponents receive points for defeating you. The penalty for going down in your contract depends on the number of tricks by which it is defeated. (See the Appendix.)

At this point, it is only important to realize that you lose points if you bid too high and don't make your contract. This is why you shouldn't try for a game bonus with every deal. Sometimes, you have to stop in a partscore. Sometimes, rather than bid higher yourself, you have to let your opponents play in their contract and try to defeat them.

GUIDELINES FOR PLAY

The play of the cards, from the points of view of both the declarer and the defenders, is an exciting part of the game. It poses numerous challenges as to which card to play on each trick. For now, a few guidelines will get you started. The play is discussed in more detail in the *Play* text.

The Opening Lead

The play starts with the player to the left of declarer. Entire books have been written on how to make good leads. Fortunately, there are a few simple rules that work well to get you going.

⇨   When leading against a notrump contract, it is usually best to lead a card from your longest suit. Long suits can be a good source of tricks. When choosing the card to lead, lead the top card if you have three or more high cards (A, K, Q, J or 10) that are touching (*e.g.*, K–Q–J or Q–J–10). If you don't have touching high cards, lead a low card (*e.g.*, the 5 from K–10–7–5).

⇨   When leading against a suit contract, you can sometimes take advantage of your trumps by leading a short suit of one or two cards. You hope that when the suit is led again, you will be able to win a trick by ruffing (playing a trump when you are out of the suit led). When leading from a two-card suit, lead the higher-ranked card first.

⇨   Another good choice is a suit in which you have touching high cards. Lead the top of two or more touching high cards (*e.g.*, K–Q or Q–J–10). Otherwise, lead a low card from a long suit.

Suppose you have the following hand:

♠ Q 6 3
♥ 5 2
♦ K Q J 7 6
♣ 9 5 3

If you are leading against a notrump contract, pick your longest suit, diamonds. Since you have touching high cards, lead the top card, the ♦ K. If you are leading against a contract with hearts as trump, the ♦ K would still be a good lead.

Suppose you have this hand:

♠ K J 6 3
♥ 9 5 4 2
♦ J 6 5 3
♣ 7

If you are leading against a notrump contract, lead your longest suit. With a choice of long suits, it is usually best to pick your strongest suit. In this case, it would be spades. Since your high cards are not touching, lead low, the ♠3. If you are leading against a contract with hearts as trump, you also might lead a low spade. However, another good choice is the ♣7. You hope the club suit will be led again, and you will be able to win a trick by ruffing with one of your low trumps.

Subsequent Leads

When you win a trick and have to lead to the next trick, the situation is different from the opening lead. In addition to your own cards, you can now see dummy's cards. You might also be able to remember some of the cards that have been played to previous tricks.

If you are defending and your partner was the opening leader, it is a good idea to return the suit that your partner led originally, unless you have a valid reason for not doing so.

If you are the declarer in a notrump contract, it's a good idea to lead a card from the longest combined suit between your hand and the dummy at your earliest opportunity. In a trump contract, you often lead the trump suit first and continue leading trumps until the opponents have none left.

Second-Hand Play

If the opponent on your right leads a card, you have to play the second card to the trick. A general piece of advice is to play a low card, second hand low, when you are not sure what to do.

The advantage of playing low is that your partner will be the last to play to this trick. Partner will be in a better position to decide whether to play a high or low card after seeing the cards played by both opponents.

Third-Hand Play

If your partner leads a card, you will contribute the third card to the trick. If it doesn't look as though partner's card will win the trick, it is usually up to you to try to win the trick for your side by playing a high card, third hand high.

You only need to play as high a card as is necessary to win the trick. For example, if you have both the king and the queen, and two low cards have been played, you play the queen. Either it will win the trick or it will force your left-hand opponent to play the ace, since you have the king. If either your partner or your RHO (right-hand opponent) has already played the ace, you don't need to play a high card. Play a low card instead.

Fourth-Hand Play

Usually it is easiest to decide what to do when you are the last to play to a trick. You can see what has already been played, and you can decide whether you need to play a high card to win the trick or a low card if you can't (or don't wish to) win the trick. Don't forget to watch what your partner has played. Only one of you needs to win the trick, not both!

SUMMARY

Four players sit down to play a game of bridge and divide themselves into two partnerships, North and South against East and West. The cards are dealt out clockwise and face down. The players pick up their hands and sort the cards into suits.

The dealer starts the auction by making a bid or by saying "pass." A bid consists of a level, which denotes the number of tricks to be taken (in addition to the six tricks called the book), and a strain, which denotes clubs, diamonds, hearts, spades or notrump. The auction continues clockwise. Each player either makes a bid that is higher on the Bidding Scale than the previous bid or says "pass." The auction ends when a bid is followed by three passes. The last bid becomes the final contract.

In the partnership that wins the auction, the player who first mentions the strain of the final contract becomes the declarer. The player on declarer's left makes the opening lead, and then declarer's partner, the dummy, puts the dummy's hand face up on the table.

The declarer plays both of the partnership's hands and tries to take enough tricks to fulfill the contract. The opponents (the defenders) try to take enough tricks to defeat the contract. At the end of the deal, the partnerships are awarded a score depending upon whether the contract was made.

There are bonuses awarded for bidding and making special contracts. Most important are the game contracts of 3NT, 4♥, 4♠, 5♣ and 5♦. There are special bonuses for making small slams and grand slams.

Exercise One — Taking Tricks
Dealer: North

Deal the cards face down starting with the player on your left. Continue around the table clockwise until all of the cards are dealt. Each player will have 13 cards.

The players pick up their hands and sort them into suits. The player to the left of the dealer leads any card by placing it face up on the table. All of the other players follow suit by playing a card of the same suit. If a player can't follow suit, a card from another suit should be placed on the trick.

The highest-ranking card played of the suit led wins the trick. The player who wins leads to the next trick. If you win a trick, place your card vertically face down on the table in front of you. If you lose a trick, place it horizontally face down on the table in front of you. Try to take as many tricks as you can.

Exercise Two — Predicting Your Winners
Dealer: East
Leader: South

After you have sorted your hand into suits, estimate the cards in each suit that might win tricks. From the first exercise, you know that high cards and sometimes low cards from long suits win tricks. You can write an "x" rather than the specific low card you think will be a winner. Here is an example:

YOUR HAND	YOUR ESTIMATE	
♠ A K 4 3 2	♠ A K x	(3) (three)
♥ K Q 8	♥ K or Q	(1) (one)
♦ 9 8	♦ —	(0) (zero)
♣ Q J 10	♣ Q	(1) (one)

After you have played the deal, turn over your winners and compare them with your estimate.

Exercise One *Answers* — Taking Tricks

Sometimes one of your high cards doesn't take a trick. This happens when an opponent has a higher card that captures it. It also happens because you can't get the lead and end up having to throw it away on one of the opponents' winners. Low cards, however, sometimes will take tricks, especially when they are part of a long suit. Your low card may be the only card left in the suit, and the opponents have to discard since they can't follow suit.

Exercise Two *Answers* — Predicting Your Winners

There are always surprises — that's what makes the game so interesting. A card may be a winner depending on when you get to play it. For example, if you have a king and are the last to play to the trick, you have a good chance of making your king a winner. If the ace is played before you, then your king is high — all you have to do is get the lead and enjoy your winner later. If the ace isn't played, then your king is a winner on that trick. Predicting the cards you think will be winners helps improve your memory.

Exercise Three — The Opening Lead

Each player takes the cards for one of the suits and helps construct the following hand in the middle of the table:

♠ A 3 2
♥ A
♦ K Q J 10 9 8
♣ A 3 2

1) What would you lead if it were your turn? _____

2) How many tricks would you expect to take with this hand? _____

Exercise Four — Playing with a Partner

Dealer: South
Leader: West

Work with the person sitting opposite you to take as many tricks as you can. When West leads, all of the other players turn their hands over and take a moment to look at the lead.

1) What is West's longest suit? _____

2) How many cards, at least, does West hold in that suit? _____

3) What does the card led tell you about other cards West might hold in the suit? _____

4) Did you like working with a partner? _____

5) What other things would you like to know that would help you when working with a partner? _____

_____

Exercise Three *Answers* — The Opening Lead

1) Lead a diamond. You want your opponent to play the ace so your remaining diamonds will be winners. Keep your aces in the other suits so you can win the next trick and have the opportunity to play your diamonds.

2) You can expect to take eight tricks.

Exercise Four *Answers* — Playing with a Partner

1) West will lead from length.

2) This means West has at least three other cards in the suit led.

3) If West leads an honor, then it is the top of a sequence. A low card means there is no sequence in the suit, but there may be one or two high cards nevertheless.

4) Working with a partner has advantages and disadvantages. It is pleasant because you now are on a team; you have someone sitting opposite you who is helping you take tricks. It is more difficult because you can't see each other's cards.

5) You would like to know not only the long suits partner has but where partner's strength lies.

Exercise Five — Playing in a Trump Contract

Dealer: West
Leader: North

The heart suit is wild or trump. Work with your partner to take as many tricks as you can. You must follow suit. When you can't, play a trump. Cards in the trump suit rank higher than cards in any of the other suits.

What did you think about playing in a trump suit?_____

Why is having short suits valuable when playing in a trump suit?

_____

Exercise Six — The Language of Bidding

How many tricks does each of the following bids represent?

1) 2♣ _____　2) 4♠ _____　3) 7NT_____

4) 3NT _____　5) 5♦ _____　6) 1♥ _____

7) 6♣ _____

Exercise Seven — Trick Scores for Partscores and Games

What trick score would be given for making each of the following contracts?

1) 2♠ _____　2) 4♥ _____　3) 4♠ _____

4) 5♣ _____　5) 3♦ _____　6) 1♥ _____

7) 3NT _____　8) 4♣ _____　9) 5♦ _____

Circle the contracts with a trick score of at least 100 points. These are called game contracts.

Exercise Five **Answers** — Playing in a Trump Contract

Short suits are important when playing in a trump contract. When you have no cards left in a suit, you can use the trump cards to ruff the opponents' winners.

Exercise Six **Answers** — The Language of Bidding

1) 8	2) 10	3) 13
4) 9	5) 11	6) 7
7) 12		

Exercise Seven **Answers** — Trick Scores for Partscores and Games

1) 60	2) 120	3) 120
4) 100	5) 60	6) 30
7) 100	8) 80	9) 100

Game contracts: 4♥ (2), 4♠ (3), 5♣ (4), 3NT (7) and 5♦ (9).

Exercise Eight — The Bidding

(E–Z Deal Cards: #1, Deal 1 — Dealer, North)

The Bidding

Each partnership uses a bidding conversation to agree on a trump or notrump contract.

Which suit do North and South like best? Who would suggest this suit first? Why would it benefit them to find they like this suit?

How many tricks can North estimate taking? How about South? How many tricks can North and South take as a partnership?

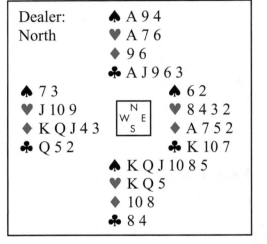

```
Dealer:        ♠ A 9 4
North          ♥ A 7 6
               ♦ 9 6
               ♣ A J 9 6 3
♠ 7 3                        ♠ 6 2
♥ J 10 9        N            ♥ 8 4 3 2
♦ K Q J 4 3   W   E          ♦ A 7 5 2
♣ Q 5 2         S            ♣ K 10 7
               ♠ K Q J 10 8 5
               ♥ K Q 5
               ♦ 10 8
               ♣ 8 4
```

Answer all of the above questions for East and West.

Which partnership predicted the most tricks? In which contract?

Exercise Nine — The Play

The Play

Play the deal in Exercise Eight.

Who first mentioned the suit that is trump?

Who is the declarer? Who makes the opening lead?

Which hand is dummy?

What is the declarer's plan to make the contract?

Exercise Eight *Answers* — The Bidding

The Bidding

- N–S like the spade suit best.
- South would suggest spades first.
- North has only three spades and might find it difficult to agree that spades should be trump.
- North can estimate taking three tricks.
- South can estimate taking six tricks at least and maybe seven.
- North and South can predict taking 10 tricks.
- E–W like the diamond suit best.
- West would likely suggest diamonds first.
- East can estimate taking one or two tricks.
- West can estimate taking three or four tricks.
- E–W can predict taking six tricks.
- N–S predicted the higher number of tricks.
- The contract would be 3♠ or 4♠.

Exercise Nine *Answers* — The Play

The Play

- South mentioned the suit that ended up being trump. South is the declarer.
- West, the player to the left of the declarer, leads.
- North's hand is the dummy and is placed face up on the table.
- South starts playing the trump suit until the opponents have none left. Then South takes the winners in the partnership's combined hands. South should end up with 10 tricks.

Exercise Ten — Bidding and Playing a Complete Deal

(E–Z Deal Cards: #1, Deal 2 — Dealer, North)

The Bidding

Do North and South have a suit they would like to be trump? Do East and West have a suit they would like to be trump? If a partnership can't agree on a trump suit, how do they decide on the final strain for the contract?

```
Dealer:        ♠ J 5 2
North          ♥ K Q J 8
               ♦ 9 3
               ♣ 10 8 6 4
    ♠ A K 8                    ♠ 9 7 3
    ♥ 10 7 5       N           ♥ A 9 3
    ♦ A K Q     W     E        ♦ 7 5 4 2
    ♣ 9 5 3 2      S           ♣ A K Q
               ♠ Q 10 6 4
               ♥ 6 4 2
               ♦ J 10 8 6
               ♣ J 7
```

How many tricks can North estimate taking? How many tricks can South estimate taking? What is the total number of tricks predicted by North and South? How many tricks can East estimate taking? How many tricks can West estimate taking? What is the total number of tricks predicted by East and West?

Which partnership predicted the higher number of tricks? What would the final contract be?

The Play

Which partner first suggested the strain of the contract? This player will be the declarer.

The player to the left of the declarer makes the opening lead. The hand of the declarer's partner, the dummy, is placed face up on the table. The declarer tries to take the tricks the partnership contracted for. How many tricks should the declarer end up with?

Exercise Ten *Answers* — Bidding and Playing a Complete Deal

The Bidding

- No, N–S do not have a suit they would like to have as trump.
- E–W also have no suit they would like to have as trump.
- The strain would be notrump.
- North can estimate two or three tricks.
- South can estimate one trick — maybe.
- N–S can predict only three or four tricks.
- East can estimate four tricks.
- West can estimate five tricks.
- E–W can predict nine tricks.
- E–W predicted the higher number of tricks.
- The contract would be 3NT.

The Play

- East or West would first mention the strain of the contract (notrump).
- The declarer (East or West) should end up with nine tricks.

CHAPTER 2
Objectives

Hand Valuation

The Golden Rules

The Roles of the Partners

Opening the Bidding

The Bidding Messages

Guidelines for Play

Summary

The Finer Points

Exercises

Sample Deals

You and your partner work together to reach your best contract. Through bidding, you decide the level to which you can afford to bid and the strain, suit or notrump, that the partnership prefers. To make these decisions, you and your partner need to know the combined strength and the distribution of your hands. Then, you see how this strength and distribution relate to having a reasonable chance of making the various contracts on the Bidding Scale. The strength of your hand may be determined by using the *point-count* system (popularized by Charles Goren).

HAND VALUATION

Tricks are taken with high cards and low cards in long suits. *Hand valuation* takes both into consideration. The features of your hand are assigned points. They are totaled together to give an estimate of the strength of your hand.

High-card Points

Points are awarded for each of the four highest cards in a suit (ace, king, queen and jack) on a 4–3–2–1 scale. These are referred to as *high-card points* or *HCP.*

Ace	4 points
King	3 points
Queen	2 points
Jack	1 point

Distribution Points

In addition, *distribution points (or long-suit points)* are assigned for each suit of five cards or longer. One point is added for every card over four:

five-card suit	1 point
six-card suit	2 points
seven-card suit	3 points
eight-card suit	4 points

Hand Value

By adding together your high-card points and distribution points, you arrive at a total point count for your hand. Let's see how this works:

	High-card Points	Distribution Points	Total Points
♠ A K 7	7	0	7
♥ Q J 10 9 8 7	3	2	5
♦ Q 7	2	0	2
♣ 10 9	0	0	0
	12	2	14

The value of the hand is 14 total points.

	High-card Points	Distribution Points	Total Points
♠ 10 9 8 6 5	0	1	1
♥ A Q 8 7 4	6	1	7
♦ A K	7	0	7
♣ A	4	0	4
	17	2	19

The value of the hand is 19 total points.

Shape

The shape of your hand is also important. There are two general shapes — *balanced* and *unbalanced*. A balanced hand has no *voids* (zero cards in a suit), no *singletons* (one card in a suit) and no more than one *doubleton* (two cards in a suit).

The following three hand patterns are balanced:

x x x x	x x x x	x x x x x
x x x	x x x x	x x x
x x x	x x x	x x x
x x x	x x	x x
4–3–3–3	4–4–3–2	5–3–3–2

The numbers beneath each pattern refer to the number of cards in each suit: 4–3–3–3 means there are four cards in one suit and three cards in each of the other three suits. It doesn't matter which suit has the four cards. The second pattern, 4–4–3–2, describes a hand with four cards in each of two suits, three cards in one suit and two cards in one suit. The last pattern, 5–3–3–2, describes a hand with one five-card suit, two three-card suits and one two-card suit.

A hand that does not have one of the above hand patterns is said to be unbalanced.

THE GOLDEN RULES

The Game Bonus

Before considering how you and your partner exchange information about the strength and shape of your hands, let's look back at your objectives in the bidding. Bidding and making a game contract may give your partnership a bonus. This goal is often within the reach of one of the pairs. Seeking the game bonus is a priority for your partnership. How many points in the combined partnership hands are needed for you to take enough tricks to make a game contract? Experience suggests the following guideline:

5 ♦ or 5 ♣ (minor suits)	29 combined total points
4 ♠ or 4 ♥ (major suits)	25 combined total points
3NT	25 combined total points

You may wonder why you need 25 combined total points for a 10-trick contract in the major suits, spades and hearts, and also for the nine-trick contract of 3NT. Because of the power of the trump suit, it is usually possible to take one extra trick in a trump contract with hands of equal strength. To make 5 ♦ or 5 ♣, however, requires 29 combined points, since you need 11 tricks, two more tricks than you need to fulfill a 3NT contract.

The Golden Fit

A bid is composed of two parts — the level and the strain. The level is generally determined by the combined strength of the partnership hands. The strain represents the choice to play in a trump suit or in notrump.

This decision is based on the partnership's combined distribution in each suit.

To name a suit as trump, you and your partner want a comfortable majority of cards in that suit. There are 13 cards in each suit. If you have six or fewer in the combined partnership hands, the opponents have the majority. Such a suit is unlikely to make a good trump suit for your side. If you have seven, the opponents have only six and you have a small majority. This might be adequate but cuts things a little close. If you have eight or more, you have a comfortable majority, since the opponents have five or fewer.

When you and your partner have at least eight combined cards in a suit, think of it as a *Golden Fit.* If you are going to play in a trump suit, you generally want to play in a Golden Fit. If you don't have an eight-card or longer fit in any suit, you generally want to play in notrump.

Partscores and the Golden Fit

If you have fewer than 25 combined total points, you do not have enough strength for a game contract. You want to play in the best partscore contract. If you have a Golden Fit, play in that suit at as low a level as possible.

Games and the Golden Fit

With 25 or more combined total points, you would like to try for a game bonus. With a Golden Fit in hearts or spades, you can bid 4 ♥ or 4 ♠.

Suppose, however, you have between 25 and 28 combined total points, and your only Golden Fit is in clubs or diamonds?

You are presented with an awkward choice. You could play in your Golden Fit in a partscore contract. This would be safe, but you would give up the opportunity for a game bonus. You could play in your Golden Fit at the game level. This would be risky, since you generally need at least 29 points to make a contract of 5 ♣ or 5 ♦. A third choice is to play in a game contract of 3NT even though you have a Golden Fit in a minor suit. This should be about right as far as the strength goes, but it would ignore the principle of playing in a Golden Fit when you have one.

Experience has shown that you will achieve better results in the long run if you make the third choice. Play in 3NT when you have 25 or more combined total points — even when you have a Golden Fit in a minor suit. There will be times when you can make either a partscore or a game in the minor suit and you can't make 3NT. These occasions will be more than offset by the times this principle works for you (*i.e.,* you make 3NT but can't make a minor-suit game, or you get a game bonus in notrump rather than a partscore in the minor suit). The best bid is the one that works most of the time. There are no perfect bids that work all of the time!

For this reason, the partnership should always try to reach a game contract when there are 25 or more combined total points. With a Golden Fit in hearts or spades, they should play in 4♥ or 4♠. Otherwise, they should play in 3NT.

Three game contracts are Golden:

Only rarely should you consider playing in 5♣ or 5♦.

THE ROLES OF THE PARTNERS

You and your partner work together, through the bidding, to discover whether you have enough strength and the right distribution to try for a Golden Game bonus.

The Opener

Each player has a role. The player who opens the bidding gets the first opportunity to provide information to the partnership. The opening bidder does not know anything about partner's hand. Opener's best approach is to try to tell partner something about both the strength and the distribution of the hand. The opening bidder is sometimes referred to as the *describer*. The opening bid paints a picture of the describer's hand for partner.

The Responder

The partner of the opening bidder is called the *responder*. As responder, you have the advantage of having heard your partner's first descriptive bid. You can see, in addition, what you have in your own hand, and therefore, you can take the responsibility of guiding the partnership to the best contract. The responder is sometimes referred to as the *captain*. In general, it is up to the responder, or captain, to determine the final contract.

Responder does this by keeping two questions in mind:

- What level?
- What strain?

What Level?

In deciding what level to bid to, the responder must try to do two things:

> - Estimate the combined strength of the two hands, and
> - Determine whether the partnership belongs in a partscore, game or slam contract.

Slams are relatively rare. We will consider them later. Since the partnership should be in a game contract if there are 25 or more total points, responder's decision boils down to determining whether the partnership has a combined total of 25 points. If it does, responder steers the partnership to the appropriate game contract. If it doesn't, responder steers the partnership to a partscore contract.

What Strain?

In addition to determining the appropriate level, the responder must try to estimate the combined distribution of the two hands to determine whether the partnership should play in a suit or in notrump.

If responder knows that the partnership belongs in a partscore contract, responder wants to steer the partnership into a Golden Fit, if one can be found, otherwise, into notrump. If responder knows that there is enough combined strength for game, responder wants to steer the partnership into 4♥ or 4♠, if there is a Golden Fit in a major suit, otherwise, into 3NT. Remember that the partnership is generally interested only in the Golden Games, ignoring 5♣ and 5♦.

OPENING THE BIDDING

Once you know the strength and shape of your hand, you are ready to decide whether to open the bidding. The dealer has the first opportunity and will either pass or make a bid at the one level. Since your partnership needs 25 or more combined total points for a game bonus, you need at least half of that, 13 points, to consider opening with a bid of one.

Opening a Suit at the One Level

To open a suit at the one level requires 13 to 21 total points (combining high-card points and distribution points). If you have 22 or more total points, you will make a bid at the two level. Hands with 22 or more points are uncommon and will be discussed briefly in the Appendix.

You need five or more cards in a major suit to open the bidding 1♥ or 1♠. You have seen that 4♥ and 4♠ are Golden Games. Opener wants to paint as clear a picture as possible of the cards for partner. When opener starts with 1♥ or 1♠, the bid describes a hand that has at least 13 total points and at least five cards in the suit bid.

Requirements for Opening the Bidding One in a Suit

With fewer than 13 total points, pass.

With 13 to 21 total points

- With a five-card or longer suit:
  - Bid your longest suit.
  - Bid the higher ranking of two five-card or two six-card suits.

- With no five-card or longer suit:
  - Bid your longer minor suit.
  - Bid the higher ranking of two four-card minor suits or the lower ranking of two three-card minor suits.

Let's see how this works:

High-card Points +
Distribution Points

♠ A Q J 4 3	8	You have 14 total points, enough to open the
♥ 5 3 2	0	bidding. You have a five-card suit, so open your
♦ K Q 7	5	longest suit, 1 ♠.
♣ J 7	1	
	14	

♠ A 2	4	You have 16 total points and an unbalanced
♥ K 9 8 7 3	4	hand. With two five-card suits, open the
♦ Q J 9 8 7	4	higher-ranking suit, 1 ♥.
♣ A	4	
	16	

♠ 9 8	0	You have a balanced hand with 14 total points.
♥ A K Q	9	With no five-card suit, open a minor suit. With
♦ K J 10 9	4	two four-card minor suits, bid the higher-
♣ J 10 9 8	1	ranking suit, 1 ♦.
	14	

♠ K Q 3	5	With only 6 total points, you do not have
♥ 9 8 7 6 3	1	enough to open the bidding. You would pass.
♦ 8 4 2	0	
♣ 10 6	0	
	6	

♠ Q J 10 9	3	With 13 total points and no five-card suit, open
♥ A 9 8	4	a minor suit. With a choice of three-card minor
♦ Q 4 3	2	suits, open the lower-ranking, 1♣.
♣ A 9 7	4	
	13	

♠ A 9 8 7 6	5	With enough to open the bidding and a hand
♥ 6	0	containing a five-card or longer suit, open the
♦ 4	0	longer suit, 1♣.
♣ K Q J 9 8 3	8	
	13	

Opening 1NT

Since opener is the describer, the opening bid should give as much information as possible to partner about the strength and distribution of the hand. One of the most descriptive opening bids in bridge is 1NT. A 1NT bid takes up all of the bidding room at the one level. It requires more than a minimum number of high-card points (HCP) to take the same number of tricks as a suit bid at the same level. Remember, a suit contract usually produces one more trick because of the ability of any trump to outrank all of the cards in the other three suits.

> ### Requirements for Opening
> ### the Bidding 1NT
> - 15, 16 or 17 HCP (not total points)
> - A balanced hand

The following three hands qualify as 1NT opening bids because they have both the strength and distribution required for the bid.

1) ♠ J 10 9	2) ♠ Q 9 8 7	3) ♠ J 7 3
♥ A 7 6	♥ K J	♥ A Q 9
♦ K 8 7 2	♦ A J 6 2	♦ K Q 10 8 5
♣ A K J	♣ K Q J	♣ A 9

The following hands, however, would not qualify.

4)	♠ J 10 9	5)	♠ A Q 8 7	6)	♠ J
	♥ A 7 6		♥ K J		♥ A Q 9 3
	♦ 9 8 7 2		♦ A J 6 2		♦ K Q 10 8 5
	♣ A K J		♣ K Q J		♣ A J 7

The first hand (4) is balanced but contains only 13 HCP, not enough strength to open the bidding 1NT. The second hand (5) is balanced but contains 21 HCP, too much to open 1NT. The third hand (6) contains 17 HCP, but it is not balanced since it has a singleton. Remember that opener is trying to paint a picture for responder.

THE BIDDING MESSAGES

Your partner has opened the bidding and the next hand passes. You are the responder, and it is your turn to bid. When should you pass partner's opening? If you choose to respond, how do you decide which bid to make?

There are no simple answers to these questions — the answers depend a great deal on which opening bid partner has made as well as the strength of your hand and the number of cards you were dealt in various suits.

Regardless of which opening bid was made, the responder must always be aware of what the partnership is trying to accomplish:

1. To discover which trump suit (if any) would be best for the partnership. In particular, the search for an eight-card major-suit fit (Golden Fit) is one of the primary objectives in the bidding.

2. To discover the combined strength of the partnership's hands so that a decision can be made as to whether the contract should be a partscore, game, small slam or grand slam.

Some opening bids reveal a great deal of information about the strength and distribution (the number of cards held in various suits) of the opener's hand. The more responder knows about opener's hand, the easier it will be for responder to select the best strain and level for the contract. Notrump opening bids, for example, will often tell responder at once everything necessary to select the best contract for the partnership.

Luckily, every bid carries one of three messages to your partner. These messages can be compared to a traffic light. For example, opening bids at the one level are all yellow, invitational bids. Responder may either bid or pass depending on responder's strength.

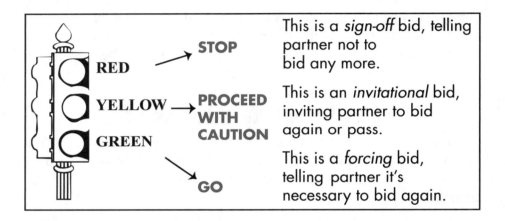

		This is a *sign-off* bid, telling partner not to bid any more.
RED	→ STOP	
YELLOW →	PROCEED WITH	This is an *invitational* bid, inviting partner to bid again or pass.
GREEN	CAUTION	
	↘ GO	This is a *forcing* bid, telling partner it's necessary to bid again.

In subsequent chapters, you will learn how to continue with the bidding conversation between the opener and responder to discover the best level and strain for the final contract. To understand bidding and the structure of the five-card major bidding system (or any system), you must recognize sign-off, invitational and forcing bids.

GUIDELINES FOR PLAY

The opening lead is made, and partner puts down the dummy. You, as declarer, have to play for the contract. How do you go about it? Playing a contract is an exciting exercise. As with all tasks of this nature, you should start by making a *plan*. The first step is to *Pause to consider your objective:* how many winners must you take, or how many losers can you afford if you are to make your contract. Then, you need to assess your current position — *Look at your winners and losers.* How close are you to fulfilling your objective? Once you have done this, you will be in a better position to decide what to do next. On many deals, you will be able to meet your objective with little extra effort.

Declarer's Objective

Declarer's objective is to make the contract by taking the required number of tricks. First, declarer must determine how many tricks are required. This is calculated by adding six tricks (book) to the level of the final contract. For example:

Contract	Number of Tricks Required
2♦	6 + 2 = 8 tricks
3NT	6 + 3 = 9 tricks
4♥	6 + 4 = 10 tricks

Counting Winners

After determining your objective, you as declarer must see how close you are to achieving it. Examine your combined holdings in each suit to see how many *sure tricks* you have. A sure trick is one that you can take without giving up the lead to your opponents.

Let's look at some examples.

DUMMY: 7 4

DECLARER: A 5

You can take one trick, the ace. Once you take the ace, the opponents have the remaining high cards in the suit.

DUMMY: A 6 4

DECLARER: K 5 2

You have two sure tricks. You can take one trick with dummy's ace, playing a low card from your hand. You can then lead one of dummy's low cards to your king.

DUMMY: Q 8 3

DECLARER: A K 4

You have three sure tricks. You can take two tricks with your ace and king, playing the low cards from dummy. Next, lead the 4 to dummy's queen. With the same number of cards in both hands, it does not matter in what order you take your sure tricks. For example, you could win the first trick with dummy's queen and the last two with your ace and king.

DUMMY: Q 8   This looks similar to the previous example,
DECLARER: A K   but you can take only two sure tricks. When
                    you play your ace and king, you will have to
follow suit by playing dummy's 8 and queen.

DUMMY: Q 8   You have three sure tricks but must be careful
DECLARER: A K 4   of the order in which you take them. If you play
                    the ace and the king first, you will have to play
dummy's queen on one of these tricks. When the suit is unevenly divided
between the two hands, you should take your sure tricks by playing the
high card from the short side first. Win the first trick with dummy's queen,
and then play the 8 to your ace and king.

Taking Your Tricks

After determining the number of sure tricks in each suit, add them
together to see if you have enough tricks to make the contract. If you do,
playing the hand is merely a matter of taking your tricks. As you saw in
the last example, you sometimes must be careful of the order in which
you take your tricks, playing the high cards from the short side first.

There is a further consideration when you are playing in a trump
contract. If you have enough tricks to make your contract, you start by
playing the trump suit until the opponents have no cards left in the trump
suit. This is referred to as *drawing trumps*. You do this to make certain
that the opponents can't play a trump on one of your sure tricks, turning
a winning trick into a losing trick.

If you add up your sure tricks and find that you don't have enough
to fulfill the contract, there is some work to do. We'll examine ways to
establish the additional tricks in later chapters.

SUMMARY

Your total hand value is calculated by combining high-card points and distribution points using the following scale:

High-card Points		Distribution Points	
Ace	4 points	five-card suit	1 point
King	3 points	six-card suit	2 points
Queen	2 points	seven-card suit	3 points
Jack	1 point	eight-card suit	4 points

Each hand is either balanced or unbalanced. There are only three balanced hand patterns. All others are unbalanced.

The Balanced Patterns

x x x x	x x x x	x x x x x
x x x	x x x x	x x x
x x x	x x x	x x x
x x x	x x	x x
4–3–3–3	4–4–3–2	5–3–3–2

One of the main objectives of the partnership is to bid to a game contract when there is sufficient combined strength.

Approximate Requirements for a Game Contract

5♦ or 5♣ (minor suits)	29 combined points
4♠ or 4♥ (major suits)	25 combined points
3NT	25 combined points

A second objective is to reach the right strain by looking for a Golden Fit of at least eight cards in hearts or spades (the major suits) in the combined hands. If there is no Golden Fit, then the contract should be played in notrump.

If you and your partner have fewer than 25 combined points, play a partscore in a Golden Fit or notrump or let the opponents play the contract. If you have 25 or more points, play in one of the Golden Games:

4♠
4♥   } GOLDEN
3NT }   GAMES

Opening the Bidding

Opener is describer. The rules for opening the bidding at the one level with 13 to 21 total points are:

- With a five-card or longer suit:
  - Bid your longest suit.
  - Bid the higher ranking of two five-card or two six-card suits.
- With no five-card or longer suit:
  - Bid your longer minor suit.
  - Bid the higher ranking of two four-card minor suits or the lower ranking of two three-card minor suits.
- With 15 to 17 HCP and a balanced hand, bid 1NT.

Responder's Decisions

Responder is the captain. Responder decides:

What level?

- With 25 or more combined points, bid a Golden Game.

What strain?

- With a Golden Fit in a major suit, play with that suit as trump in a partscore or game contract.
- With a Golden Fit in a minor suit, play with that suit as trump in a partscore contract. Play 3NT rather than a minor-suit game.

When playing a contract, first determine the number of tricks you need to make your contract. Then count the number of sure tricks in the combined hands. If you have enough tricks, take them. Be careful to play the high card from the short side first when a suit is unevenly divided between the two hands. In a trump contract, draw trumps before taking sure tricks in the other suits.

Bidding Messages

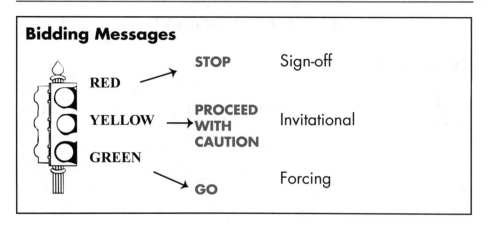

THE FINER POINTS

Distribution Points

While the use of high-card points in hand valuation is a commonly accepted standard, there are two ways of valuing distribution when opening the bidding.

In this text, we recommend that you add points for long suits (1 point for a five-card suit, 2 points for a six-card suit, *etc.*). Another method is to add points for short suits according to the following scale:

void	3 points
singleton	2 points
doubleton	1 point

This point scale is usually adjusted when you have high cards in a short suit (for example, a singleton king) and can become quite complex.

When you first pick up your hand, the value of short suits may not be apparent. It is often easier to see that long suits are valuable because of their extra trick-taking potential. Since the two methods result in approximately the same value (if you have a long suit somewhere, you have a short suit somewhere else), we suggest that you count for long suits when opening the bidding. Later in the text you will see that points are given for short suits once the partnership finds a Golden Fit.

Opening 1NT

A common variation is to open the bidding 1NT with 16, 17 or 18 HCP rather than 15, 16 or 17 HCP. Another variation is opening 16, 17 or 18 *total* point hands with 1NT. It is easy to adjust to either style (or even other ranges for 1NT), but this text is consistent with the 15 to 17 HCP range.

Some players do not like to open 1NT with two low cards in a suit (worthless doubleton) or when they have a five-card major suit. While this style has some merit, it can make later bidding awkward. For the beginning student, the more straightforward requirements in the text are recommended.

Opening a Suit at the One Level

The requirements given in the text ensure that an opening bid of 1 ♥ or 1 ♠ shows at least a five-card suit. This is the basis for a *five-card-major system* of bidding. A more classic approach is always to open the bidding in your longest suit, which sometimes means opening with a four-card major suit. While such a *four-card-major system* simplifies the rules for opening the bidding, this text has been written to conform with the more modern style of five-card majors presented in the *Learn to Play Bridge* program. Once you are familiar with the basic bidding concepts, it is easy to adjust to the style of your choice with your favorite partner.

Some authorities recommend opening the bidding with fewer than 13 total points in certain situations. Since this involves additional considerations such as opener's position at the table or the location of the high cards in specific suits, it is beyond the scope of this text. As you gain experience, you will be able to introduce more judgment into deciding when to open the bidding. When getting started, 13 total points is an excellent minimum requirement for opening the bidding.

Exercise One — Hand Valuation

Add up the high-card points (HCP) and the distribution points on each of the following hands. What is the total point value for each hand?

1) ♠ 10 9 8 6 5 3
   ♥ A K Q
   ♦ 9 8
   ♣ Q J

2) ♠ A Q J
   ♥ 9 6 4 3 2
   ♦ J 9 4 3
   ♣ 9

3) ♠ 8 6 3
   ♥ A Q J 9
   ♦ K 9 8
   ♣ A K Q

HCP:_____   HCP: _____   HCP: _____

Distr. Pts: _____   Distr. Pts: _____   Distr. Pts:_____

Total Pts: _____   Total Pts: _____   Total Pts:_____

Exercise Two — Hand Shapes

A balanced hand has no voids, no singletons and no more than one doubleton. Circle the hands that are balanced.

1) ♠ K J 7 3
   ♥ A 9 5
   ♦ Q J 6
   ♣ A J 10

2) ♠ J 7
   ♥ K 9 7 4
   ♦ K Q 10 5
   ♣ A J 8

3) ♠ K Q 3
   ♥ A
   ♦ Q 8 6 4 2
   ♣ K J 6 5

4) ♠ K 8
   ♥ A K 8 6 2
   ♦ K Q 7 3
   ♣ 9 5

5) ♠ K 8
   ♥ 9 5 2
   ♦ A Q 8
   ♣ K Q J 7 3

6) ♠ Q 6
   ♥ K 4 2
   ♦ A J 8 7 5 2
   ♣ K 3

Exercise One *Answers* — Hand Valuation

1) 12 HCP
   2 distr. pts.
   ───────
   14 total pts.

2) 8 HCP
   1 distr. pt.
   ───────
   9 total pts.

3) 19 HCP
   0 distr. pts.
   ───────
   19 total pts.

Exercise Two *Answers* — Hand Shapes

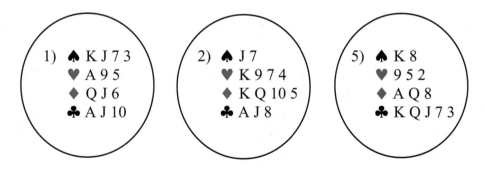

1) ♠ K J 7 3
   ♥ A 9 5
   ♦ Q J 6
   ♣ A J 10

2) ♠ J 7
   ♥ K 9 7 4
   ♦ K Q 10 5
   ♣ A J 8

5) ♠ K 8
   ♥ 9 5 2
   ♦ A Q 8
   ♣ K Q J 7 3

Exercise Three — What Level?

How many points do you need in the combined hands to make the following contracts?

1) 3NT _____   2) 4♥ _____   3) 4♠ _____

4) 5♣ _____   5) 5♦ _____

Exercise Four — What Strain?

Take all of the cards in a single suit (*e.g.,* the heart suit) and spread them face down on the table. By separating the cards into various groupings, discuss the following questions as a group.

1) How many cards must a partnership hold to have a majority of the cards in the suit?

2) Would a minimum majority of cards in a suit be adequate in a trump suit? Why?

3) How many cards of a suit should a partnership hold to be comfortable making it the trump suit?

4) In how many ways can eight cards in a suit be divided between the partnership hands?

5) Are the specific high cards you hold in a suit important when choosing the trump suit? (You might try turning the cards face up when answering the last question.)

Exercise Three *Answers* — What Level?

1) 25   2) 25   3) 25   4) 29   5) 29

Exercise Four *Answers* — What Strain?

1) The partnership needs seven cards in the combined hands to have the majority of cards in the suit.

2) No. A minimum majority would not be adequate, since the opponents would have six trump cards, nearly as many as you.

3) When the partnership holds eight or more trumps, they can be comfortable with the trump suit.

4) The eight cards could be divided in this manner: eight in one hand and none in the other, although this is very rare; seven in one hand and one in the other (also rare); six in one hand, two in the other; five in one hand, three in the other; four in one hand, four in the other.

5) The specific high cards are not as important as the length of the trump suit.

Exercise Five — Opening the Bidding

How many total points are in each of the following hands? Determine the proper opening bid.

1) ♠ 9 6 4
   ♥ Q J 9 8
   ♦ A K 4
   ♣ A Q J

HCP:_____

Distr. Pts: _____

Total Pts: _____

Bid:_____

2) ♠ A J 9 8 7
   ♥ K 7
   ♦ K J 8 2
   ♣ 9 8

HCP: _____

Distr. Pts: _____

Total Pts: _____

Bid: _____

3) ♠ 10 9 8
   ♥ Q 9 8 7 6
   ♦ A Q J
   ♣ 8 5

HCP: _____

Distr. Pts:_____

Total Pts: _____

Bid: _____

4) ♠ 3
   ♥ A J 8 6 5
   ♦ K 4
   ♣ A K J 7 3

HCP:_____

Distr. Pts: _____

Total Pts: _____

Bid:_____

5) ♠ A Q 7 3
   ♥ A 9 5
   ♦ 7 6
   ♣ K J 6 2

HCP: _____

Distr. Pts: _____

Total Pts: _____

Bid: _____

6) ♠ A J 6 3
   ♥ 5
   ♦ K J 9 4
   ♣ A 8 6 2

HCP: _____

Distr. Pts:_____

Total Pts: _____

Bid: _____

7) ♠ K 4 3
   ♥ A K 8 6
   ♦ A J 5
   ♣ K J 2

HCP:_____

Distr. Pts: _____

Total Pts: _____

Bid:_____

8) ♠ Q 8 5 3
   ♥ Q 9 6 3
   ♦ A J 10
   ♣ A 6

HCP: _____

Distr. Pts: _____

Total Pts: _____

Bid: _____

9) ♠ 4
   ♥ A Q 9 6 3
   ♦ 5
   ♣ A K 10 7 5 2

HCP: _____

Distr. Pts:_____

Total Pts: _____

Bid: _____

Exercise Five *Answers* — Opening the Bidding

Remember your decision on whether or not to open 1NT should be based on high card points and not total points.

1) 17 HCP
    <u> 0</u> distr. pts.
    17 total pts.
    1NT

2) 12 HCP
    <u> 1</u> distr. pt.
    13 total pts.
    1♠

3)   9 HCP
    <u> 1</u> distr. pt.
    10 total pts.
    Pass

4) 16 HCP
    <u> 2</u> distr. pts.
    18 total pts.
    1♥

5) 14 HCP
    <u> 0</u> distr. pts
    14 total pts.
    1♣

6) 13 HCP
    <u> 0</u> distr. pts
    13 total pts.
    1♦

7) 19 HCP
    <u> 0</u> distr. pts.
    19 total pts.
    1♣

8) 13 HCP
    <u> 0</u> distr. pts.
    13 total pts.
    1♦

9) 13 HCP
    <u> 3</u> distr. pts.
    16 total pts.
    1♣

Exercise Six — Responder, the Captain, Decides What Level and What Strain

Your partner opens the bidding 1 ♥. You as responder decide at what level and in what strain to play the contract. On the following hands, would you play at a game, partscore or possibly a game? What strain would you choose? What type of bidding message do you want to convey to the opener?

1) ♠ K 9 8	2) ♠ Q J 9	3) ♠ A 7 5
♥ 10 7 2	♥ K 5 3 2	♥ K J
♦ 10 8 7 6	♦ 9 7 5	♦ A 8 6 2
♣ J 9 4	♣ 8 3 2	♣ J 9 6 3

_____   _____   _____

Exercise Seven — Responder, the Captain, Decides What Level and What Strain

Your partner opens the bidding 1NT. You, as responder, decide the level and strain. What type of bidding message do you want to convey to the opener with your bid?

1) ♠ 8 2	2) ♠ 9 8 3	3) ♠ A K 9 7 4
♥ 10 9	♥ K Q 10 7 6 2	♥ Q 7
♦ A K 8 7 6	♦ 6 3	♦ J 7 6
♣ Q J 9 8	♣ K 4	♣ Q 9 8

_____   _____   _____

Exercise Eight — Counting Winners

How many sure tricks can you take with each of the following suit combinations?

DUMMY:	1) A 7 2	2) K 6 4	3) A 4	4) Q 5
DECLARER:	9 6 3	A Q 5	K Q	A K 6

_____   _____   _____   _____

Exercise Six *Answers* — Responder, the Captain, Decides What Level and What Strain

1) Partscore in hearts. Bidding message is sign-off.

2) Possibly game in hearts. Bidding message is invitational.

3) Game most likely is notrump unless opener has six hearts. Bidding message is forcing.

Exercise Seven *Answers* — Responder, the Captain, Decides What Level and What Strain

1) Game in notrump. Bidding message is sign-off.

2) Game in hearts since opener must have at least two hearts. Bidding message is sign-off.

3) Game in either spades or notrump. Bidding message is forcing.

Exercise Eight *Answers* — Counting Winners

    1) 1   2) 3   3) 2   4) 3

Exercise Nine — Taking Tricks

(E-Z Deal Cards: # 2, Deal 1 — Dealer, North)

You know how to value both hands of the partnership, and you know that you need 25 combined points to make a Golden Game. Let's see how this works. Turn up all of the cards on the first pre-dealt deal. Put each hand dummy style at the edge of the table in front of each player.

The Bidding

How many combined points are there in each partnership? Does one partnership have enough combined strength for a Golden Game? Does the partnership have a Golden Fit in a major suit?

```
Dealer:      ♠ A 7
North        ♥ K 5 2
             ♦ A K Q J
             ♣ 6 5 4 2

♠ 8 4 3 2              ♠ K Q J 10 9
♥ Q J 10 4    N        ♥ A 9 6
♦ 10 8 4    W   E      ♦ 5 3
♣ 10 8        S        ♣ 9 7 3

             ♠ 6 5
             ♥ 8 7 3
             ♦ 9 7 6 2
             ♣ A K Q J
```

North is the dealer. Who would open the bidding? What would the opening bid be? Which player would be the describer? Which player would be the responder? Which player would be the captain? What should the contract be? Which player would be the declarer?

The Play

Suppose that North is the declarer in a contract of 3NT. Who would make the opening lead? What would the opening lead be? How many tricks must declarer take to fulfill the contract?

Look at each combined suit in the North and South hands and determine how many sure tricks there are. There is a bridge saying, ***take your tricks and run,*** that applies to this deal. Why would this be good advice? What might happen if you do not take your tricks when you have the opportunity?

Exercise Nine *Answers* — Taking Tricks

The Bidding

- N–S have 27 combined points; E–W have 14 combined points (13 HCP plus 1 for length in spades).
- N–S have enough for a Golden Game.
- N–S do not have a Golden Fit in a major suit.
- North opens the bidding with 1NT.
- North is the describer.
- South is the responder and the captain.
- The contract should be 3NT.
- North is the declarer.

The Play

- East makes the opening lead.
- East leads the ♠K.
- Declarer needs nine tricks.
- Declarer has nine sure tricks.
- *Take your tricks and run* is good advice, because declarer can be assured of making the contract by taking the nine winners.
- If the defenders get the lead, they could take four spades and the ♥A — more tricks than declarer can afford to lose.

Exercise Ten — High Card from the Short Side

(E-Z Deal Cards: # 2, Deal 2 — Dealer, East)

When a partnership has fewer than 25 combined points, they should play in a partscore. If there is no Golden Fit, the partnership should play in notrump. Let's see how this works. Turn up all of the cards on the second pre-dealt deal and arrange them as in the previous exercise.

The Bidding

How many points are there in each partnership? Does either partnership have enough strength for a Golden Game? Does either partnership have a Golden Fit? Which partnership has the majority of the strength?

East is the dealer. Who would open the bidding? What would the opening bid be? Which player would be the describer? Which player would be the responder? Which player would be the captain?

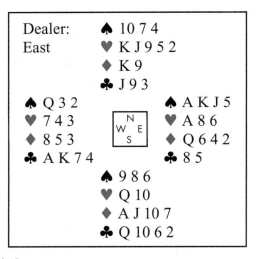

Dealer: ♠ 10 7 4
East   ♥ K J 9 5 2
           ♦ K 9
           ♣ J 9 3

♠ Q 3 2   ♠ A K J 5
♥ 7 4 3   ♥ A 8 6
♦ 8 5 3   ♦ Q 6 4 2
♣ A K 7 4   ♣ 8 5

         ♠ 9 8 6
         ♥ Q 10
         ♦ A J 10 7
         ♣ Q 10 6 2

If East and West bid to a contract, should it be a game contract or a partscore contract? What should be the strain of the contract? What might be a reasonable contract? Must East end up as the declarer? If not, how might West become declarer?

The Play

Suppose that West is the declarer in a contract of 1NT. Who would make the opening lead? What would the opening lead be? How many tricks must declarer take to fulfill the contract?

Look at each combined suit in the East and West hands and determine how many sure tricks there are. There is a bridge saying, *play the high card from the short side*, that applies to this deal. Why would this be good advice? What might happen if declarer does not follow this advice?

Exercise Ten *Answers* — High Card from the Short Side

The Bidding

- N–S have 18 combined points; E–W have 23 combined points.
- Neither partnership has enough strength for a Golden Game.
- Neither partnership has a Golden Fit.
- E–W have the majority of the strength.
- East opens the bidding with 1 ♦.
- East is the describer.
- West is the responder and the captain.
- E–W should be in a partscore.
- The strain should be notrump.
- 1NT would be a reasonable contract.
- The opening bidder does not necessarily end up as the declarer.
- West could be the declarer by first mentioning the strain of the contract. For example, West could mention notrump first.

The Play

- North makes the opening lead.
- North leads a low card from hearts, the longest suit.
- Declarer needs seven tricks to fulfill the contract.
- E–W have seven sure tricks.
- ***Play the high card from the short side*** applies to the spade suit. This is good advice. Declarer should win the first trick with the ♠Q. Declarer still has a low card to lead to the ♠A K J. Declarer needs to be careful to play spades in the correct order to win four tricks in the suit.

Exercise Eleven — Playing in a Golden Fit

(E-Z Deal Cards: #2, Deal 3 — Dealer, South)

The partnership needs eight or more cards in a suit for a Golden Fit. Let's see how this works. Turn up all of the cards on the third pre-dealt deal and arrange them as in the previous exercise.

The Bidding

How many points are there in each partnership? Does either partnership have enough combined strength for a Golden Game? Does either partnership have a Golden Fit? Which partnership has the majority of the strength?

South is the dealer. Does the dealer always open the bidding? Who would open the bidding? What would the opening bid be?

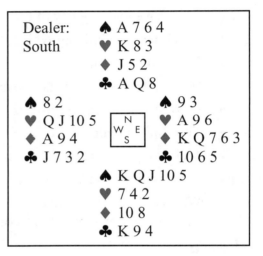

Dealer:
South

♠ A 7 6 4
♥ K 8 3
♦ J 5 2
♣ A Q 8

♠ 8 2
♥ Q J 10 5
♦ A 9 4
♣ J 7 3 2

♠ 9 3
♥ A 9 6
♦ K Q 7 6 3
♣ 10 6 5

♠ K Q J 10 5
♥ 7 4 2
♦ 10 8
♣ K 9 4

If North and South bid to a contract, should it be a game contract or a partscore contract? What should the strain of the contract be? What might be a reasonable contract?

The Play

Suppose that South is the declarer in a contract of 2♠. Who would make the opening lead? What would the opening lead be? How many tricks must declarer take to fulfill the contract?

Look at each combined suit in the North and South hands. Determine how many sure tricks there are. What is the advantage of playing in a Golden Fit? What might happen if North and South played in a notrump contract instead of their Golden Fit?

Exercise Eleven *Answers* — Playing in a Golden Fit

The Bidding

- N–S have 24 combined points; E–W have 18 combined points.
- Neither partnership has enough strength for a Golden Game.
- N–S have a Golden Fit in spades and the majority of the strength.
- E–W have a Golden Fit in diamonds.
- The dealer does not have to open the bidding.
- North opens the bidding with 1♣.
- N–S want to reach a partscore contract in spades.
- A reasonable contract is 2♠.

The Play

- West makes the opening lead.
- West leads the ♥Q.
- Declarer must take eight tricks.
- There are eight sure tricks between North and South.
- The advantage of playing in a Golden Fit is that you can stop the opponents from taking too many tricks in any one suit.
- If N–S played this deal in notrump, the opponents could take four tricks in hearts and five tricks in diamonds.

Exercise Twelve — Drawing Trumps

(E-Z Deal Cards: #2, Deal 4 — Dealer, West)

When the partnership has 25 or more combined points and a Golden Fit in a major suit, it should play in a Golden Game contract in the major suit. Let's see how this works.

Turn up all of the cards on the fourth pre-dealt deal and arrange them as in the previous exercise.

The Bidding

How many points are there in each partnership? Does either partnership have enough strength for a Golden Game? Does either partnership have a Golden Fit? Which partnership has the majority of the strength?

West is the dealer. Who would open the bidding? What would the opening bid be? After West's opening bid, how does East know there is enough com-

```
Dealer:        ♠ K Q 10
West           ♥ 4
               ♦ 8 7 4 3 2
               ♣ A 6 4 3
  ♠ A 7 6 3           ♠ 9 5
  ♥ A K 7      N      ♥ Q J 10 9 8 6
  ♦ K 10 6   W   E    ♦ A Q 9
  ♣ K 8 2      S      ♣ 7 5
               ♠ J 8 4 2
               ♥ 5 3 2
               ♦ J 5
               ♣ Q J 10 9
```

bined strength for a game contract? How does East know there is a Golden Fit in a major suit? What contract would East steer the partnership to?

The Play

Suppose that East is the declarer in a contract of 4 ♥. Who would make the opening lead? What would the opening lead be? How many tricks must declarer take to fulfill the contract?

Look at each combined suit in the East and West hands. Determine how many sure tricks there are. Another saying, **get the kiddies off the street** (play the trump suit as soon as you get the lead), applies to this deal. Why? What would happen if declarer did not play the trump suit before trying to take the other sure tricks?

Exercise Twelve *Answers* — Drawing Trumps

The Bidding

- N–S have 15 combined points; E–W have 28 combined points.
- E–W have enough points for a Golden Game.
- E–W have a Golden Fit in hearts.
- N–S have a Golden Fit in clubs.
- E–W have the majority of strength.
- West opens the bidding with 1NT.
- East knows that there is enough combined strength for a game contract because East has 11 total points and West has at least 15 HCP — a combined total of at least 26 points.
- East knows there is a Golden Fit in hearts because West must have at least two hearts to open the bidding with 1NT.
- The contract should be 4 ♥.

The Play

- South leads the ♣Q.
- Declarer needs 10 tricks.
- There are 10 sure tricks.
- Declarer should draw trumps to take away the opponents' trump cards.
- If declarer did not do this, the opponents could score a low trump when South ruffs the third diamond trick.

CHAPTER 3
Responses to 1NT Opening Bids

Responder's General Approach

Responder's Decision with 0 to 7 Total Points

Responder's Decision with 8 or 9 Total Points

Responder's Decision with 10 to 15 Total Points

Opener's Rebid after a 1NT Opening Bid

Guidelines for Play

Summary

Exercises

Sample Deals

RESPONDER'S GENERAL APPROACH

If your partner opens the bidding, you as responder have a picture of opener's hand. You also know what you have in your own hand. Your objective is to put this information together and decide both the level and the strain of the final contract.

If opener starts the bidding with 1NT, that bid gives responder a very clear description of opener's hand — 15, 16 or 17 HCP and a balanced shape (distribution). Let's see how responder can use this information.

Responder Decides What Level

When your partner opens the bidding 1NT, you as responder know that opener has 15, 16 or 17 HCP. By adding your strength to that of opener's, you can usually tell whether the partnership has at least 25 combined points, enough for a game contract, or fewer than 25 combined points, enough for only a partscore contract.

Please note that while a 1NT opener shows 15 to 17 HCP, responder uses *total* points to value the hand.

Let's look at some sample hands you might hold as responder:

HCP +
Distribution Points

♠ A 8 7	4	
♥ A Q 8 7 6 3	8	
♦ 8 6 2	0	
♣ 7	0	
	12	

With 12 total points, responder knows the combined strength is either 27 (12 + 15), 28 (12 + 16) or 29 (12 + 17) points. Responder is sure there is enough combined strength for game and should steer the partnership toward a Golden Game.

♠ J 10 9	1	
♥ 9 8 7	0	
♦ Q 9 7 4	2	
♣ K 4 2	3	
	6	

With 6 total points, responder knows that the combined strength lies between 21 (6 + 15) to 23 (6 + 17) points. The partnership has fewer than the 25 points needed for a game contract. Responder passes because responder knows the contract should be a partscore.

♠ Q 8 5	2	With 9 total points, responder knows
♥ K 6	3	the combined strength is as little as 24
♦ K J 4 2	4	(9 + 15) points or as much as 26 (9 + 17)
♣ 10 9 5 3	0	points. Responder will have to get more
	$\overline{9}$	information from opener before decid-

ing whether the partnership should be in
game. Bid 2NT.

Responder Decides What Strain

In addition to deciding the level of the contract, responder decides the strain. To do this, responder must first determine whether there is a Golden Fit.

It is important to recall that an opening 1NT bid shows one of three hand patterns: 4–3–3–3, 4–4–3–2 or 5–3–3–2 (see page 31). When opener bids 1NT, opener promises at least two cards in each suit and usually at least three cards. **Sometimes opener has four or more cards in a suit and occasionally five cards.** Let's look at some examples to see how responder uses this information to decide if there is a Golden Fit.

♠ J 9 8 7 4 2
♥ Q J 2
♦ A K
♣ 7 4

Responder has a six-card spade suit. Opener has at least two cards in spades, so responder can be sure that there is a Golden Fit in spades. Bid 4♠.

♠ 9 6 3
♥ J 8 5
♦ 8 7 5
♣ Q 7 6 3

Since opener seldom has a five-card suit, it is unlikely that there is a Golden Fit in spades, hearts or diamonds. There is some possibility that opener has a four-card club suit, but responder can't be very sure of a Golden Fit. Pass.

♠ A 4
♥ K Q 9 7 6
♦ J 6 3
♣ 9 8 3

With a five-card heart suit, it's very likely that there's a Golden Fit. Only when opener has a doubleton heart will there not be a Golden Fit. Bid 3♥.

Responder Decides What Level and What Strain

Let's see how responder puts the pieces together to steer the partnership to an appropriate contract.

HCP +
Distribution Points

♠ J 8	1
♥ K Q J 9 8 2	8
♦ 9 2	0
♣ K 8 3	3
	12

With 12 total points, responder knows the combined strength is at least 27 (12 + 15) points, more than enough for a game contract. With a six-card heart suit, responder knows there is a Golden Fit in hearts. Responder takes the partnership directly to its final contract of 4 ♥.

♠ J 5 3	1
♥ 10 7	0
♦ J 8 7 5 4 2	3
♣ 9 8	0
	4

With only 4 total points, responder knows that there are at most 21 (4 + 17) points, only enough for a partscore. With a six-card diamond suit, responder is assured of a Golden Fit and confidently puts the partnership in a safe contract of 2 ♦.

♠ J 2	1
♥ 9 3	0
♦ A K 9 6 4 2	9
♣ 8 6 3	0
	10

Holding 10 total points, responder knows that there are at least 25 (10 + 15) points, enough for game. With a six-card diamond suit, responder can be assured of a Golden Fit in diamonds. However, 5 ♦ is not one of the Golden Games. Instead, responder steers the partnership into a final contract of 3NT.

RESPONDER'S DECISION WITH 0 TO 7 TOTAL POINTS

What Level?

When responder has 0 to 7 total points, the contract should be played in a partscore. Even if opener has 17 HCP and responder has a maximum of 7 total points, there are only 24 ($17 + 7 = 24$) combined points, not enough for game.

What Strain?

Responder wants to play a partscore in a Golden Fit if one can be found; otherwise, in notrump. If there is a Golden Fit, the cheapest level available for bidding is the two level. After an opening 1NT bid, there are no one-level bids available on the Bidding Scale. If responder determines there is no Golden Fit, responder can pass and leave the contract in 1NT.

With only 0 to 7 total points, you, as responder, can't afford to get the partnership higher than the two level. This limits your options. You can't make any exploratory bids that might uncover a Golden Fit. You must decide immediately on the best partscore contract. To do this, you look at the long suits in your hand and decide whether there is likely to be a Golden Fit.

If you have a six-card suit, you are certain that there is a Golden Fit. Opener has promised a balanced hand with a minimum of two cards in each suit.

If you have a five-card suit, a Golden Fit is highly likely. As we saw in Chapter Two, opener is most likely to hold three or more cards in a given suit. Since there is no room on the Bidding Scale to make an exploratory bid, you assume there is a Golden Fit. Even if you happen to find opener with only a doubleton, the partnership will still have a majority of the trump suit ($5 + 2 = 7$).

If you have only a four-card suit, opener would also need at least a four-card suit to have a Golden Fit. This is less likely than opener's having two or three cards in the suit. With 0 to 7 total points, your hand is so weak that you can't afford the bidding space to get more information about opener's hand. You will have to make an on-the-spot decision and go with the odds. Settle for a partscore in notrump by passing.

If you have fewer than four cards in a suit, there is virtually no chance of a Golden Fit. You should leave the strain in notrump.

2♣, The Stayman Convention

There is another point responder must take into account when deciding the strain. A bid of 2♣ in response to an opening bid of 1NT is reserved for a special purpose, the *Stayman convention*. The use of this bid is described in Chapter 9. For now, you only need to know that a 2♣ response after a 1NT opening bid has nothing to do with the club suit.

Therefore, you do not respond 2♣ with 0 to 7 total points even when you know there is a Golden Fit in clubs. Instead, you pass and play a partscore in 1NT.

Put It All Together

When Responding to a 1NT
Opening Bid with 0 to 7 Total Points

- Bid 2♠, 2♥ or 2♦ with a five-card or longer suit (2♣ is reserved for the Stayman convention).

- Otherwise, pass.
Note: These are partscore sign-off bids.

Your partner opens the bidding 1NT, and you hold:

♠ J 8 7 5 4 2 ♥ Q 10 2 ♦ J 7 6 ♣ 9	You know you belong in a partscore, so play in your Golden Fit. Your partnership has at least eight cards in spades in the combined hands since opener has at least two. Respond 2♠.
♠ J 5 3 ♥ Q 7 3 ♦ K 9 8 7 2 ♣ 10 4	You have at least a seven-card fit in diamonds and very likely eight or more. Quite often opener will have three or more diamonds. Respond 2♦.

♠ Q 6 2
♥ 8 7 4
♦ J 10 8 2
♣ 9 7 3

With only one four-card suit, it is unlikely there is a Golden Fit. Opener will have four or more diamonds less than half the time. Pass and play in 1NT.

♠ Q 6
♥ J 4
♦ 9 6 5 3
♣ 10 8 7 6 2

As in the second example, you are likely to have a Golden Fit. You have a five-card club suit, but you can't play a partscore in 2♣ (Stayman convention). Pass and play in 1NT.

RESPONDER'S DECISION WITH 8 OR 9 TOTAL POINTS

What Level?

When responder has 8 or 9 total points opposite opener's 15, 16 or 17 HCP, there may be enough points for a game contract. The partnership has a combined strength of 23, 24, 25 or 26 total points. Half of the time, there are 25 or more combined points. Responder needs more information. Responder would like to know whether opener has specifically 15, 16 or 17 HCP.

A 2NT response is used to ask opener to tell responder more about opener's hand. With 15 HCP, opener should pass, and the partnership will stay safely in partscore. With 17 HCP, opener will definitely bid 3NT. With 16 HCP, opener needs to exercise some judgment as to whether or not to bid game – is there a five-card suit that might produce extra tricks or 10's and 9's in suits that could be promoted to winners.

What Strain?

By bidding 2NT, responder is heading toward a Golden Game in notrump. If there are 25 or more combined points, responder wants to play 3NT, even if there is a Golden Fit in diamonds or clubs.

If there is a Golden Fit in spades or hearts, however, responder would like to play in a major-suit game. In addition to more information about opener's strength, responder also might like more information about opener's length in the major suits. But, when responder holds only 8 or 9 total points, bidding space is limited. The Stayman convention would come in handy here. Responder can first bid 2♣ to ask if opener has four or more cards in one or both of the major suits. Opener answers at the two level. There is still room to ask the next question: what is the exact strength of opener's hand?

For now, a *raise* to 2NT can be used to show any hand with 8 or 9 total points. You can read about the Stayman convention in Chapter 9 (the bonus chapter) and learn to use it at your leisure.

Put It All Together

```
When Responding to a 1NT
Opening Bid with 8 or 9 Total Points

• Bid 2NT.*

• Bid 2♣, Stayman.

  * Note: This is an invitational bid.
```

Your partner opens the bidding 1NT, and you hold:

♠ K 8 7
♥ A 3
♦ J 9 8 7
♣ J 10 9 8

With 9 total points, you can't rule out the possibility of a game contract. You don't have enough points, however, to bid game without further information from opener. Respond 2NT to ask opener to further describe the strength of opener's hand.

♠ Q 8
♥ A 10 9
♦ J 3
♣ 10 9 8 6 5 3

With 9 total points, you want to look for a Golden Game. Ignore the Golden Fit in your minor suit, since there can't be enough combined strength to make 5♣. Respond 2NT.

♠ 9 8 5
♥ Q 7 6
♦ J 9 8 4 3
♣ A 7

With 8 total points, respond 2NT to try to reach a Golden Game.

RESPONDER'S DECISION WITH 10 TO 15 TOTAL POINTS

What Level?

When responder has 10 or more points, there are enough combined points for game even if opener has only 15 points. With more than 15 total points, responder is probably interested in a slam contract. Slam bidding is briefly discussed in the Appendix. In the meantime, let's consider the range of 10 to 15 total points for which responder wants to choose one of the Golden Games — 4♠, 4♥ or 3NT.

What Strain?

Responder's first choice is to play in a major-suit game if there is a Golden Fit (eight or more cards in the suit). If not, responder wants to play in 3NT.

If you, as responder, have a six-card or longer major suit, you know for sure there is a Golden Fit. In this case, you can bid game directly — 4♥ or 4♠.

If you have a five-card major suit, you know there will be a Golden Fit if opener has three or more cards in the suit. Unlike the situation when you had 0 to 7 total points and merely had to assume that there was a Golden Fit, here you have some room to explore on the way to your game contract. You can bid at the three level, 3♥ or 3♠. These bids are *forcing* and ask opener to bid game in the major suit with three or more cards and to bid 3NT with only two. Opener may not pass a forcing bid. Thus, responder is assured of getting to the right Golden Game.

When you have a four-card major suit, opener must have at least four cards for there to be a Golden Fit. Once again you start to run out of bidding room. You can't bid your major at the two level since that would show 0 to 7 total points. You can't bid it at the three level since, as you've just seen, that shows a five-card suit. You can't bid it at the four level since that shows a six-card or longer suit (and also gets the partnership past 3NT).

This is another situation in which the Stayman convention could be used. A 2♣ response asks whether opener has four or more cards in one or both of the major suits. If opener does have a four-card major, opener bids it at the two level, and responder bids on accordingly. The details of this convention are discussed in Chapter 9, The Stayman convention (bonus chapter). You only need to know that responder has a way to find out whether opener has a four-card major suit. In the meantime, until you understand this convention, you can assume that there is no Golden Fit and bid game in notrump.

When responder has three or fewer cards in a major suit, a Golden Fit is highly unlikely. Responder bids game in 3NT.

Put It All Together

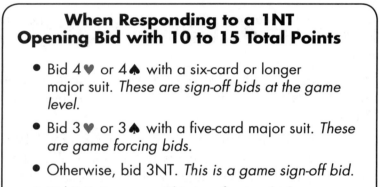

> ### When Responding to a 1NT
> ### Opening Bid with 10 to 15 Total Points
>
> * Bid 4♥ or 4♠ with a six-card or longer major suit. *These are sign-off bids at the game level.*
> * Bid 3♥ or 3♠ with a five-card major suit. *These are game forcing bids.*
> * Otherwise, bid 3NT. *This is a game sign-off bid.*
> * Bid 2♣ Stayman. *This is a forcing bid.*

Your partner opens 1NT, and you hold the following hands:

♠ A K 9 7 5 4   With 12 total points, you want to play in a game
♥ Q 7 6   contract. With a six-card spade suit, you know you
♦ J 9   have a Golden Fit. Place the final contract in 4♠.
♣ 8 7

♠ 10 9   You have 11 total points, enough for game. With
♥ Q 2   only two cards in each major, there is no possibility
♦ A 9 8 6 4   of a Golden Fit in a major suit. Respond 3NT.
♣ K J 5 3

♠ 9 8 6
♥ A J 9 6 2
♦ K Q 3
♣ Q 7

With 13 total points and a five-card major suit, you want to play game in 4♥ if opener has three or more; otherwise in 3NT. Respond 3♥. This bid asks opener to bid 4♥ with three or more hearts; otherwise, to bid 3NT.

♠ A Q J 8
♥ J 10 9
♦ Q 9 8 4
♣ 3 2

With 10 total points and a four-card major suit, you could use the Stayman convention, 2♣, to ask if opener has a four-card major. Since this bid hasn't been discussed in detail yet, assume there is no Golden Fit in a major suit and respond 3NT.

♠ A 9
♥ K 7 6
♦ Q J 9 8 5 4
♣ 10 2

With 12 total points and no likely major-suit fit, respond 3NT. Ignore the Golden Fit in diamonds, since 5♦ isn't one of the Golden Games. In fact, just raise 1NT to 3NT.

OPENER'S REBID AFTER A 1NT OPENING BID

Opener's second bid is called *opener's rebid.* If responder makes a sign-off bid, opener passes at the next turn. If responder makes an invitational bid, opener may either pass or bid again. If responder makes a forcing bid, opener must bid again.

Suppose you open the bidding 1NT with the following hand:

♠ K Q 8 5
♥ A K 3
♦ K J 2
♣ J 6 3

If responder bids 2♠, you pass. Even though you have attractive spades, you can't bid more. Partner has made a sign-off bid and expects you to pass. If responder bids 2NT, you may either pass or bid 3NT. Responder is making an invitational bid. With 17 HCP, you bid 3NT. If responder bids 3♥, this is a forcing bid, and you must bid again. Since you have three hearts, bid a game in hearts, 4♥. If you held only two hearts, you would bid 3NT.

GUIDELINES FOR PLAY

In the previous chapter, we saw that declarer makes a plan by first pausing to consider the objective (how many tricks are needed to make the contract) and then by looking at the winners and losers (counting the number of sure tricks in the combined hands). If there are enough sure tricks to make the contract, declarer can go ahead and take them. On most deals, however, there will not be enough sure tricks, and declarer will have to *Analyze the alternatives* to figure out how to develop the extra tricks that are needed. One of the techniques for developing extra tricks is through the promotion of high cards.

Developing Tricks through Promotion

A card is *promoted* into a sure trick when all of the higher-ranking cards in the suit have been played. Sometimes the opponents will promote some tricks for you by taking their sure tricks in a suit, but usually you will have to do the work. Let's look at some examples.

DUMMY: 5 4

DECLARER: K Q

You don't have a sure trick. You can lead the king (or queen) to make an opponent play the ace in order to win the trick. Your remaining high card is now promoted into a sure trick.

DUMMY: Q 6

DECLARER: K J 5

You can develop two sure tricks. Lead one of your high cards to drive out the opponents' ace; your two remaining high cards are promoted into winners. Because the suit is unevenly divided between the two hands, you should follow the principle of playing the high card from the short side first — the queen in this example.

DUMMY: Q J 10

DECLARER: 8 5 3

You can develop one trick. Lead the queen to drive out the opponents' ace or king. When you have another opportunity to lead, play the jack to drive out the opponents' remaining high card. You have now promoted your 10 into a trick.

DUMMY: 7 5 4 2

DECLARER: J 10 9 8

You have a lot of work to do — the opponents have the ace, the king and the queen. Lead one of your high cards at every opportunity and you eventually can promote a trick.

Losing Tricks to the Opponents

When developing tricks through promotion, you have to give the lead to the opponents. There is nothing wrong with losing a trick to the opponents, provided that they can't take enough tricks to defeat your contract. You often have to lose tricks to the opponents, either because you have no choice or because you are trying to develop the tricks needed to make your contract.

If you have to give up the lead while developing additional tricks, you want to be able to regain the lead to take the tricks you have developed. It's generally a good idea to keep sure tricks in other suits to help you regain the lead and maintain control. In other words, when developing tricks in a suit, follow the guideline "take your losses early" while you still have winning tricks in other suits. Don't take all of your sure tricks in other suits first — your action might develop sure tricks for your opponents.

SUMMARY

Responses to 1NT

After your partner opens the bidding, put your hand in one of three categories based on your total points:

0 to 7	Bid 2 ♦, 2 ♥ or 2 ♠ with a five-card or longer suit. (2 ♣ is reserved for the Stayman convention.) Otherwise, pass.
8 or 9	Bid 2NT (2 ♣ can uncover an eight-card major-suit fit).
10 to 15	Bid 4 ♥ or 4 ♠ with a six-card or longer suit. Bid 3 ♠ or 3 ♥ with a five-card suit. Otherwise, bid 3NT (2 ♣ can uncover an eight-card major-suit fit).

Each bid carries one of three possible bidding messages:

The Bidding Messages in Response to a 1NT Opening Bid

Sign-off:	Invitational:	Forcing:
• Pass	• 2NT	• 3 ♥, 3 ♠
• 2 ♦, 2 ♥, 2 ♠		• 2 ♣ (the Stayman convention)
• 3NT, 4 ♥, 4 ♠		
• 5 ♣, 5 ♦ (Rarely)		

Rebids by Opener after a 1NT Opening Bid

After responder's sign-off:
- Pass.

After responder's invitational bid of 2NT:
- Pass with 15 HCP.
- With 16 HCP opener should use judgment to decide whether to bid 3NT or to pass opener's invitational bid.
- Bid 3NT with 17 HCP.

After responder's forcing bid of 3 ♥ or 3 ♠:
- Bid four of the major with three or more cards in the major.
- Bid 3NT with two cards in the major.

Developing Tricks through Promotion

You sometimes need to develop additional tricks in order to make your contract. One technique for doing this is promotion: playing high cards to drive out the opponents' higher-ranking cards until your lower-ranking cards become sure tricks. Promotion involves giving up the lead to the opponents. It is a useful technique as long as you have enough sure tricks in other suits to regain the lead before the opponents can take enough tricks to defeat the contract.

Exercise One — Responding with 0 to 7 Total Points

You are the responder after your partner opens 1NT. Value the hand and decide the level, the strain and the response for each of the following hands:

1) ♠ 10 8 6 5 4 2	2) ♠ J 9 8	3) ♠ Q J
♥ J 7 5	♥ A 9 6 2	♥ 9 8
♦ 8	♦ J 7 6	♦ Q 9 8
♣ J 6 2	♣ 10 9 4	♣ 10 9 7 6 3 2

Points: _____   Points: _____   Points:_____

Level: _____   Level:_____   Level: _____

Strain:_____   Strain: _____   Strain: _____

Response: _____   Response: _____   Response: _____

What do all of the hands have in common? _____

_____

Exercise Two — Responding with 10 to 15 Total Points

You are the responder after your partner opens 1NT. Value the hand and decide the level, the strain and the response for each of the following hands.

1) ♠ Q J 9 7 6 4	2) ♠ A 8 2	3) ♠ Q J
♥ K 8 6	♥ A Q 9 8 3	♥ K Q
♦ K 4 3	♦ 9 4 2	♦ Q 9 8
♣ 5	♣ 10 9	♣ J 9 7 6 3 2

Points: _____   Points: _____   Points:_____

Level: _____   Level:_____   Level: _____

Strain:_____   Strain: _____   Strain: _____

Response: _____   Response: _____   Response: _____

What do all of the hands above have in common? _____

_____

Exercise One *Answers* — Responding with 0 to 7 Total Points

1)	4 total points	Partscore	Spades	2♠
2)	6 total points	Partscore	Notrump	Pass
3)	7 total points	Partscore	Notrump	Pass — 2♣ is a conventional response.

    All of the hands are in the 0 to 7 total-point range, so responder knows that the partnership belongs in partscore.

Exercise Two *Answers* — Responding with 10 to 15 Total Points

1)	11 total points	Game	Spades	4♠
2)	11 total points	Game	Maybe hearts	3♥
3)	13 total points	Game	Notrump	3NT

    All of the hands have at least 10 total points, so responder knows that the partnership belongs in game.

Exercise Three — Responding with 8 or 9 Total Points

You are the responder after your partner opens the bidding 1NT. Construct a hand with which you would respond 2NT.

♠ _____   ♥ _____   ♦ _____   ♣ _____

Exercise Four — The Bidding Messages

Each bid has a message. Your partner opens the bidding 1NT.

1. What are seven sign-off responses you can make?_____

_____

2. What invitational response can you make?_____

3. What are two forcing responses you can make?_____

Exercise Five — Playing in the Golden Fit

Construct the following hands for North and South:

Randomly deal the remaining cards to East and West. Have South play as declarer in a contract of 1NT. Record the number of tricks taken by South. Then, have North play as declarer in a contract of 2♠. Record the number of tricks taken by North.

When the opening bid is 1NT, why is it important that responder, holding 0 to 7 total points, steer the partnership into a Golden Fit whenever possible?

NORTH
♠ J 10 9 8 7 6
♥ 7 3 2
♦ 8 7
♣ 4 3

SOUTH
♠ Q 5
♥ A K 4
♦ A 6 5 3
♣ A 8 6 2

Exercise Six — Promoting Tricks

How many tricks can be developed with each of the following suit combinations?

DUMMY:	1) K Q J	2) K 5	3) J 8 4	4) 10 8 6 3
DECLARER:	7 4 2	Q 4	Q 10 3	J 9 5 2

_____   _____   _____   _____

Exercise Three *Answers* — Responding with 8 or 9 Total Points

Any hand with 8 or 9 total points.

Exercise Four *Answers* — The Bidding Messages

1. The seven sign-off bids are: pass, 2 ♦ , 2 ♥ , 2 ♠ , 3NT, 4 ♥ , 4 ♠ .
2. The invitational response is 2NT.
3. Two forcing responses are 3 ♥ and 3 ♠ .

Exercise Five *Answers* — Playing in the Golden Fit

It is important for responder to steer the partnership into a Golden Fit whenever possible because the trump cards prevent the opponents from taking winners in their strong suits.

Exercise Six *Answers* — Promoting Tricks

1) 2   2) 1   3) 1   4) 1

Exercise Seven — Promoting Winners in Notrump

(E-Z Deal Cards: #3, Deal 1 — Dealer, North)

Turn up all of the cards on the first pre-dealt deal. Put each hand dummy style at the edge of the table in front of each player.

The Bidding

North is the dealer. Who would open the bidding? What would the opening bid be? Which player would be the describer? Which player would be the responder? Which player would be the captain?

Look at responder's hand. At what level should the contract be played? In what strain should the contract be played? What would the response be? What is the bid-

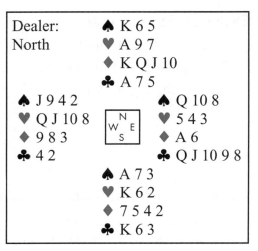

```
Dealer:        ♠ K 6 5
North          ♥ A 9 7
               ♦ K Q J 10
               ♣ A 7 5
♠ J 9 4 2              ♠ Q 10 8
♥ Q J 10 8     N       ♥ 5 4 3
♦ 9 8 3      W   E     ♦ A 6
♣ 4 2          S       ♣ Q J 10 9 8
               ♠ A 7 3
               ♥ K 6 2
               ♦ 7 5 4 2
               ♣ K 6 3
```

ding message given by responder's bid? What would opener do? What would the contract be? Who would be the declarer?

The Play

Who would make the opening lead? What would the opening lead be?

How many tricks must declarer take to fulfill the contract? How many sure tricks does declarer have? Which suit provides declarer with the opportunity to develop the additional tricks needed to make the contract? Which suit should declarer play after winning the first trick? Why?

Bid and play the deal. Did declarer make the contract?

Exercise Seven *Answers* — Promoting Winners in Notrump

The Bidding

- North opens the bidding with 1NT.
- North is the describer.
- South is the responder and the captain.
- The contract should be in game.
- The strain is notrump.
- The response would be 3NT.
- Responder makes a sign-off bid and opener should pass.
- The contract is 3NT.
- North is the declarer.

The Play

- East makes the opening lead.
- East leads the ♣Q.
- Declarer needs nine tricks.
- Declarer has six sure tricks.
- The diamond suit provides the best opportunity to develop the additional tricks needed to make the contract.
- Declarer should play diamonds after taking the first trick because declarer wants to set the suit up right away while there are still winners in the other suits.
- Declarer should make the contract.

Exercise Eight — Promoting Winners in a Suit Contract

(E-Z Deal Cards: #3, Deal 2 — Dealer, East)

Turn up all of the cards on the second pre-dealt deal and arrange them as in the previous exercise.

The Bidding

East is the dealer. Who would open the bidding? What would the opening bid be? Which player would be the describer? Which player would be the responder? Which player would be the captain?

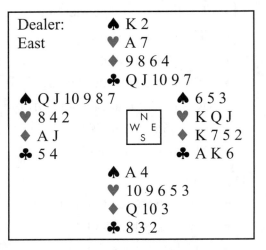

```
Dealer:        ♠ K 2
East           ♥ A 7
               ♦ 9 8 6 4
               ♣ Q J 10 9 7
♠ Q J 10 9 8 7        ♠ 6 5 3
♥ 8 4 2          N    ♥ K Q J
♦ A J         W   E   ♦ K 7 5 2
♣ 5 4            S    ♣ A K 6
               ♠ A 4
               ♥ 10 9 6 5 3
               ♦ Q 10 3
               ♣ 8 3 2
```

Look at responder's hand. At what level should the contract be played? In what strain should the contract be played? What would the response be? What is the bidding message given by responder's bid? What would opener do? What would the contract be? Who would be the declarer?

The Play

Who would make the opening lead? What would the opening lead be?

How many tricks must declarer take to fulfill the contract? How many sure tricks does declarer have? How can declarer develop the tricks needed to make the contract? Which suit should declarer develop first? Why? What would happen if declarer played the other suits first?

Bid and play the deal. Did declarer make the contract?

Exercise Eight *Answers* — Promoting Winners in a Suit Contract

The Bidding

- East opens the bidding with 1NT.
- East is the describer.
- West is the responder and the captain.
- The contract should be in game.
- The strain should be spades.
- The response should be 4♠.
- The responder gives a sign-off message.
- Opener should pass.
- The contract would be 4♠.
- West is the declarer.

The Play

- North leads the ♣Q.
- Declarer needs 10 tricks, but has only four sure tricks.
- Declarer can develop the extra tricks in spades (four) and hearts (two).
- Declarer should play the spades first because that is the trump suit.
- If declarer plays the other suits first, declarer's winners may be ruffed by the opponents.
- Declarer should make the contract.

Exercise Nine — High Card from the Short Side

(E-Z Deal Cards: #3, Deal 3 — Dealer, South)

Turn up all of the cards on the third pre-dealt deal and arrange them as in the previous exercise.

The Bidding

South is the dealer. Who would open the bidding? What would the opening bid be?

Look at responder's hand. At what level should the contract be played? In what strain should the contract be played? What would the response be? What is the bidding message given by responder's bid? What would opener do? What would the contract be? Who would be the declarer?

```
Dealer:          ♠ 7 6 2
South            ♥ 8 7
                 ♦ K J 10 6 3
                 ♣ A 4 2
♠ Q J 10 8                ♠ 9 4
♥ K 10 3          N       ♥ Q J 9 5
♦ A 2         W     E     ♦ 9 8 7 4
♣ 10 8 5 3        S       ♣ Q 9 7
                 ♠ A K 5 3
                 ♥ A 6 4 2
                 ♦ Q 5
                 ♣ K J 6
```

The Play

Who would make the opening lead? What would the opening lead be?

How many tricks must declarer take to fulfill the contract? How many sure tricks does declarer have? How can declarer develop the tricks needed to make the contract? Which suit should declarer play after winning the first trick? Which card should declarer play first in the suit? Why? What might happen if declarer played the suit differently?

Bid and play the deal. Did declarer make the contract?

Exercise Nine *Answers* — High Card from the Short Side

The Bidding

- South opens the bidding with 1NT.
- Maybe the contract should be a game.
- The strain would be notrump.
- The response would be 2NT.
- Responder makes an invitational bid.
- Opener holding 17 HCP — the maximum 1NT range — would bid again.
- The contract would be 3NT.
- South is the declarer.

The Play

- West makes the opening lead.
- West leads the ♠Q.
- Declarer needs nine tricks and has five sure tricks.
- The extra tricks can be developed in diamonds.
- Diamonds should be played after winning the first trick.
- Declarer should play the ♦Q first — the high card from the short side.
- If declarer plays the suit differently, declarer may not be able to get to the dummy to enjoy the diamond winners.
- Declarer should make the contract.

Exercise Ten — Patience when Promoting

(E-Z Deal Cards: #3, Deal 4 — Dealer, West)

Turn up all of the cards on the fourth pre-dealt deal and arrange them as in the previous exercise.

The Bidding

West is the dealer. Who would open the bidding? What would the opening bid be?

Look at responder's hand. At what level should the contract be played? In what strain should the contract be played? What would the response be? What is the bidding message given by responder's bid? What would opener do? What would the contract be? Who would be the declarer?

```
Dealer:        ♠ 7 4 3
West           ♥ 8 7 3
               ♦ K 2
               ♣ K Q J 10 8
♠ A K 5 2              ♠ 9 6
♥ K Q J         N      ♥ 6 5 4
♦ 8 4        W     E   ♦ Q J 10 9 7 6
♣ A 9 3 2         S    ♣ 6 4
               ♠ Q J 10 8
               ♥ A 10 9 2
               ♦ A 5 3
               ♣ 7 5
```

The Play

Who would make the opening lead? What would the opening lead be?

How many tricks must declarer take to fulfill the contract? How many sure tricks does declarer have? How can declarer develop the tricks needed to make the contract? Which suit should declarer play after winning the first trick? How often will declarer have to give up the lead before developing sure tricks in the suit?

Would it be better to play the hand in a notrump contract? If not, why not?

Bid and play the deal. Did declarer make the contract?

Exercise Ten *Answers* — Patience when Promoting

The Bidding

- West opens the bidding with 1NT.
- The level of the contract should be a partscore.
- The strain should be diamonds.
- The response is 2♦.
- Responder gives a sign-off bid.
- Opener must pass.
- The contract would be 2♦.
- East is the declarer.

The Play

- South makes the opening lead.
- South leads the ♠Q.
- Declarer needs to take eight tricks to fulfill the contract.
- Declarer has three sure tricks.
- The extra tricks can be developed in diamonds, the trump suit, and the heart suit.
- After winning the first trick, declarer plays diamonds.
- Declarer will have to give up the lead two times before developing sure tricks in the diamond suit. Declarer should then work to develop the extra trick in hearts.
- Diamonds will play better than notrump because there isn't enough protection in the other suits. Declarer would lose too many tricks in notrump.
- Declarer should make the contract.

CHAPTER 4
Responses to Opening Bids of One in a Suit

Responder's General Approach

Responder's Decision with 0 to 5 Total Points

Responder's Decision with 6 to 9 Total Points

Responding to a Major Suit

Responder's Decision with 10 or 11 Total Points

Responder's Decision with 12 or More Total Points

Guidelines for Play

Summary

The Finer Points

Exercises

Sample Deals

RESPONDER'S GENERAL APPROACH

When partner has opened the bidding with one of a suit and the next hand passes, you are the responder and it is your turn to bid

This chapter will help you decide what to bid (if at all), keeping in mind what your partnership is trying to accomplish:

1. To discover which trump suit (if any) would be best.

2. To discover the combined strength of the two hands to determine the level of the final contract.

When the opening bid is one of a suit, opener could have anywhere from 13 to 21 total points, balanced or unbalanced. Before deciding the best place to play the contract, responder needs more information from opener. The more responder knows about the opener's hand, the easier it will be to select the best strain and level for the contract. While most of responder's bids are considered forcing (waiting for opener to give a more specific description of the hand), there are three types of bidding messages the responder can give to the opener.

Responder's Use of the Bidding Messages

Sign-off Bid: After an opening bid of one in a suit, the only sign-off bid a responder can make holding a very weak hand (0 to 5 total points) is pass. There is no likelihood of a game contract. Responder doesn't know enough about opener's strength and distribution to be able to make a decision about the level and strain of the contract. In addition, responder doesn't hold enough points to ask opener to further describe the hand.

Invitational Bid: With a minimum hand (6 to 9 total points), responder may want to make an invitational bid. This would give opener a chance to bid again or accept the option to pass. When responder makes an invitational bid, responder must be willing to play at the level and the strain of that bid because opener may pass. Responder can make an invitational bid (1) by showing support for opener's suit at the cheapest available level or (2) by bidding notrump at the cheapest available level.

Forcing Bid: Most of the time, responder makes a forcing bid. Responder usually wants more information from opener. Responder does this by bidding a new suit. With a minimum hand, 6 to 9 total points, responder can afford to bid a new suit only at the one level. With a stronger hand (10 or more total points), responder can afford to bid a new suit at the two level.

How Responder Categorizes Strength

As responder, you put your hand into one of four categories according to its total point value:

$$0 \quad \text{to} \quad 5$$
$$6 \quad \text{to} \quad 9$$
$$10 \quad \text{or} \quad 11$$
$$12 \quad \text{or} \quad \text{more}$$

Once you have categorized your strength, we'll see how you go about steering the partnership to the appropriate level and strain when you hold each of these point ranges.

Roles of the Partners

Opener is the describer and the responder is the captain. The conversation works best when opener paints a picture for responder and responder makes the decision. Responder's bids are designed to get more information from the opener, so responder can make an appropriate decision.

RESPONDER'S DECISION WITH 0 TO 5 TOTAL POINTS

What Level?

When responder has 0 to 5 total points, the contract will be a partscore. Opener shows from 13 to 21 total points, so there is only a remote chance (if opener has specifically 20 or 21 points) that the partnership has 25 combined points.

What Strain?

After an opening bid of one of a suit — a new suit by responder is forcing, not sign-off. This means that even with a long suit, responder should pass with 0 to 5 points and leave opener to play the contract in the suit opener bid. After all, opener's suit could be as long as or longer than responder's suit. Responder has no bidding room to find out without getting the partnership too high. Remember the only sign-off bid with 0–5 total points is pass.

Put It All Together

> **When responding to an opening bid of one in a suit with 0 to 5 points:**
> • Pass.

Let's look at an example. Your partner opens the bidding 1 ♥, and you have the following hand:

♠ J 9 8 5 3 2   Even though you have six spades, pass. A new-suit
♥ 5 2   bid by responder is forcing, and opener would bid
♦ 9 5 4   again. This probably would get the partnership too
♣ 8 2   high.

RESPONDER'S DECISION WITH 6 TO 9 TOTAL POINTS

What Level?

Until responder has more information from opener, the level is unknown. Opener has from 13 to 21 total points; responder has from 6 to 9 total points. Even if responder has a minimum response, there is still a chance for the game bonus if opener has the top range for an opening bid at the one level. On the other hand, even if responder has the top of the range, there will not be enough combined strength for game if opener has a minimum hand.

Responder must keep the auction going when holding 6 to 9 total points in case there is a game. Responder can't afford to get the partnership too high until more is known about opener's hand.

What Strain?

The main priority when searching for the right strain is to uncover a major-suit Golden Fit if one exists. A suit contract is usually better than notrump when there is a major-suit Golden Fit.

When opener starts the bidding with 1♥ or 1♠, responder knows opener has a hand with at least five cards in the major suit and from 13 to 21 total points. To be sure there is a Golden Fit, responder needs at least three cards in opener's major. With three or more cards in opener's major, responder raises, or *supports*, the major suit. For example, if partner opens 1♥, responder could raise to 2♥ to show a Golden Fit. The level to which responder raises depends on the strength of responder's hand.

When opener starts the bidding with 1♣ or 1♦, responder knows that opener has at least three cards in the minor suit and from 13 to 21 total points. Responder should not raise a minor-suit opening bid with fewer than four-card support. Five-card support is preferred so that an eight-card fit is guaranteed. Opener could have four cards in a major suit, however, and since finding a Golden Fit in a major suit is important, responder must look for one before raising opener's minor. In fact, raising a minor-suit opening bid should be seen as a low priority. Responder should try to bid a major suit or notrump in preference to raising a minor.

Because of the difference involved when responding to opening bids of one of a major suit and one of a minor suit, we will look at the two cases separately.

RESPONDING TO A MAJOR SUIT

Dummy Points

Suppose your partner is the dealer, and this is your hand:

♠ —
♥ J 7 5 3
♦ K 9 6 4 2
♣ 10 8 6 3

If partner opens 1 ♠, your hand is not as valuable as it would be if partner opened 1 ♥. Valuing your hand with *dummy points,* also called *short-suit points,* takes this into consideration. If hearts are trump, the void in the spade suit is very useful. The void is more useful than the ♠A would be. Having a singleton or a doubleton is also an advantage after you have discovered a Golden Fit.

When counting dummy points, value your distribution as follows:

DUMMY POINTS

Void	5 Points
Singleton	3 Points
Doubleton	1 Point

Use dummy points instead of distribution points for length when raising partner's major suit. By adding your high-card points and dummy points, you arrive at a total point count value for your responding hand.

Let's see how this is done.

Partner opens the bidding 1 ♥, and you hold the following hand:

	High-card Points	Dummy Points	Total Points
♠ —	0	5	5
♥ J 7 5 3	1	0	1
♦ K 9 6 4 2	3	0	3
♣ 10 8 6 3	0	0	0
	4	5	9

Once you see that your hand is suitable for a raise of partner's major, value your hand using dummy points before deciding what response to make.

RESPONDING TO A MAJOR SUIT WITH 6 TO 9 TOTAL POINTS

When your partner opens 1 ♥ or 1 ♠ and you have 6 to 9 total points, you have three choices in order of priority.

The First Choice

Your first priority with three or more cards in partner's major is to raise or support partner's major. With only 6 to 9 total points, raise to the cheapest level, the two level. This is an invitational bid. If opener has a minimum hand, opener will pass. With additional strength, opener may bid again.

For example, your partner opens 1 ♥, and you have the following hand:

♠ 6 4	You know there is a Golden Fit in hearts since part-
♥ Q J 9	ner's opening bid shows at least five hearts. You
♦ 10 8 2	have 6 high-card points and 1 point for the doubleton
♣ K 8 7 5 3	in spades, a total of 7 points. Raise to the cheapest
	level, 2 ♥.

The Second Choice

If you don't have support for partner's major suit, you may bid a new suit — but only at the one level, since your hand is minimum (6 to 9 total points). If partner has opened the bidding 1 ♥, the only suit you can bid at the one level is spades. If partner has opened 1 ♠, you won't be able to bid a new suit at the one level.

To bid a new suit at the one level, you need a four-card or longer suit. Let's look at an example. Your partner opens the bidding 1 ♥, and you have the following hand:

♠ J 9 7 3   Your first choice is to support partner's hearts if you
♥ Q 7   can, but you have only two hearts. Your next choice
♦ A 6 4 3 2   is to bid a new suit at the one level. With a four-card
♣ 10 6   spade suit, you can bid 1 ♠. This is a forcing bid and
               opener will bid again.

The Third Choice

If you can't support partner's major and you can't bid a new suit at the one level, your only remaining option is to bid 1NT. It shows a hand with 6 to 9 total points with which you are unable to raise partner's major or bid a new suit at the one level.

This 1NT response *does not* promise a balanced hand. The 1NT response sends opener the message that the responder has enough total points to keep the bidding going, but no other bid to make.

For example, your partner opens the bidding 1 ♠, and you have the following hand:

♠ 10 5   You can't support spades or bid a new suit at the one
♥ J 8 6 5 3 2 level. The hearts are attractive, but you don't have
♦ A 7   enough strength to bid a new suit at the two level.
♣ 6 3 2   The only choice left is 1NT. Unlike an opening bid
               of 1NT, a response of 1NT does not describe a bal-
anced hand. Instead, it shows a minimum hand of 6 to 9 total points.

Put It All Together

> ### Rules for responding to a major-suit opening bid with 6 to 9 total points
> - Raise partner's major suit to the two level with at least three-card support.
> - Bid a new suit at the one level.
> - Bid 1NT.

Let's look at some examples. Your partner opens the bidding 1 ♥, and you hold the following:

♠ 10 9 7 3
♥ Q J
♦ A 7 3
♣ J 10 6 3

You can't support hearts since you have only two hearts. Your second choice, bidding a new suit at the one level, is possible because you have a four-card spade suit. Respond 1 ♠.

♠ 7 5 4
♥ K 6
♦ Q J 9 8 6 4
♣ J 8

You don't have the requirements to either support partner's heart suit or bid a new suit at the one level. You have an attractive-looking diamond suit, but you may not bid it at the one level. With only 9 total points, respond 1NT.

♠ A 9 8 7
♥ K 6 3 2
♦ 9 8 6
♣ 10 3

You could bid a new suit at the one level, but your first priority is to support partner's major. With 7 high-card points and 1 point for the doubleton club, bid 2 ♥, telling partner there is a Golden Fit.

RESPONDING TO A MINOR SUIT WITH 6 TO 9 TOTAL POINTS

The First Choice

The priorities in bidding revolve around uncovering a Golden Fit in a major suit — at the partscore or game level. This priority guides your thinking after an opening bid in a minor suit. Suppose your partner opens 1♦ and you have the following hand:

♠ K 7 6 3
♥ 8 5
♦ J 7 6 5 3
♣ A 2

You have diamond support, but supporting partner's minor suit is not a priority. You can afford to bid a new suit at the one level, and you have a four-card major suit. Bid 1♠. This keeps the search for a major suit open. Since a new-suit bid by responder is forcing, opener must bid again. Thus, you will still have an opportunity to support diamonds if you can't find a fit in a major suit.

In summary, when your partner starts the bidding with 1♣ or 1♦, your first priority is to bid a new suit at the one level if you can. If you have a choice of suits, there are guidelines:

> • Bid your longest suit.
> • Bid the higher-ranking of two five-card suits.
> • Bid the lower-ranking of two four-card suits.

Your partner opens 1♣. What do you do with the following hands?

♠ Q 8 6 5 3
♥ A 8 7 4
♦ J 7
♣ 6 3

You have two suits that you could bid at the one level. In this case, you bid the longer suit, 1♠.

♠ 8
♥ K 10 8 5 2
♦ A 7 5 4 2
♣ 5 4

With a choice of two five-card suits to bid at the one level, bid the higher-ranking. Respond 1♥.

♠ J 8 6 4
♥ A 9 7 6
♦ K 2
♣ 10 9 5

With a choice of two four-card suits to bid at the one level, bid the lower-ranking. Respond 1♥.

The Second Choice

If you can't bid a new suit at the one level, your second priority is to bid 1NT. It shows 6 to 9 total points. It tells partner that you can't bid a new suit at the one level.

For example, partner opens 1♦ and you have the following hand:

♠ K 7 6
♥ Q 8 2
♦ J 5
♣ Q 9 6 4 2

You don't have a four-card or longer suit to bid at the one level, and you have stoppers in the other suits. Your hand looks like notrump, so bid it. Respond 1NT.

The Third Choice

If you can't bid a new suit at the one level, and your hand isn't suited for a 1NT bid, your third choice is to support your partner's minor suit. Remember that partner may have only three cards in the suit when opening with a minor. You should *prefer* to have five-card support when you raise to the two level.

For example, your partner opens 1♦ and you have the following hand:

♠ 8 3
♥ K 9 7
♦ Q 10 8 7 4
♣ K J 3

You don't have a four-card or longer suit to bid at the one level. You don't have a stopper in spades, so you prefer not to bid notrump. However, you do have five cards in partner's minor suit. Bid 2♦.

Put It All Together

> ### Rule for responding to a minor-suit opening bid with 6 to 9 total points
>
> - Bid a new suit at the one level.
> - Bid 1NT.
> - Raise partner's minor suit.

    You can see that the priorities are different than those for responding to a major suit. Also, to raise a major suit to the two level, you need only three cards in the suit; to raise a minor suit to the two level, you prefer five. Remember that raising a minor-suit opening bid should be seen as a low priority for responder. Responder should try to bid a major suit or notrump in preference to raising a minor.

    Here are examples after partner opens 1♣:

♠ 9 8 6 5
♥ Q 10 8 6 3
♦ K 5
♣ Q 6

Your first priority is to bid a new suit at the one level if you can. With a choice of suits, bid your longer suit, 1 ♥.

♠ K 9 3
♥ Q 10 8
♦ A 10 2
♣ 7 5 4 2

With no suit to bid at the one level, bid 1NT.

♠ 8 5
♥ Q J 7
♦ J 9 3
♣ K 10 8 7 3

You can't bid a new suit at the one level and your hand is not suitable for notrump (no spade stopper). With five-card support for partner's suit, move to your third choice and raise to 2♣.

RESPONDER'S DECISION WITH 10 OR 11 TOTAL POINTS

With 10 or 11 total points, responder knows the partnership has at least 23 (10 + 13 = 23) points and is close to the strength required for game. Responder's first priority is to support opener's major suit. If responder can't support opener's major, responder can bid a new suit — at the two level if necessary.

Partner Opens a Major Suit

Suppose opener bids 1 ♠, and responder has the following hand:

♠ 9 8 7 3   With support for opener's major suit, responder
♥ K 6   values the hand using dummy points. There are 10
♦ Q J 10 4   HCP plus 1 point for the doubleton heart. With 11
♣ A 9 4   total points, responder can bid 3 ♠. This is an invitational bid. It tells opener three things: responder has support for opener's suit, responder is too strong to raise to 2 ♠ (6 to 9 total points) and responder is not strong enough to commit the partnership to game. If opener has a minimum hand of 13 total points, opener should pass and play in the partscore. With more, opener can bid on to game.

Suppose opener bids 1 ♠, and responder holds this hand:

♠ 7 3   Responder can't support opener's major but does
♥ A Q 9 8 3   have a suit that is biddable. With 11 total points,
♦ 10 6 3   responder has enough strength to bid at the two
♣ K J 10   level and may respond 2 ♥. Because responder has not previously passed and 2 ♥ is a new-suit bid, it's forcing and opener will have to bid again.

Partner Opens a Minor Suit

If opener bids a minor suit, responder's priority is still to look for a major suit. Responder will bid a four-card or longer major suit rather than bid notrump or raise opener's minor suit.

For example, suppose the opening bid is 1 ♦, and responder holds the following hand:

♠ J 9 7 5	Responder bids a new suit, 1 ♠, and waits to hear a
♥ J 4	further description of opener's hand. If there is no
♦ Q 10 8 5 3	Golden Fit in spades, responder will show diamond
♣ A Q	support at the next opportunity. Bidding notrump

with this hand is not acceptable because of the questionable heart stopper. Responder should rebid by raising diamonds to the three level to show 10 or 11 total points, inviting opener to bid game in notrump with more than 13 total points or game in the minor with 18 or more total points.

If responder doesn't have a new suit to bid, responder can raise opener's minor suit to the three level with 10 or 11 total points, inviting opener to bid game in notrump with more than 13 total points or game in the minor with 18 or more total points.

For example, suppose the opening bid is 1 ♣, and responder has the following hand:

♠ 9 6	Responder raises opener's suit to the three level, 3 ♣,
♥ 7 4 2	to show 10 or 11 total points and to invite opener to
♦ A J 7	bid game in notrump with more than 13 total points,
♣ K Q 9 7 5	or game in the minor with 18 or more total points.

RESPONDER'S DECISION WITH 12 OR MORE TOTAL POINTS

What Level?

When responder has at least 12 points, responder knows there are enough points for a game contract. As captain, responder must make sure the partnership doesn't stop below the level of game. If responder bids below the level of game, the bid must be a forcing bid.

Since responder raises opener's major to the two level with 6 to 9 total points and to the three level with 10 or 11 total points, it would seem natural to raise to the four level when responder has support and 12 or more total points. While this is the most natural approach, it uses up a lot of room on the Bidding Scale. Opener has little opportunity to finish describing the hand. This can be important when opener is interested in reaching a slam contract, for which there is a big bonus. The more modern approach is for responder to bid a new suit first and show support for opener's suit at responder's next opportunity to call. (Actually, the immediate raise to the game level is made with a very special kind of hand. Check The Finer Points in this chapter to learn more.)

Partner Opens a Major Suit

Opposite an opening bid of one of a major, responder has three choices with 12 or more total points:

- With a balanced hand, bid 2NT with 13–15 HCP.

- With a balanced hand, bid 3NT with 16–18 HCP.
  When making the suggestion of a notrump game to the opener, the responder should evaluate the hand using high-card points. Remember when there is no trump suit, you need to have enough high cards to take the required number of tricks. This is different when responding 1NT to an opening bid. The 1NT response to an opening bid is more of a denial bid than a suggestion of notrump as a good strain for the contract. Showing the differences between the points in responder's hand will allow the partnership to more accurately evaluate slam possibilities.

- Bid a new suit.

With 12 or more total points, responder makes forcing bids until game is reached.

Let's look at some examples in response to a 1 ♠ opening bid:

♠ Q 10   With 14 HCP points and a balanced hand, responder
♥ K J 10   can bid 2NT. This is a forcing bid.
♦ A K 5 4
♣ J 10 6 3

♠ 3
♥ A 3
♦ A K J 9 7 4
♣ Q 10 8 3

Responder doesn't have a balanced hand and bids a new suit, 2♦. After hearing opener's next bid, responder will be in a better position to decide on the strain and level of the contract.

♠ Q J 9 3
♥ 8 7
♦ A J 9 8
♣ A Q 3

With 15 total points, counting 1 point for the doubleton heart, responder could support opener's spades, but 15 total points is too much to raise to the three level. A raise to the four level wouldn't leave the partnership much room to explore the possibility for a slam contract. Instead, responder bids a new suit, 2♦, giving opener the opportunity to further describe the hand. Responder will show spade support by jumping to game at the next opportunity to call.

Partner Opens a Minor Suit

Responder's first priority is to bid a new suit, a major if possible, looking for a Golden Fit. With 12 or more total points, responder has enough strength to explore.

Responder has the following choices.

- Bid a new suit, a major if possible.
- With a balanced hand, bid 2NT with 13–15 HCP.
- With a balanced hand, bid 3NT with 16–18 HCP.

All of responder's bids under game are forcing. Let's look at some examples in response to an opening bid of 1♦:

♠ A Q 8 7
♥ K 3
♦ K J 9 5 2
♣ 7 5

Responder could support opener's diamonds. Looking for a Golden Fit in a major, however, takes priority. Responder should bid a new suit, preferring a major if one is available. Bid 1♠.

♠ A J 10
♥ K J 9
♦ K 10 7 3
♣ Q 9 6

With no new suit to bid and a balanced hand, responder bids 2NT with this 14-HCP hand. This is a forcing bid, and opener may not pass.

GUIDELINES FOR PLAY

Declarer often needs to *Analyze the alternatives* to develop additional tricks in order to make the contract. As we saw in the previous chapter, one method for developing extra tricks is through the promotion of high cards. Another common technique makes use of the power of long suits.

Developing Tricks through Length

Each suit contains 13 cards. The more cards your side has in a suit, the fewer the opponents have. After a suit has been led a couple of times, it is possible that the opponents will have no cards remaining in the suit. In that case, whenever the opponents are out of trumps or the contract is notrump, any remaining cards you have in the suit will be sure tricks, even if they are low cards. Let's look at some examples.

DUMMY: 7 6 4 3
DECLARER: A K Q J 2

You have nine cards and the opponents have four (13 − 9 = 4). Even if one opponent has all four of the missing cards, that opponent will not have any left after you play the ace, the king, the queen and the jack. The 2 will be a sure trick, and you will take five tricks in the suit.

DUMMY: 5 4 3 2
DECLARER: A K Q 6

You have eight cards and the opponents have five (13 − 8 = 5). When you play the ace, the king and the queen, the remaining card, the 6, will be a sure trick if one of the opponents started with three cards and the other with two cards in the suit. If one opponent started with four or five cards, the 6 will not be a winning trick.

DUMMY: 5 4 3 2
DECLARER: A K 7 6

You have eight cards. The best you can hope for is that one opponent has three and the other has two. In that case, you play the ace and the king and lead the suit again, giving up a trick to the opponents' remaining high card. The remaining card will have become a winning trick.

DUMMY: 9 5 3

DECLARER: A 8 6 4 2

It is possible to develop two additional tricks if the opponents' cards are divided three and two. Play the ace and lead the suit a second time, losing a trick to the opponents. After regaining the lead, give up another trick to the opponents. Both of your remaining cards will have become sure tricks. Remember to maintain your high cards in the side suits for entries while establishing your long suit. With few or no entries in the side suits, declarer may preserve the ace in the long suit as an entry by losing two tricks first and playing the ace on the third lead of the suit.

Giving Up the Lead

As the last couple of examples show, you often have to give one or more tricks to the opponents when developing additional tricks through length. This is not a problem, provided the opponents can't take enough tricks to defeat your contract when they get the lead. Also, you must have sure tricks in other suits. You will need to regain the lead in order to play the winners you have developed.

This is similar to the situation we saw in the last chapter when you were promoting high cards. You want to keep your sure tricks in other suits whenever possible while developing the extra tricks you need. Once again, the guideline *take your losses early* is useful when developing tricks.

Distribution of the Opponents' Cards

When developing tricks through length, the way in which the missing cards are distributed in the opponents' hands can be very important. For example, if you are missing five cards, you may have to hope that the missing cards are divided favorably: three in one hand and two in the other. This is called a 3–2 *break* or *split*.

Sometimes the opponents' cards will break unfavorably. For example, five missing cards could break 4–1 or 5–0. As you play the suit, you should watch to see how the missing cards are divided. In general, an odd number of missing cards will usually divide as evenly as possible. An even number of missing cards will usually divide slightly unevenly. You can see this in the following table:

Number of Missing Cards	Most Likely Distribution
3	2–1
4	3–1
5	3–2
6	4–2
7	4–3
8	5–3

Here are examples:

DUMMY: 6 4 2

DECLARER: A K Q 3

You are missing six cards. The most likely distribution of the opponents' cards is 4–2. After you play the ace, the king, and the queen, the 3 will not be a sure trick unless you are lucky and the opponents' cards break 3–3.

DUMMY: A K 7 4 2

DECLARER: 6 5 3

You normally can expect to take four tricks with this suit. After you play the ace and the king, you can give up a trick. (High cards in the side suits will be needed for entries.) The remaining cards will be winners if the opponents' cards break 3–2. If the opponents' cards break 4–1, you will have to give up two tricks, and you will end up with only three tricks. If the suit breaks 5–0 — too bad!

SUMMARY

Responses to Opening Bids of One of a Suit

0 to 5*   Responding to a major or a minor suit
- Pass.

6 to 9*   Responding to a major suit
- Raise to the two level with three-card or longer support.
- Bid a new suit at the one level.
- Bid 1NT.

Responding to a minor suit
- Bid a new suit at the one level.
- Bid 1NT.
- Raise to the two level with preferably five-card or longer support.

10 or 11*   Responding to a major suit
- Raise to the three level with three-card or longer support.
- Bid a new suit.

Responding to a minor suit
- Bid a new suit.
- Raise to the three level with five-card or longer support.

12 or more* Responding to a major suit
- Bid 2NT with a balanced hand and 13–15 HCP.
- Bid 3NT with a balanced hand and 16–18 HCP.
- Bid a new suit.

Responding to a minor suit
- Bid a new suit.
- Bid 2NT with a balanced hand and 13–15 HCP.
- Bid 3NT with a balanced hand and 16–18 HCP.

One way to develop additional tricks is to take advantage of your long suits. If the missing cards in the opponents' hands are distributed favorably, you often can develop tricks by continuing to play the suit, even if you have to give up one or more tricks to the opponents.

total points

THE FINER POINTS

Dummy Points when Raising Partner's Minor Suit

Because 5 ♣ and 5 ♦ are not Golden Games, the partnership will usually play in 3NT with 25 or more combined points. In a notrump contract, a short suit is a disadvantage rather than an advantage. This explains why responder uses high-card points when suggesting a notrump contract at the game level. The partnership does not want to reach 3NT with only 25 points when some of the points come from valuing short suits.

If the partnership is not headed for a notrump contract, however, dummy points can be used when supporting partner's minor suit. This is the case in these situations: when the partnership is going to play in a partscore contract in a minor suit, when the partnership is going to play game in a minor suit because the combined hands are not suited for notrump and when the partnership is going to play a slam contract in a minor suit.

Raising Partner's Suit — Forcing Raises

When responder has support for partner's suit, the text recommends the following framework based on the total value of responder's hand:

0 to 5		Pass.
6 to 9		Raise to the two level.
10 or 11		Raise to the three level.
12 or more		Bid a new suit, intending to raise partner's suit later.

A popular style in many areas is to reverse the last two actions, so the framework becomes:

0 to 5		Pass.
6 to 9		Raise to the two level.
10 or 11		Bid a new suit, intending to raise partner's suit later.
12 or more		Raise to the three level.

The major difference is in the message given by the immediate raise to the three level. In the first framework, the raise to the three level is only an invitational (yellow) bid. Since responder is limited to at most

11 points, opener doesn't need to carry on with only a minimum opening bid. This style is referred to as a *limit raise*.

In the second framework, responder says that there is enough combined strength for a game contract. This is a forcing (green) bid, and opener must bid again. This style is referred to as a *forcing (jump) raise*.

The choice of styles is a matter of partnership preference. Each has advantages and disadvantages. While the text is consistent with the more modern approach of limit raises, it is simple to adapt to the style that is popular in your area or that your partner prefers.

Even within the two frameworks, there are many possible variations. Most authorities recommend that responder always have four-card support when raising to the three level. Others give special meanings to certain responses to fill out the framework. Such special conventions and treatments are not recommended for new players.

In addition, it is not uncommon to use a slightly different point range for responder's responses. The most common responses when opener bids one of a major is:

0	to	5	Pass.
6	to	10	Raise to the two level.
11	to	12	Raise to the three level.
13	or	more	Bid a new suit, intending to raise partner's suit later.

If you wish to use these ranges, just be aware of the bidding messages you are sending to partner on the way to deciding the level and strain of the final contract.

It might seem that the simplest framework for raising opener's suit is the following:

0	to	5	Pass.
6	to	9	Raise to the two level.
10	or	11	Raise to the three level.
12	or	more	Raise to the four level.

This is certainly a playable system, but the classic use of the raise to the four level is as a preemptive bid, showing fewer than 9 points and at least five-card support. Preemptive bids are discussed briefly in the

Appendix but are beyond the scope of this text.

When to Respond 2NT

With no support for opener's suit and 13 to 15 HCP, responder has two options. Responder can bid a new suit or bid 2NT. With an unbalanced hand, responder always bids a new suit. With a balanced hand, responder has a choice. For example, if the opening bid is 1 ♥, does responder bid 2NT or a new suit (2♣) with this hand?

> ♠ A J 3
> ♥ 10 5
> ♦ K 9 7 5
> ♣ A K 10 3

Responder can use the following guidelines:

- With a five-card suit, bid the suit.
- With a four-card suit, bid the suit if it can be bid at the one level.
- Otherwise, bid 2NT.

Thus, on the above hand, responder would bid 2NT.

Responder's Jump Shift

When responder bids a new suit, the text indicates that responder always bids it at the cheapest available level. With very strong hands, usually 17 or more points, responder can show the extra strength by jumping a level. Since responder is changing (shifting) the suit and jumping a level, this is referred to as a *jump shift*. For example, in response to an opening bid of 1 ♥, responder could jump shift by bidding 2♠, 3♣ or 3 ♦. The jump shift is a forcing (green) bid. It tells opener that the partnership belongs at least at the game level and likely at the slam level.

A jump shift occurs rarely, and, since a new suit by responder is forcing even when responder does not jump, it is not needed even when responder has a powerful hand. However, in the next chapter, you will see that opener often makes use of the jump shift to show a powerful opening bid.

Exercise One — Responding to a Major-Suit Opening with 6 to 9 Total Points

Partner opens the bidding 1 ♥. Add up the high-card points and the dummy or distribution points on each of the following hands, and decide what you would respond.

1)	♠ 3	2)	♠ J 10 7 6	3)	♠ K 3 2
	♥ Q J 10		♥ Q 3		♥ J 10
	♦ Q 8 7 6 2		♦ K Q 8 7 4		♦ Q J 9 6 4
	♣ J 10 9 8		♣ 9 6		♣ 5 3 2

HCP:_____   HCP: _____   HCP: _____

Dummy   Dummy   Dummy
Distr. Pts: _____   Distr. Pts: _____   Distr. Pts:_____

Total Pts: _____   Total Pts:_____   Total Pts: _____

What do all three hands have in common? _____

For which of the three hands do you count dummy points?_____

Exercise Two — Priorities when Responding with 6 to 9 Total Points

If partner opens the bidding with one of a major, you have three choices with 6 to 9 total points. Arrange the following choices in order of their priority:

1) a) Bid 1NT.
   b) Bid a new suit at the one level.
   c) Raise partner's major suit to the two level.

If partner opens the bidding with one of a minor suit, your priorities change. Arrange the following choices in order of their priority:

2) a) Raise partner's minor suit to the two level.
   b) Bid a new suit at the one level.
   c) Bid 1NT.

Exercise One *Answers* — Responding to a Major-Suit Opening with 6 to 9 Total Points

1) 6 HCP   3 dummy points   9 total points   2♥
2) 8 HCP   1 distribution point   9 total points   1♠
3) 7 HCP   1 distribution point   8 total points   1NT

- All three hands fall in the 6 to 9 point range.
- Count dummy points for the first hand because you can support partner's major suit.

Exercise Two *Answers* — Priorities when Responding with 6 to 9 Total Points

1) c) Raise partner's major suit to the two level with at least three-card support.
   b) Bid a new suit at the one level.
   a) Bid 1NT.

2) b) Bid a new suit at the one level.
   c) Bid 1NT.
   a) Raise partner's minor suit to the two level with at least five-card support.

Exercise Three — Responding to a Minor-Suit Opening with 6 to 9 Total Points

Your partner opens the bidding 1 ♦ . What would you respond with each of the following hands?

1) ♠ 9 8 4 2
   ♥ Q 8 7
   ♦ K J 4 3
   ♣ J 3

   _____

2) ♠ J 10
   ♥ J 4 3
   ♦ Q 9 8
   ♣ K 9 7 5 3

   _____

3) ♠ 9 5 3
   ♥ Q J 10 8 7
   ♦ Q 6
   ♣ J 5 3

   _____

Exercise Four — Responding with 10 or 11 Total Points

Your partner opens the bidding with 1 ♠. What would you respond with each of the following hands?

1) ♠ 10 9
   ♥ A Q J 6 5
   ♦ K 4
   ♣ 8 6 4 3

   _____

2) ♠ J 9 8 4
   ♥ K Q
   ♦ J 6 3
   ♣ K 10 7 5

   _____

3) ♠ 8
   ♥ 10 6 3
   ♦ Q J 10 8 6
   ♣ A Q J 9

   _____

It is important to remember the roles of each player. What role does the responder have?_____

What will the opener do on the next bid? _____

Exercise Three *Answers* — Responding to a Minor-Suit Opening with 6 to 9 Total Points

1) 1♠   2) 1NT   3) 1♥

Exercise Four *Answers* — Responding with 10 or 11 Total Points

With 10 or 11 total points, responder raises partner's major with three-card or longer support; otherwise, responder bids a new suit.

1) 2♥   2) 3♠   3) 2♦

- Responder is the captain.
- Opener will further describe the hand on the next bid.

Exercise Five — Responding with 12 or More Total Points

If responder has 12 or more total points, what will the level of the contract be? _____

What bidding message will responder give with all responses?

_____

Your partner opens the bidding 1♠. What would you respond with each of the following hands?

1)	♠ A Q 8 3	2)	♠ J 7	3)	♠ 8
	♥ A 5		♥ K Q 10		♥ K 5 3
	♦ Q J 10 6		♦ A J 8 4		♦ A Q 10 8 6
	♣ 7 6 4		♣ K J 6 3		♣ K 9 6 3

_____   _____   _____

In the first example, how can responder be certain opener will not pass and leave the partnership to play in diamonds rather than spades?

_____

Exercise Six — Developing Tricks through Length

How many tricks can be developed with each of the following suit combinations if the opponents' cards are divided as favorably as possible?

DUMMY:	1) A 9 6 3	2) A 7 6 4 2	3) K 7 4	4) 7 4
DECLARER:	K 8 4 2	9 5 3	A Q 6 3	A K 8 6 5 2

_____   _____   _____   _____

Exercise Five *Answers* — Responding with 12 or More Total Points

- The level will be game.
- Responder will force opener to bid until game is reached.
- 1) 2♦   2) 2NT   3) 2♦
- A new suit by responder is a forcing bid, and opener must bid again.

Exercise Six *Answers* — Developing Tricks through Length

1) 3   2) 3   3) 4   4) 5

Exercise Seven — Developing Winners in Notrump

(E–Z Deal Cards: #4, Deal 1 — Dealer, North)

Turn up all of the cards on the first pre-dealt deal. Put each hand dummy style at the edge of the table in front of each player.

The Bidding

North is the dealer. Who would open the bidding? What would the opening bid be?

Look at responder's hand. Can responder support opener's suit? Can responder bid a new suit? What would responder bid? What is the bidding message given by responder's bid? Does opener have to bid again? If opener does not bid again, what will the contract be? Who will be the declarer?

```
Dealer:        ♠ 8 5 4
North          ♥ A 10 5
               ♦ 9 7 4
               ♣ A 9 5 2
 ♠ 7 6 2               ♠ Q J 10 9
 ♥ K Q 9 7    ┌─────┐   ♥ J 8 4 3
 ♦ Q J 10 8   │  N  │   ♦ K 3
 ♣ Q 10       │W   E│   ♣ J 8 4
              │  S  │
              └─────┘
               ♠ A K 3
               ♥ 6 2
               ♦ A 6 5 2
               ♣ K 7 6 3
```

The Play

Suppose that North is declarer in a contract of 1NT. Who would make the opening lead? What would the opening lead be?

How many tricks must declarer take to fulfill the contract? How many sure tricks does declarer have? Which suit provides declarer with the opportunity to develop the additional tricks needed to make the contract? Which suit should declarer play after winning the first trick? Why?

Bid and play the deal. Did declarer make the contract?

Exercise Seven *Answers* — Developing Winners in Notrump

The Bidding

- South opens the bidding with 1♦.
- Responder can't support opener's suit nor bid a new suit at the one level.
- The response would be 1NT and is invitational.
- Responder has 6 to 9 points and no four-card major.
- Opener does not have to bid again.
- The contract would be 1NT.
- North is the declarer.

The Play

- East makes the opening lead.
- The opening lead would be the ♠Q.
- Declarer needs seven tricks to fulfill the contract.
- Declarer has six sure tricks.
- The additional trick could be developed in clubs.
- Declarer should play clubs as quickly as possible after winning the first trick to develop the extra trick needed. Meanwhile, declarer keeps the winners in the other suits to prevent the opponents from taking tricks.
- Declarer should make the contract.

Exercise Eight — Developing Winners in the Trump Suit

(E–Z Deal Cards: #4, Deal 2 — Dealer, East)

Turn up all of the cards on the second pre-dealt deal and arrange them as in the previous exercise.

The Bidding

East is the dealer. Who would open the bidding? What would the opening bid be?

Look at responder's hand. Can responder support opener's suit? What is the value of responder's hand? What would responder bid? What is the bidding message given by responder's bid? Does opener have to bid again? If opener does not bid again, what will the contract be? Who will be the declarer?

	Dealer:	♠ K J
	East	♥ 9 8 7 5
		♦ Q J 10 9
		♣ K 7 6

♠ A 8 7 3 2		♠ 9 6 5 4
♥ A 6 4	N W E S	♥ K 3 2
♦ A 8		♦ K 7 6
♣ J 5 3		♣ 9 4 2

	♠ Q 10
	♥ Q J 10
	♦ 5 4 3 2
	♣ A Q 10 8

The Play

Suppose that West is declarer in a contract of 2 ♠. Who would make the opening lead? What would the opening lead be?

How many tricks must declarer take to fulfill the contract? How many sure tricks does declarer have? Which suit provides declarer with the opportunity to develop the additional tricks needed to make the contract? Which suit should declarer play after winning the first trick? Will declarer have to be lucky to make the contract? If so, why?

Bid and play the deal. Did declarer make the contract?

Exercise Eight *Answers* — Developing Winners in the Trump Suit

The Bidding

- The opening bid would be 1♠ by West.
- Responder can support opener's suit.
- The value of the hand is 6 points.
- Responder would bid 2♠.
- This is an invitational bid and opener doesn't have to bid again.
- The contract is 2♠ and West is the declarer.

The Play

- North makes the opening lead.
- The lead would be the ♦Q.
- Declarer needs to take eight tricks.
- Declarer has five sure tricks.
- The best opportunity to develop additional tricks is in the spade suit.
- After winning the first trick, declarer should play the spades.
- Declarer needs to be lucky to make the contract because declarer can afford to lose only one trick in the spade suit. The opponents' spades need to be divided 2–2.
- Declarer should make the contract.

Exercise Nine — Developing a Side Suit

(E–Z Deal Cards: #4, Deal 3 — Dealer, South)

Turn up all of the cards on the third pre-dealt deal and arrange them as in the previous exercise.

The Bidding

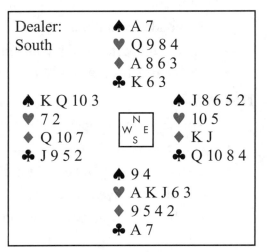

South is the dealer. Who would open the bidding? What would the opening bid be?

Look at responder's hand. What is the value of responder's hand? Although responder can support South's major, what would responder bid first to show the strength of the hand? What is the bidding message given by responder's bid? What would opener rebid? What would the final contract be, most likely? Who would be the declarer?

Dealer:	♠ A 7
South	♥ Q 9 8 4
	♦ A 8 6 3
	♣ K 6 3

♠ K Q 10 3   ♠ J 8 6 5 2
♥ 7 2   ♥ 10 5
♦ Q 10 7   ♦ K J
♣ J 9 5 2   ♣ Q 10 8 4

♠ 9 4
♥ A K J 6 3
♦ 9 5 4 2
♣ A 7

The Play

Suppose that South is declarer in a contract of 4 ♥. Who would make the opening lead? What would the opening lead be?

How many tricks must declarer take to fulfill the contract? How many sure tricks does declarer have? Which suit provides declarer with the opportunity to develop the additional tricks needed to make the contract? Which suit should declarer play after winning the first trick?

Bid and play the deal. Did declarer make the contract?

Exercise Nine *Answers* — Developing a Side Suit

The Bidding

- South opens the bidding with 1 ♥.
- The value of responder's hand is 14 total points — 1 point for the doubleton spade.
- Responder first bids 2 ♦.
- This bid is forcing.
- Opener would show support by raising to 3 ♦.
- The final contract would be 4 ♥ because responder puts the contract back into hearts.
- South is the declarer.

The Play

- West makes the opening lead.
- The lead would be the ♠ K.
- Declarer needs to take 10 tricks to make the contract.
- Declarer has nine sure tricks.
- The diamond suit provides the best chance for the extra trick.
- After winning the first trick, declarer should draw the trumps. That will take two rounds on this deal. Then, declarer goes about trying to get the extra trick in the diamond suit.
- Declarer should make the contract.

Exercise Ten — Patience when Developing a Long Suit

(E–Z Deal Cards: #4, Deal 4 — Dealer, West)

Turn up all the cards on the fourth pre-dealt deal and arrange them as in the previous exercise.

The Bidding

West is the dealer. Who would open the bidding? What would the opening bid be?

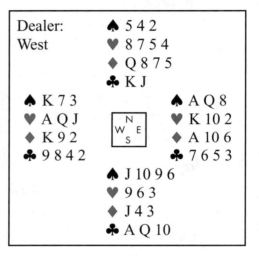

```
Dealer:          ♠ 5 4 2
West             ♥ 8 7 5 4
                 ♦ Q 8 7 5
                 ♣ K J
♠ K 7 3                        ♠ A Q 8
♥ A Q J          ┌─────┐       ♥ K 10 2
♦ K 9 2          │ N   │       ♦ A 10 6
♣ 9 8 4 2        │W   E│       ♣ 7 6 5 3
                 │  S  │
                 └─────┘
                 ♠ J 10 9 6
                 ♥ 9 6 3
                 ♦ J 4 3
                 ♣ A Q 10
```

Look at responder's hand. What is the value of responder's hand? Can responder support opener's suit? Can responder bid a new suit? What would responder bid? What is the bidding message given by responder's bid? Does opener have to bid again? If opener has to bid again, what would the contract be, most likely? Who would be the declarer?

The Play

Suppose that East is declarer in a contract of 3NT. Who would make the opening lead? What would the opening lead be?

How many tricks must declarer take to fulfill the contract? How many sure tricks does declarer have? Which suit provides declarer with the opportunity to develop the additional trick needed to make the contract? Which suit should declarer play after winning the first trick? What will have to happen for declarer to make the contract?

Bid and play the deal. Did declarer make the contract?

Exercise Ten *Answers* — Patience when Developing a Long Suit

The Bidding

- The opening bid would be 1♣ by West.
- Responder has 13 points.
- Responder can't support the opening minor suit because responder holds only four clubs and holds a hand suitable for notrump.
- Responder has no suit to show.
- Responder would bid 2NT.
- This is a forcing bid and opener must bid again.
- Opener is likely to continue on in notrump, making the contract 3NT with East as the declarer.

The Play

- South makes the opening lead.
- The lead would be the ♠J.
- Declarer needs to take nine tricks.
- Declarer has eight sure tricks.
- The club suit provides declarer with the opportunity to develop an extra trick.
- A club should be played right after winning the first trick.
- The opponents' clubs have to divide 3–2.
- Declarer should make the contract.

CHAPTER 5
Rebids by Opener

Opener's General Approach to the Second Bid

Opener's Rebid after Responder Makes an Invitational Bid

Opener's Rebid after Responder Makes a Forcing Bid

Guidelines for Play

Summary

The Finer Points

Exercises

Sample Deals

OPENER'S GENERAL APPROACH TO THE SECOND BID

Opener's first bid of one of a suit paints a broad picture. It shows a hand between 13 and 21 total points that could be balanced or unbalanced. Responder does not have enough information to decide the level and the strain of the contract. Opener's hand could have as few as 13 points or as many as 21 total points. It could have a wide range of distributional patterns.

Opener's second bid, the rebid, gives responder a clearer picture of the strength (point-count value) and shape (whether it is balanced or unbalanced) of opener's hand. Opener categorizes the hand according to its strength and shape.

Opener Categorizes the Strength

Opener puts the hand into one of three categories according to its point count:

Minimum Hand	13 to 15 total points
Medium Hand	16 to 18 total points
Maximum Hand	19 to 21 total points

The more points opener has for the opening bid, the higher opener can go when making a rebid.

Opener Categorizes the Shape

Opener puts the hand into one of two categories according to the shape of the hand.

Balanced	No voids, no singletons and no more than one doubleton.
Unbalanced	A void, a singleton or more than one doubleton.

With a balanced hand, it would seem that opener should always rebid notrump. Responder is interested in uncovering any Golden Fit, however, to help decide the strain of the contract. Thus, if a Golden Fit has not yet been found, opener will bid a new suit of at least four cards at the one level if possible. Otherwise, opener will rebid in notrump and let responder take it from there.

With an unbalanced hand, if a Golden Fit has not yet been found, opener will show a second suit of four cards or longer when there is one that can be shown without getting the partnership too high on the Bidding Scale. Otherwise, opener will rebid the suit with which the auction was started.

Opener's Use of the Bidding Messages

Opener is the describer. Opener watches the bidding messages that responder, the captain, gives.

Sign-off Bids: If opener starts the bidding with 1NT, many of responder's bids are sign-off bids asking opener to pass. The opening bid is so specific, 15 to 17 HCP and a balanced shape, that responder can usually decide the level and the strain without further information from opener.

An opening bid of one in a suit is made on many different kinds of hands, so responder needs more information before making a decision. None of responder's bids are sign-offs, and opener is never in the position of being forced to pass on the second time it's opener's turn to bid.

Invitational Bids: There are three invitational bids that responder can make. Two such invitational bids are raises of opener's suit. For example:

OPENER	RESPONDER
1 ♥	2 ♥

OPENER	RESPONDER
1 ♥	3 ♥

When responder holds either a minimum hand with 6 to 9 total points and supports opener's suit with a simple raise to the two level or a medium hand of 10 or 11 total points and supports opener's suit with a limit raise to the three level, responder can't insist that opener pass on the second round of bidding. Responder doesn't know the strength of opener's hand. Opener could have a hand as big as 21 total points. Therefore, a single raise or a double raise (limit raise) of opener's suit *invites* opener either to pass or bid again depending on the strength of opener's hand.

The third invitational bid that responder can make is 1NT. For example:

OPENER	RESPONDER
1♦	1NT

This bid shows a minimum hand of 6 to 9 total points. Opener is invited to pass if opener is content with the contract of 1NT, or to bid again if not.

Forcing Bids: Most of the time, responder is looking for more information from opener. The bid of a new suit by responder is forcing when responder has not previously passed. For example:

OPENER	RESPONDER
1♥	1♠

Responder's hand is no longer limited to 6 to 9 total points. Responder could have as few as 6 total points but might have 12 or more. Opener is being asked to bid again; opener must continue to describe the hand.

Another forcing bid by responder is a jump to 2NT:

OPENER	RESPONDER
1♥	2NT

Responder's bid shows a balanced hand with 13 to 15 HCP with only two hearts.

The Role of the Players

The role of each player is important. After opener hears responder's bidding message, opener focuses on the best descriptive rebid. Responder, the captain, will put the pieces of the puzzle together. Responder will consider opener's description and combine it with the known strength and shape of responder's hand. After consulting the Bidding Scale for what is required for the various bids, responder will decide the level and strain and steer the partnership to a contract (Chapter 6).

Keep It Simple

It would be easy, at this point, to become so concerned with the memory work involved that the joy of the game of bridge would escape. Just remember to keep it simple — the more strength opener has for the opening bid, the further opener can move up the Bidding Scale on the rebid. At the same time, opener tries to describe the shape of opener's hand to responder. Opener always keeps the goals of the partnership in mind: to find out whether or not there is a Golden Game and a Golden Fit.

OPENER'S REBID AFTER RESPONDER MAKES AN INVITATIONAL BID

Responder Raises a Major-Suit Opening

Consider opener's action after responder has made a single raise of opener's bid of one of a major suit. For example:

OPENER	RESPONDER
1 ♠	2 ♠

The strain for the contract has been decided. Opener suggested a major suit, and responder confirmed that there is a Golden Fit. Opener doesn't need to show another suit or describe whether the hand is balanced or unbalanced. There is no need to search further for the strain. Responder's only uncertainty is whether the contract should be a partscore or game. To decide this, responder may need more information about the strength of opener's hand.

♠ A K 10 9 8 2   Opener has 11 HCP plus 2 points for the six-card
♥ J 10 9   suit, a total of 13 points. This is a minimum hand
♦ 5 3   (13 to 15 points). Responder's raise is invitational,
♣ K 3   and opener may pass or bid again. On this hand,
                   opener has no extra strength and will pass, leaving
the partnership in a partscore. Even if responder has as many as 9 total points, there won't be enough combined strength for game.

♠ A Q J 7 4 2   Opener has 15 HCP plus 2 points for the six-card
♥ A 9   suit, a total of 17 points. This is a medium hand (16 to
♦ 7 4 2   18 points). With some extra strength, opener moves
♣ A 6   higher on the Bidding Scale to three. The decision
                 as to whether there is enough combined strength for
                 game will be left to responder. If responder has 6
or 7 total points, there won't be enough combined strength for game. If
responder has 8 or 9 total points, the partnership will have enough.

♠ K Q 10 7 6 2   Opener has 21 total points, 19 HCP plus 2 points
♥ Q 4   for the six-card suit. This is a maximum hand (19
♦ A K   to 21 total points). With this much extra strength,
♣ A J 8   opener can jump one level on the bidding scale and
                 rebid 4♠, putting the partnership in game. Even if
responder has as few as 6 total points, there will be enough combined
strength for a game contract.

The more strength opener has for the original opening bid, the higher
opener rebids. After responder raises a major-suit opening bid to the two
level, opener passes with a minimum hand (13 to 15 total points), raises
to the three level with a medium hand (16 to 18 total points) and jumps
to the four level (game) with a maximum hand (19 to 21 total points).

Similarly, consider opener's action after responder raises the opening
bid to the three level. For example:

OPENER   RESPONDER
1 ♥   3 ♥

Again, the strain has been decided. Responder is making an invitational bid. The only decision left is whether there is enough combined
strength for game:

♠ K 9 5   Opener has 12 HCP plus 1 point for the five-card suit.
♥ K J 7 5 3   Since responder has at most 11 total points, there will
♦ A 8 2   not be enough combined strength for game. Opener
♣ J 7   must decline responder's invitation and pass.

♠ 10 6
♥ A Q 10 6 5 3
♦ A Q J 8
♣ 5

With 13 HCP plus 2 points for the six-card suit, opener has enough to accept the invitation. Opener bids 4♥. There is no need to bid another suit, since the strain has already been decided.

When responder raises opener's major suit to the three level, opener passes with a minimum of 13 total points but bids game with 14 or more. Actually, 14 total points only works if responder has 11 total points, not 10 total points. Unfortunately, the opener cannot find out through the bidding (there's not even room on the bidding scale) if responder has 10 or 11 total points. Opener decides to proceed based on the "quality" of the hand. This is a subtle difference that becomes easier to see with experience. See The Finer Points on page 158 for more information.

Responder Raises a Minor-Suit Opening

Consider opener's action after responder has made a single raise of opener's bid of one of a minor suit. For example:

OPENER	RESPONDER
1♦	2♦

In this case, the strain for the contract has not yet been decided. Opener suggested a minor suit. Responder has confirmed a Golden Fit in the minor suit and probably doesn't have a Golden Fit in a major suit. (Responder would have bid a four-card or longer major suit at the one level if responder had one.) If the contract is to be a partscore, playing in the minor suit Golden Fit will be fine. However, if the contract is to be game, it probably should be played in 3NT rather than 5♦. Opener will need to keep this in mind when choosing a rebid.

♠ Q 9 7
♥ J 10
♦ A 9 8 7 6 3
♣ K Q

Opener has 12 HCP plus 2 points for the six-card suit, a total of 14 points. This is a minimum hand (13 to 15 total points). Responder's raise is invitational, and opener may pass or bid again. On this hand, opener has no extra strength and will pass, leaving the partnership in a partscore. Even if responder has as much as 9 total points, there won't be enough combined strength for game.

♠ 9 8   Opener has 15 HCP plus 2 points for the six-card
♥ 9 7   suit, a total of 17 points. This is a medium hand
♦ K Q J 6 4 2   (16 to 18 total points). With some extra strength,
♣ A K Q   opener moves higher on the Bidding Scale to 3 ♦.
                     The decision on whether or not there is enough com-
                     bined strength for game will be left to responder. If
responder has only 6 or 7 total points, there won't be enough combined
strength for game. If responder has at least 8 total points, the partnership
should have enough for the Golden Game of 3NT.

♠ A K 7   Opener has 19 HCP. This is a maximum hand (19
♥ K 10 4   to 21 points). With this much extra strength, opener
♦ K J 10 7   wants to be in game and should jump to 3NT, the
♣ K Q 9   Golden Game, rather than 5 ♦. Unless responder
                     has the maximum of 10 total points, it is unlikely
there will be enough combined strength for a 5 ♦ contract. The jump
rebid to 3NT is called a jump shift. A jump shift means "jumping" a
level and "shifting" the strain to a new one not previously mentioned in
the bidding.

Opener's rebid when responder raises a minor suit to the two level is
similar to that when responder raises a major suit to the two level. Opener
passes with a minimum hand, raises to the three level with a medium
hand, and jumps to game (3NT) with a maximum hand.

Similarly, when responder raises opener's minor suit to the three
level, opener passes with only 13 total points but bids game (3NT) with
14 or more.

Responder Bids 1NT

After an opening bid of one in a suit, a 1NT response shows 6 to 9
total points. It is an invitational bid, and opener can either pass or bid
again. This time, however, the strain has not been decided, so opener
has to consider both the strength and shape of the hand when making
the next bid.

Suppose the auction starts this way:

OPENER	RESPONDER
1 ♥	1NT

The following hands for opener fall into the minimum range (13 to 15 total points). Opener can't move too far up the Bidding Scale because opener does not want to show responder any extra strength. At the same time, opener wants to describe the shape of opener's hand as accurately as possible.

♠ K 7 3   Opener has 12 HCP plus 1 point for the five-card suit,
♥ A Q 10 9 5   a total of 13 points. Opener knows there is no Golden
♦ K 10 3   Fit in hearts because responder would have raised to
♣ 8 2   2♥ with three or more. Since the contract is already in notrump and opener has a balanced hand with no extra strength, opener's best action is to pass. The partnership probably can't make game since responder has a maximum of 9 total points.

♠ Q 9 8   Opener has 13 total points. The hand is unbalanced,
♥ K Q 6 4 3   since opener has a singleton club. To finish describ-
♦ A J 8 4   ing the hand, opener rebids 2♦, showing the second
♣ 3   suit. Responder can now choose whether to pass or bid 2♥.

♠ 9 6 2   Opener has 12 HCP plus 2 points for the six-card suit,
♥ A K 10 8 6 2   making a total of 14 points. Opener's hand is unbal-
♦ A J 4   anced, but there is no second suit to show. Opener
♣ 6   rebids the original suit, 2♥. The rebid of the heart suit after a 1NT bid by responder definitely shows a six-card suit.

♠ K 10 6 4   Opener has a minimum hand of 14 total points.
♥ A Q J 7 6 3   Opener has a second suit, spades, which might be
♦ Q 10   shown. There are two reasons, however, why opener
♣ 5   should not show this suit. First, if opener bids 2♠ to show the second suit and an unbalanced hand, responder will have to choose between spades and hearts. If responder prefers hearts, responder must bid 3♥ and, with both partners having minimum hands, the partnership might be too high on the Bidding Scale. Second, opener knows there can't be a Golden Fit in spades since responder would have bid 1♠ with four or more spades rather than 1NT. Opener should rebid the original suit, 2♥.

The last example illustrates a general principle. When holding a minimum hand, opener should not rebid at the two level a suit that ranks higher than the original suit bid by opener. It is all right to bid a lower-ranking suit, as in the second example.

When opener has a medium-strength hand (16 to 18 total points) and responder bids 1NT, there is still some possibility of a game contract if responder has the top of the range (8 or 9 total points). If responder is at the bottom of the range (6 or 7 total points), game is unlikely, and the partnership should rest in a partscore contract.

Suppose the auction starts this way:

OPENER	RESPONDER
1 ♦	1NT

♠ 2
♥ A 8 3
♦ A K J 9 7 6
♣ A 4 2

Opener has 16 HCP plus 2 points for the six-card suit, a total of 18 points. Opener has an unbalanced hand with no second suit. To describe the shape of the hand, opener must rebid the original suit. With extra strength, however, opener does not rebid the suit at the two level as opener would holding a minimum-strength hand. Instead, opener jumps to the three level and bids 3 ♦. This bid promises a six-card diamond suit.

♠ 9
♥ A K 7 2
♦ K J 10 8 4
♣ A J 5

Opener has 16 HCP plus 1 point for the five-card suit, a total of 17 points. This puts the hand in the medium-strength category. Again the hand is unbalanced, but this time opener has a second suit. Opener can show this by bidding 2 ♥ to tell responder this is an unbalanced hand with at least five diamonds and four hearts. Opener also shows a medium-strength hand by bidding a higher-ranking suit at the two level. Opener wouldn't do this with a minimum-strength hand. Opener has enough strength to allow the partnership to play at the three level if necessary.

♠ 4
♥ K J 5
♦ K Q 10 6 3
♣ A Q J 8

This hand is similar to the previous example, except that opener's second suit is lower-ranking than the original suit. Opener, with 16 points plus 1 point for the five-card suit, describes the hand by rebidding 2 ♣. This shows an unbalanced hand. It will sound exactly the same to responder as if opener has a minimum-strength hand with diamonds and clubs. Unfortunately, there is no way around this. If opener jumps to 3♣ to show the extra strength, the partnership might get too high on the Bidding Scale. We'll see in the next section that a jump in a new suit is used to show a maximum hand.

The previous examples contain no balanced hands with 15 to 17 HCP. On these hands, as you know, the bidding will be opened with 1NT. With a balanced 18 or 19 HCP hand, you will begin the bidding with one of a suit and make a jump rebid (jump shift) in notrump. For more information, see The Finer Points on page 158.

When opener has a maximum-strength hand (19 to 21 totals points) and responder shows a minimum-strength hand of 6 to 9 total points, the partnership has enough combined strength for game.

Opener's rebid will guarantee that the partnership reaches a game contract.

Suppose the auction starts as follows:

OPENER	RESPONDER
1♠	1NT

♠ A K J 8 7
♥ 10 4 2
♦ A Q 7
♣ A 10

Opener has 18 HCP plus 1 point for the five-card suit, a total of 19 points. Opener has a balanced hand and shows this by jumping to 3NT.

♠ K Q J 9 7 6 3
♥ 5
♦ A J
♣ A Q J

With 18 HCP plus 3 points for the seven-card suit, opener has 21 total points. With an unbalanced hand and no second suit to show, opener rebids the original suit but jumps right to a game of 4♠ to show the great strength.

♠ A Q 10 5 3
♥ 9 5
♦ A K J 6
♣ A 3

Opener has 19 total points — 18 HCP plus 1 point for the five-card suit. This is a maximum-strength unbalanced hand with a second suit that can be shown. To show this, opener rebids 3♦. Again, this jump is called a jump shift. It is a forcing bid by opener describing a maximum-strength unbalanced hand. Responder will use this information to determine the appropriate contract.

In the last example, opener's second suit was lower-ranking than the original suit, and opener jumped to show the extra strength. If opener's second suit were higher-ranking than the original suit, it would take up a lot of room on the bidding scale if opener were to jump. For example:

OPENER	RESPONDER
1 ♦	1NT
3 ♠	

Responder, having responded 1NT rather than 1 ♠, is known not to have four spades. If responder now wanted to show diamond support, the bid would have to be 4 ♦, getting the partnership past 3NT. As you saw in the discussion on medium-strength hands, opener can show extra strength by bidding a suit higher-ranking than the original suit at the two level. Opener just needs to bid 2 ♠ in the above example to show extra strength. Responder will not know whether opener has a medium- or maximum-strength hand but will bid again to give opener an opportunity to further describe the hand.

Put It All Together

When the opening bid is one of a suit and responder makes an invitational response, opener chooses a rebid following these guidelines:

Opener's Rebid after Responder Raises Opener's Major Suit to the Two Level

With 13 to 15 total points (minimum hand):
- Pass.

With 16 to 18 total points (medium hand):
- Raise to the three level.

With 19 to 21 total points (maximum hand):
- Jump raise to the four level (game).

Opener's Rebid after Responder Raises Opener's Minor Suit to the Two Level

With 13 to 15 total points (minimum hand):
- Pass.

With 16 to 18 total points (medium hand):
- Raise to the three level.

With 19 to 21 total points (maximum hand):
- Jump to 3NT (game).

Opener's Rebid after Responder Raises Opener's Suit to the Three Level

With 13 total points (minimum hand):
- Pass.

With 14 or more total points:
- Bid game.

Opener's Rebid after Responder Bids 1NT

With 13 to 15 total points (minimum hand):
- Pass with a balanced hand of 13 or 14 HCP. *Remember, with a balanced hand of 15 HCP, you will open 1NT.*
- Bid a second suit of four cards or longer if it is lower-ranking than the original suit.
- Rebid the original suit at the two level.

With 16 to 18 total points (medium hand):
- Bid a second suit of four cards or longer, even if it is higher-ranking than the original suit.
- Rebid the original suit at the three level.

With 19 to 21 total points (maximum hand):
- Bid 3NT with a balanced hand and 18 or 19 HCP.
- Bid a second suit of four cards or longer, jumping a level (jump shift) if it is lower-ranking than the original suit.
- Rebid the original suit, jumping to game.

Let's see how this works.

OPENER	RESPONDER
1♠	2♠

♠ K J 9 8 5 4
♥ A 8 6
♦ K 9
♣ Q 4

With 13 HCP plus 2 points for the six-card suit, you have a minimum hand of 15 points. Pass and rest in a partscore.

♠ A K J 7 5 3
♥ K Q
♦ A Q 8
♣ 5 3

With 19 HCP plus 2 points for the six-card suit, you have a maximum hand of 21 points. Jump to game, 4♠.

♠ K Q 10 9 6 2
♥ 5 4
♦ K Q 8
♣ A J

With 15 HCP plus 2 points for the six-card suit, you have a medium hand of 17 points. Raise to 3♠ and leave the final decision to responder.

What do you rebid with the following hands when the auction starts:

OPENER	RESPONDER
1♣	2♣

♠ A Q 8 5
♥ K 10 6 3
♦ J 9
♣ Q J 2

With a minimum hand of 13 HCP, pass and stop in a partscore. Remember that responder will hold five clubs when raising your minor suit, so you will be playing in a Golden Fit.

♠ K 3 2
♥ A 7 3
♦ 3
♣ A K J 8 6 2

With a medium hand of 17 total points — 15 HCP plus 2 points for the six-card suit — raise to the three level, 3♣. Responder will decide whether to stay in a partscore or carry on to game.

♠ A J 10
♥ K J
♦ 9 7 3
♣ A K Q J 8

With a maximum hand of 20 total points — 19 HCP plus 1 point for the fifth club — jump to game. Rebid 3NT, not 5♣, since 3NT is a Golden Game.

What do you rebid with the following hands when the auction starts:

OPENER	RESPONDER
1♦	1NT

♠ 9 3
♥ A
♦ A 10 8 7 3
♣ K Q 6 4 3

You have 13 HCP plus 1 point for each of the five-card suits. That puts this hand in the minimum range. With an unbalanced hand and a second suit that is lower-ranking than your original suit, rebid 2♣.

♠ A 5
♥ K J 9
♦ A K 7 3 2
♣ A 5 2

You have 19 HCP plus 1 point for the five-card suit and a balanced hand that was too strong to open 1NT. You can show the strength on your rebid by jumping to 3NT.

♠ A Q 3
♥ J 8 7
♦ A K Q 10 6 3
♣ 6

This is a medium-strength unbalanced hand of 18 total points – 16 HCP and 2 points for the six-card suit. With no second suit, show your strength by jumping in your original suit, 3 ♦. Rebidding your original suit also shows extra length.

♠ Q J 10 9
♥ A 3
♦ K Q 9 7 6 4
♣ 5

With 12 HCP plus 2 points for the six-card suit, your hand falls in the minimum category. It is an unbalanced hand, but you are not strong enough to bid a second suit at the two level that is higher-ranking than your first suit. Instead, rebid your first suit, 2 ♦.

Again, this rebid in your original suit shows extra length.

♠ A Q
♥ 6 2
♦ A Q J 8 7
♣ K Q J 9

This hand contains 20 total points — 19 HCP plus 1 point for the five-card suit — putting it in the maximum category. With an unbalanced hand, you want to show your second suit. To do this, you jump shift to 3 ♣, telling responder you are in the maximum range.

♠ K 7
♥ Q J 9 2
♦ A 8 7 4
♣ Q J 3

You have a minimum hand, 13 points, that is balanced. You can describe your hand best with a pass, leaving the contract in notrump at the cheapest level. Remember that the response of 1NT is invitational only, not forcing.

OPENER'S REBID AFTER RESPONDER MAKES A FORCING BID

Responder Bids a New Suit at the One Level

A new-suit bid by responder is forcing if responder has not previously passed. Opener can no longer show a minimum hand by passing. Responder has at least 6 total points but could have considerably more. Since opener can't tell how many points responder has, opener must continue to describe the hand. The partnership's priority is still to look for a Golden Game, in spades or hearts with a Golden Fit, otherwise in notrump. Without enough combined points for a game contract, the partnership settles for a partscore in a Golden Fit or notrump.

Opener uses the familiar guidelines. Opener classifies the strength and shape of the hand and describes them with a carefully selected rebid.

When planning to raise responder's major, opener falls into the position of becoming a dummy for partner. When classifying the strength of the hand, opener should then use dummy points (short suit points) for shortness in place of distributional points for length.

DUMMY POINTS	
Void	5 Points
Singleton	3 Points
Doubleton	1 Point

This is similar to the case where responder raises opener's major (Chapter 4). Since opener is showing a five-card suit by opening the bidding in a major suit, responder needs only three-card support to raise. When responder bids a major suit at the one level, however, responder may have only four cards in the suit. Thus, opener needs four-card support to raise.

Suppose the auction starts:

OPENER	RESPONDER
1 ♦	1 ♥

Let's see how opener approaches the rebid when holding a minimum-strength hand (13 to 15 total points).

♠ A 9 3
♥ K 7 6 4
♦ A J 7 3 2
♣ 9

Opener has started the bidding with 1 ♦. On hearing the response of 1 ♥, opener knows the partnership has a Golden Fit in a major suit. Opener's first priority is to inform responder of opener's support for hearts. Since opener is planning to support responder's major suit, opener revalues the hand using dummy points. Opener has 12 HCP plus 3 points for the singleton — a total of 15 points. Opener raises to the cheapest level, bidding 2 ♥. Note that opener does not pass, knowing the partnership has found a Golden Fit. Responder's bid is forcing, and opener must keep the auction going to allow responder to determine the appropriate level for the contract.

♠ Q J 9 4
♥ J 8 2
♦ A K J 4
♣ Q 5

Opener can't support responder's major suit. Responder may have only a four-card suit, so opener needs four-card support to ensure a Golden Fit. However, opener does not give up on the search for a Golden Fit in a major suit. Opener can conveniently show the spade suit at the one level and rebids 1 ♠. It is quite possible that responder has a four-card spade suit and a four-card heart suit (or even a five-card heart suit). With four hearts and four spades, responder would have bid hearts first, showing the suits up the line (Chapter 4).

♠ K J 10
♥ J 5
♦ A J 10 9 4
♣ A 6 2

Opener can't raise responder's major suit and does not have another suit to bid at the one level. However, the hand is a minimum-strength balanced hand. Opener can describe this type of hand by rebidding 1NT. Since opener would have started the bidding with 1NT holding a balanced hand with 15 to 17 HCP, this sequence tells responder that opener has a minimum balanced hand, too weak to open 1NT.

♠ A 10 8
♥ 5
♦ K Q 10 7 3
♣ A J 4 2

Opener has a minimum-strength hand, but it is not balanced. Opener can describe the hand by rebidding 2♣, showing the second suit. As discussed in the section on rebids by opener after a 1NT response, it is all right for opener to bid a second suit at the two level with a minimum-strength hand if it is lower-ranking than the original suit. Opener would need a medium-strength hand if the second suit were a higher-ranking suit.

♠ A 10
♥ 10 4
♦ A Q J 8 5 3
♣ 7 5 4

Opener has a minimum unbalanced hand with no second suit to bid. In this case, opener can rebid the original suit at the cheapest available level, 2♦. Rebidding the suit without a jump tells responder that opener is in the minimum range.

Suppose the auction starts this way:

OPENER	RESPONDER
1 ♣	1 ♠

Let's see the effect on opener's rebid when opener holds a medium hand (16 to 18 total points).

♠ A K 6 4   Having heard partner's response of 1♠, opener
♥ 9 3   intends to describe the hand further by showing sup-
♦ J 8   port for partner's suit. But before raising responder's
♣ A K J 6 3   major, opener values the hand using dummy points.
Opener has 16 HCP plus 1 point for each of the
doubletons, a total of 18 points. With more than minimum strength,
opener can describe the hand to responder by jumping a level and raising to 3♠. Responder, knowing that opener has medium strength, will
decide whether there is enough combined strength for game.

♠ 7 2   This hand is worth 17 total points, 16 HCP plus 1
♥ A Q J 5   point for the five-card suit. It is unbalanced. Opener
♦ K 5   wants to show the second suit whenever possible
♣ K Q J 10 8   to give responder a good description of the hand.
Opener can bid 2♥ because there is extra strength.
Even if responder has only 6 points and prefers clubs to hearts, the partner-
ship should not be too high on the Bidding Scale in a contract of 3♣.

♠ 10 4   Opener has a medium-strength unbalanced hand
♥ A K 6   with no second suit to show. In this case, opener
♦ J 2   rebids the original suit with a jump, 3♣. This tells
♣ A K J 9 6 2   responder about the extra strength, since with a
minimum hand opener would have rebid 2♣. This
bid also shows extra length in the club suit.

With a medium-strength hand, opener sometimes will be able to
describe the shape by bidding a second suit at the one level or bidding
a lower-ranking second suit at the two level. When opener does this, responder will assume that opener has a minimum-strength hand. It is not
always possible for opener to describe both the strength and the shape.
As the auction continues, opener may get an opportunity to show the
extra strength.

Opener does not have to worry about what to rebid with a balanced
hand with 15 to 17 HCP. All such hands would be opened 1NT (Chapter
3). See the Finer Points on page 158 for more information.

Let's move on to opener's rebid when holding a maximum-strength
hand (19 to 21 total points). Suppose the auction starts:

OPENER	RESPONDER
1 ♥	1 ♠

♠ K Q 9 3
♥ A Q J 7 5
♦ A 4
♣ K 2

Hearing a response of 1 ♠, opener knows there is a Golden Fit in a major suit. Before deciding how high to raise responder's suit, opener revalues the hand using dummy points. With 19 HCP plus 1 point for each doubleton, opener has 21 total points. To show this much strength, opener jumps all the way to game, 4 ♠. Even if responder has only 6 total points, there should be enough combined strength for the partnership to make game.

♠ A Q 10
♥ K Q J 10 5
♦ K 9 3
♣ K J

Opener has a balanced hand and can't support responder's suit (responder may have a four-card suit). Opener can show this by jumping a level to 2NT. It may seem strange that opener does not jump all the way to game, 3NT, but remember that opener is merely describing the hand. Responder will make the decision of where to play the contract after getting sufficient information about opener's hand.

♠ A Q
♥ A K J 8 2
♦ K Q 10 6 3
♣ 5

Opener, with a maximum-strength unbalanced hand and a second suit to show, jump shifts to 3 ♦. Responder will know that opener has a hand in the range of 19 to 21 total points and will ensure that the partnership reaches a game contract.

♠ A 4
♥ A Q J 9 7 5 3
♦ K 3
♣ K 2

Opener has 17 HCP plus 3 points for the seven-card suit, a maximum hand. With no second suit to show, opener rebids the original suit with a jump to game, 4 ♥, to show a hand in the maximum range.

Responder Bids a New Suit at the Two Level

To bid a new suit at the two level, responder must have at least 10 total points. As with a new suit at the one level, responder's bid is forcing — opener can't pass. Opener uses the same principles in choosing a rebid, but, since the auction is already at the two level, opener's rebid is often higher on the Bidding Scale than if responder had bid at the one level. This can be illustrated with a few examples.

Suppose the auction starts this way:

OPENER	RESPONDER
1♠	2♥

♠ A K 9 8 4　Since opener can support responder's major, opener
♥ Q J 8 6　　revalues the hand using dummy points. With 13 HCP
♦ K 5　　　　plus 1 point for each of the doubletons, opener has
♣ 10 2　　　　15 total points. Since responder shows at least 10
　　　　　　　total points to bid at the two level, opener should
bid game, 4♥.

♠ A Q 10 7 4　Opener has a medium-strength hand of 18 total
♥ A Q 9 3　　points in support of responder's suit — 16 HCP
♦ K J　　　　plus 1 point for each doubleton. To show the extra
♣ 9 3　　　　strength, opener jumps one level and bids 4♥. This
　　　　　　　gets the partnership to game when opener has only
a medium hand, but responder must have at least 10 total points to have
bid a new suit at the two level.

♠ K J 10 8 4　Opener has a minimum hand but can't raise re-
♥ J 7　　　　sponder's suit. With a balanced hand, opener can
♦ K J 9　　　rebid notrump at the cheapest available level, 2NT.
♣ A 10 2　　　Since opener did not jump, responder will know that
　　　　　　　opener has a minimum-strength balanced hand, too
　　　　　　　weak to open 1NT.

♠ A J 9 7 4　Opener has a maximum-strength hand of 19 total
♥ A J　　　　points. However, this is a balanced hand with 18
♦ K Q 6　　　HCP. To show this, opener jumps to 3NT. Responder
♣ Q J 10　　　knows that opener has a balanced hand that was too
　　　　　　　strong to open 1NT.

Responder Jumps to 2NT

By jumping to 2NT in response to an opening bid of one in a suit,
responder shows a balanced hand of 13 to 15 HCP without support for
opener's major suit (if opener bid a major). Responder has announced
that the partnership holds enough combined strength for a game contract.
Even though responder's bid has left room for opener to further describe
the hand, responder is strongly suggesting notrump as the final strain in

this sequence. Therefore, responder's point count is based on high-card points.

Suppose the auction starts this way:

OPENER	RESPONDER
1 ♠	2NT

♠ A J 7 6 3
♥ K 9 5
♦ 8 4 2
♣ A 3

Opener has a minimum-strength hand of 13 points — 12 HCP plus 1 point for the five-card suit. With a balanced hand, opener can simply raise to 3NT. Note that opener can't pass, since responder's bid is forcing. Opener also knows that there is no Golden Fit in spades, because responder did not raise them.

♠ A J 7 6 3
♥ K 9 5 4 2
♦ 8
♣ A 3

Opener has a minimum-strength hand, but it is unbalanced. Opener can rebid 3 ♥, showing the second suit and leaving it up to responder to place the contract.

♠ A J 7 6 3 2
♥ K 9 5
♦ 8 4 2
♣ A

Opener has a minimum-strength unbalanced hand but knows there is a Golden Fit in spades. Responder is showing a balanced hand and can't have a singleton spade. Opener can simply bid a game contract in the known fit, 4 ♠.

Put It All Together

When responder makes a forcing response, opener can't pass. Opener considers the strength and shape of the hand and rebids accordingly.

Suppose you open the bidding 1 ♣ and your partner responds 1 ♠.

♠ 10 9 7 3
♥ A Q 5
♦ 4 3
♣ A K 6 2

You have support for partner's major suit, so revalue the hand using dummy points. You have 13 HCP plus 1 point for the doubleton diamond, making a total of 14 points. With a minimum hand, raise to the cheapest available level, 2 ♠.

♠ Q 6 3
♥ A J 4 2
♦ J 8 7
♣ A Q 5

With a minimum-strength hand, you can't support responder's spades with only three, and you can't bid a new suit that is higher-ranking than your original suit at the two level. You describe a minimum balanced hand by rebidding 1NT.

♠ 3 ♥ K 10 2 ♦ J 8 4 ♣ A K Q 7 5 3	You have an unbalanced hand with no second suit, and it lies in the minimum range. Describe this to responder by rebidding your suit at the cheapest available level, 2♣.
♠ A J 10 6 ♥ — ♦ K 9 3 ♣ A Q J 7 5 3	You can support responder's major suit. You have a maximum-strength hand worth 20 points counting dummy points — 15 HCP plus 5 points for the void in hearts. Raise to game, 4♠.
♠ K 3 ♥ A Q J ♦ Q 10 5 ♣ A K 9 3 2	With a 19 HCP balanced hand, jump to 2NT to describe your strength and shape.
♠ 4 2 ♥ Q 2 ♦ A Q ♣ K Q J 8 6 3 2	With a medium-strength unbalanced hand and no second suit, rebid your original suit, jumping a level. Bid 3♣.

GUIDELINES FOR PLAY

When you don't have enough tricks to make your contract, you have to *Analyze your alternatives.* Sometimes, you can try to win a trick with one of your high cards even if the opponents have a higher-ranking card. To do this, you will need a little luck. The higher-ranking card must be favorably placed in an opponent's hand. If it is, careful play will let you develop an extra trick.

The Finesse

Consider the following suit:

DUMMY: K 4

DECLARER: 3 2

If you had the queen, you could lead the king to drive out the opponents' ace. The queen would be promoted to a sure trick. Without the queen, leading the king will do no good. The opponents will win the ace, and now their queen will be a sure trick. In such situations, you can sometimes get a trick by leading toward the high card. This is called taking a finesse. You have to hope that the opponents' cards are favorably placed.

For example:

K 4

A J 9 7 5   W N E   Q 10 8 6
                S

3 2

When you (South) lead from your hand toward dummy, you will be able to take a trick if the opponent on your left holds the ace. Your left-hand opponent has to play before dummy plays. If the ace is played, you play the 4 from dummy, and the king has become a sure trick. If the ace isn't played, you play dummy's king. It will win the trick because the opponent on your right doesn't have the ace.

A finesse will not always work. For example, the opponents' cards could be placed in this fashion:

K 4

J 9 7 5   W N E   A Q 10 8 6
                S

3 2

You lead a low card toward dummy. The opponent on your left plays a low card, and you try a finesse by playing dummy's king. Unfortunately, the opponent on your right wins the trick with the ace, and your finesse fails. However, you gave it your best shot. You couldn't take a trick no matter how you played the suit. The ace was unfavorably placed.

Here is another example of a finesse:

DUMMY: A Q   You always have one sure trick, the ace. If
DECLARER: 3 2   you need two tricks from this suit, you follow
                      the principle of leading toward high cards by
                      leading toward the ace and queen. If the op-
ponent on your left plays a low card, you play dummy's queen. You are
hoping that your left-hand opponent holds the king.

For example:

```
                    A Q
                   ┌─────┐
       K J 8 7     │ W N E│    10 9 6 5 4
                   │   S  │
                   └─────┘
                    3 2
```

The player on your right does not have a higher card than your queen, and you win the trick. Of course, if your right-hand opponent did have the king, your finesse would lose. You would be back to the one sure trick you started with.

Entries

In the above examples, you had to lead from the appropriate hand to give yourself the best chance to get an extra trick. There are many times when you want the lead to be in a specific hand. For example, if you have sure tricks in one hand, you want to be able to get to that hand in order to take them.

A card, or a combination of cards, which lets you get from one hand to the other is called an *entry*. There are two parts to an entry — you need a sure trick in one hand and a lower card of the same suit in the other hand. The lower card enables you to cross to the other hand. Here is a simple example:

DUMMY: A   This combination of cards provides an entry to
DECLARER: 2   dummy's hand. You have a low card in your hand which you can lead to the sure trick in dummy.

Here is another example:

DUMMY: K 4 2   This suit provides an entry to either hand. You
DECLARER: A 6 5   can play one of your low cards to dummy's king, or you can lead one of dummy's low cards to your ace.

Entries are very useful. They let you to be in the right place at the right time. As declarer, you should always watch your entries, being careful not to squander them.

SUMMARY

When making a rebid, opener puts the hand into one of the following categories according to the point-count value. (Remember to use dummy points only if you plan to support responder's major suit.)

Minimum Hand	13 to 15 total points
Medium Hand	16 to 18 total points
Maximum Hand	19 to 21 total points

Next, opener chooses the rebid that best describes the hand. Opener takes into account the nature of responder's bid, using the following guidelines.

Opener's Rebid after Responder Raises Opener's Major Suit to the Two Level

With 13 to 15 total points (minimum hand):
- Pass.

With 16 to 18 total points (medium hand):
- Raise to the three level.

With 19 to 21 total points (maximum hand):
- Jump raise to the four level (game).

Opener's Rebid after Responder Raises Opener's Minor Suit to the Two Level

With 13 to 15 total points (minimum hand):
- Pass.

With 16 to 18 total points (medium hand):
- Raise to the three level.

With 19 to 21 total points (maximum hand):
- Jump to 3NT (game).

Opener's Rebid after Responder Raises Opener's Suit to the Three Level

With 13 total points:
- Pass.

With 14 or more total points:
- Bid game.

Opener's Rebid after Responder Bids a New Suit at the One Level

With 13 to 15 total points (minimum hand):

- Raise partner's major to the cheapest available level with four-card support (count dummy points). **First priority is to show support.**
- Bid a second suit of four cards or longer if it can be bid at the one level. A lower-ranking suit than the original one may be bid at the two level. **Second priority is to try to find a trump fit.**
- Rebid the original suit at the cheapest available level. **Third priority is to show extra length.**
- Bid notrump with a balanced hand at the cheapest available level. A notrump rebid says none of the above.

With 16 to 18 total points (medium hand):

- Raise partner's major, jumping one level, with four-card support (count dummy points). **First priority is to show support.**
- Make a jump rebid in notrump (a special bid to show a balanced 18-19 HCP). **Second priority is to limit your hand.** When opener was minimum, rebidding notrump was opener's last priority.
- Rebid the original suit, jumping one level. **Third priority is to show extra length.** This rebid guarantees at least a six-card suit.
- Bid a second suit of four cards or longer, even if it is higher-ranking than the original suit and must be bid at the two level. This is still a common rebid, despite it being the last priority.

With 19 to 21 total points (maximum hand):

- Raise partner's major, jumping two levels, with four-card support (count dummy points). **First priority is to show support.**
- Bid a second suit of four cards or longer, jumping one level (jump shift)

- Bid 3NT — a double jump. **This third priority suggests a specific type of hand** — one with a long solid suit and stoppers in all unbid suits.
- Rebid the original suit, jumping to game.

Opener's Rebid after Responder Bids a New Suit at the Two Level

- Opener can't pass since responder's new suit bid is forcing.
- Opener uses the same principles in choosing a rebid as with a new suit at the one level (see previous chart).
- Opener's rebid is often higher on the Bidding Scale since the auction is already at the two level.

Opener's Rebid after Responder Bids 1NT

With 13 to 15 total points (minimum hand):

- Pass with a balanced hand.
- Bid a second suit of four cards or longer if it is lower-ranking than the original suit.
- Rebid the original suit at the two level.

With 16 to 18 total points (medium hand):

- Bid a second suit of four cards or longer, even if it is higher-ranking than the original suit.
- Rebid the original suit at the three level.

With 19 to 21 total points (maximum hand):

- Bid 3NT with a balanced hand and 18 or 19 HCP.
- Bid a second suit of four cards or longer, jumping a level (jump shift), if it is lower-ranking than the original suit.
- Rebid the original suit, jumping to game.

Opener's Rebid after Responder Bids 2NT

- With a balanced hand, raise to 3NT.
- With an unbalanced hand, bid a second suit of four cards or longer or rebid the original suit.

A good guideline for when you are declarer is to lead toward the high cards. To do this, you may need an entry to allow you to get to the appropriate hand.

THE FINER POINTS

The text recommends categorizing opener's strength into one of the following even ranges:

Minimum Hand	13 to 15 total points
Medium Hand	16 to 18 total points
Maximum Hand	19 to 21 total points

Some authorities recommend a slightly uneven set of ranges:

Minimum Hand	13 to 16 total points
Medium Hand	17 or 18 total points
Maximum Hand	19 to 21 total points

Remember if you change the ranges by even a point, it changes some of the responses in trying to reach the optimum level and strain.

The Reverse

The text points out that opener can show a medium-strength hand by bidding a second suit at the two level that is higher-ranking than the original suit. For example:

OPENER	RESPONDER
1♣	1♠
2♥	

Such a sequence is called a *reverse*. The text also states that opener can reverse with a maximum-strength hand instead of jump shifting in the second suit. The jump shift is used only with a maximum hand when opener's second suit is lower-ranking than the original suit.

A reverse requires more than a minimum hand. Responder may have as few as 6 total points but will have to bid again in case opener has a maximum hand. (This will be discussed in the next chapter.) Responder will have to bid at the three level to show support for one of opener's suits. If opener could have as few as 13 total points to make such a bid, the partnership could end up at the three level with as few as 19 (13 + 6) points in the combined hands.

"Good" Hands versus "Bad" Hands – Gaining Judgment

Sometimes during the bidding both the opener and the responder may need to look to the quality of their hands to make a judgment call on how to proceed in the bidding. Rest assured this becomes easier with experience. Let's take a look at the following hands to see the basics.

	Hand #1		versus	Hand #2	
	♠	K 6 5		♠	6 5 3
	♥	A 9 8 7		♥	A K 8 7
	♦	K J 10 3 2		♦	K Q J 10 2
	♣	Q		♣	5

Both hands contain 13 HCP plus 1 extra point for the length in diamonds. However, Hand #1 is definitely a weaker hand than #2. Why? Because a hand will be stronger when its high cards are working together. Hand #2 *looks* stronger and it is — even though the total point evaluation doesn't show it.

Balanced Hand Bidding

We know that we open 1NT with a balanced hand and 15 to 17 HCP. In fact, we know that when we bid notrump, we need to rely more heavily on our high cards. By the time we are finished with learning our total bidding system, you will have a complete set of methods as opening bidder with a balanced hand. At the moment, you should recognize the following:

- With a balanced hand of 13 or 14 HCP, open one of a suit and make a non-jump rebid in notrump.

- With a balanced hand of 15 to 17 HCP, open 1NT.

- With a balanced hand of 18 or 19 HCP, open one of a suit and make a jump rebid in notrump.

Looking ahead:

Since this chapter deals with maximum rebids in the 19 to 21 total point range, you may be wondering what to do with a 20 or 21 HCP balanced hand. With a balanced 20 or 21 HCP, you will open 2NT. This will be covered in depth in the *Play of the Hand in the 21st Century* student text along with further balanced hand bidding concepts.

Exercise One — Responder Raises Your Major Suit

With each of the following hands, you open the bidding 1♥, and partner responds 2♥, which is an invitational bid. Add the high-card points and the distributional points. Put each hand in a range of minimum, medium or maximum. What is your rebid?

1) ♠ 9 7 6	2) ♠ Q 7	3) ♠ 10 7
♥ K Q J 9 8 3	♥ A Q 7 6 3 2	♥ A Q J 6 5
♦ A 5	♦ K J	♦ A K Q 2
♣ A J	♣ J 7 2	♣ A 2
HCP:_____	HCP:_____	HCP:_____
Distr. Pts.:_____	Distr. Pts.:_____	Distr. Pts.:_____
Total Pts.: _____	Total Pts.: _____	Total Pts.: _____
Range:_____	Range: _____	Range: _____
Rebid: _____	Rebid:_____	Rebid:_____

Exercise Two — Responder Raises Your Minor Suit

With each of the following hands, you open the bidding 1♣ and partner responds 2♣, which is an invitational bid. Add the high-card points and the distributional points. Put each hand in a range of minimum, medium or maximum. What is your rebid?

1) ♠ Q 8 2	2) ♠ 7 3	3) ♠ A 10 8
♥ K J 5 2	♥ K 4	♥ K Q 4
♦ A 6 3	♦ A 4 2	♦ A J
♣ K J 4	♣ A K J 6 3 2	♣ K Q 10 8 4
HCP:_____	HCP:_____	HCP:_____
Distr. Pts.:_____	Distr. Pts.:_____	Distr. Pts.:_____
Total Pts.: _____	Total Pts.: _____	Total Pts.: _____
Range:_____	Range: _____	Range: _____
Rebid: _____	Rebid:_____	Rebid:_____

Exercise One *Answers* — Responder Raises Your Major Suit

1)   15 HCP
     2 distr. pts.
    17 total pts.
    Medium
    3 ♥

2)   13 HCP
     2 distr. pts.
    15 total pts.
    Minimum
    Pass

3)   20 HCP
     1 distr. pt.
    21 total pts.
    Maximum
    4 ♥

Exercise Two *Answers* — Responder Raises Your Minor Suit

1)   14 HCP
     0 distr. pts.
    14 total pts.
    Minimum
    Pass

2)   15 HCP
     2 distr. pts.
    17 total pts.
    Medium
    3 ♣

3)   19 HCP
     1 distr. pt.
    20 total pts.
    Maximum
    3NT

Exercise Three — Responder Bids 1NT

With each of the following hands, you open the bidding 1♠ and partner responds 1NT. Add the high-card points and the distributional points. Put each hand in a range of minimum, medium, or maximum. What is your rebid?

1) ♠ K J 8 7 3
   ♥ 10 4 2
   ♦ A 9 6
   ♣ A J

HCP:_____
Distr. Pts.:_____
Total Pts.: _____
Range:_____
Rebid: _____

2) ♠ A K 9 5 3
   ♥ 6
   ♦ K Q J 5
   ♣ J 4 2

HCP:_____
Distr. Pts.:_____
Total Pts.: _____
Range: _____
Rebid:_____

3) ♠ A J 9 8 4 2
   ♥ 7 4 3
   ♦ A Q 8
   ♣ 4

HCP:_____
Distr. Pts.:_____
Total Pts.: _____
Range: _____
Rebid:_____

4) ♠ A Q J 6 4 3
   ♥ A 7 2
   ♦ 9
   ♣ K J 10

HCP:_____
Distr. Pts.:_____
Total Pts.: _____
Range:_____
Rebid: _____

5) ♠ A K J 4 2
   ♥ K 9
   ♦ A Q 4
   ♣ Q 9 5

HCP:_____
Distr. Pts.:_____
Total Pts.: _____
Range: _____
Rebid:_____

6) ♠ K Q J 8 3
   ♥ 9 4
   ♦ A
   ♣ A K 7 6 3

HCP:_____
Distr. Pts.:_____
Total Pts.: _____
Range: _____
Rebid:_____

Exercise Three *Answers* — Responder Bids 1NT

The 1NT bid is an invitational bid, and opener can pass or bid again. The strain has not yet been decided, so opener has to consider not only the strength of the hand but also the shape.

1) 13 HCP
   <u> 1</u> distr. pt.
   14 total pts.
   Minimum
   Pass

2) 14 HCP
   <u> 1</u> distr. pt.
   15 total pts.
   Minimum
   2 ♦

3) 11 HCP
   <u> 2</u> distr. pts.
   13 total pts.
   Minimum
   2 ♠

4) 15 HCP
   <u> 2</u> distr. pts.
   17 total pts.
   Medium
   3 ♠

5) 19 HCP
   <u> 1</u> distr. pt.
   20 total pts.
   Maximum
   3NT

6) 17 HCP
   <u> 2</u> distr. pts.
   19 total pts.
   Maximum
   3 ♣

Exercise Four — Raising Responder's Suit

With each of the following hands, you open the bidding 1♣ and partner responds 1♠. Add the high-card points and the dummy points. Put each hand in a range of minimum, medium or maximum. What is your rebid?

1) ♠ J 8 7 6	2) ♠ Q 7 4 2	3) ♠ A J 3 2
♥ 8	♥ 10 9	♥ —
♦ A 9 3	♦ A K	♦ Q J 9 6
♣ A K Q 7 6	♣ K 8 7 4 2	♣ A K J 7 2

HCP:_____	HCP:_____	HCP:_____
Dummy Pts.:_____	Dummy Pts.:_____	Dummy Pts.:_____
Total Pts.: _____	Total Pts.: _____	Total Pts.: _____
Range:_____	Range: _____	Range: _____
Rebid: _____	Rebid:_____	Rebid:_____

Exercise Five — Opener Bids a Second Suit at the Two Level

Examine the following auctions:

OPENER	RESPONDER		OPENER	RESPONDER
1♥	1NT		1♥	1NT
2♦			2♠	

In both cases, opener is showing an unbalanced hand with two suits. Responder usually must make a choice between opener's suits. In which auction can responder always make the choice at the two level?

In which auction might responder have to go to the three level to show a preference?

Which is higher-ranking on the Bidding Scale?
1. Hearts/ Diamonds? _____   2. Hearts/Spades? _____
What is the difference between the two auctions in terms of the rank of opener's second suit? _____

When choosing a rebid with an unbalanced hand, opener bids a new suit at the two level that is lower-ranking than the original suit even when holding a minimum hand. If the new suit is higher-ranking than the original suit, why can't opener afford to mention it at the two level unless opener holds a medium hand? _____

Exercise Four *Answers* — Raising Responder's Suit

This 1♠ bid is a forcing bid and opener must bid again. If you can support responder's suit, you need to revalue your hand using dummy points before deciding on your rebid.

1) 14 HCP	2) 12 HCP	3) 16 HCP
3 dummy pts.	2 dummy pts.	5 dummy pts.
17 total pts.	14 total pts.	21 total pts.
Medium	Minimum	Maximum
3♠	2♠	4♠

Exercise Five *Answers* — Opener Bids a Second Suit at the Two Level

- In the first auction, responder could show a preference at the two level.
- In the second auction, responder might have to go to the three level to show a preference.
- Hearts is higher ranking.
- Spades is higher ranking.
- In the first auction, the second suit is lower ranking than the first suit.
- In the second auction, the second suit is higher ranking than the first suit.
- Without extra values, opener doesn't want to force the responder to show a preference at the three level.

Exercise Six — More Rebids after Responder Bids a New Suit

With each of the following hands, you open the bidding 1♦ and partner responds 1♠. Add the high-card points and the distributional points. Put each hand in a range of minimum, medium, or maximum. What is your rebid?

1) ♠ 9 8
   ♥ K 10 4
   ♦ A J 8 6
   ♣ K Q 5 4

2) ♠ 3
   ♥ K 8 4
   ♦ K Q 9 6 2
   ♣ A J 10 6

3) ♠ K 3
   ♥ A 8 2
   ♦ A K J 8 4 2
   ♣ 9 4

HCP:_____
Distr. Pts.:_____
Total Pts.: _____
Range:_____
Rebid: _____

HCP:_____
Distr. Pts.:_____
Total Pts.: _____
Range: _____
Rebid:_____

HCP:_____
Distr. Pts.:_____
Total Pts.: _____
Range: _____
Rebid:_____

4) ♠ A J
   ♥ A J 10 9
   ♦ A K 7 5 3
   ♣ 10 2

5) ♠ K 6 2
   ♥ 4
   ♦ A K Q 8 3
   ♣ A Q J 2

6) ♠ J 3
   ♥ A Q J
   ♦ A Q 9 6
   ♣ K Q 6 3

HCP:_____
Distr. Pts.:_____
Total Pts.: _____
Range:_____
Rebid: _____

HCP:_____
Distr. Pts.:_____
Total Pts.: _____
Range: _____
Rebid:_____

HCP:_____
Distr. Pts.:_____
Total Pts.: _____
Range: _____
Rebid:_____

Exercise Six *Answers* — More Rebids after Responder Bids a New Suit

The 1♠ response is forcing. You must bid again.

1) 13 HCP
   _0_ distr. pts.
   13 total pts.
   Minimum
   1NT

2) 13 HCP
   _1_ distr. pt.
   14 total pts.
   Minimum
   2♣

3) 15 HCP
   _2_ distr. pts.
   17 total pts.
   Medium
   3♦

4) 17 HCP
   _1_ distr. pt.
   18 total pts.
   Medium
   2♥

5) 19 HCP
   _1_ distr. pt.
   20 total pts.
   Maximum
   3♣

6) 19 HCP
   _0_ distr. pts.
   19 total pts.
   Maximum
   2NT

Exercise Seven — Responder Jumps

Examine the following auctions:

OPENER	RESPONDER		OPENER	RESPONDER
1♥	3♥		1♥	2NT

How many points does responder show in each auction?

1st _____   2nd _____

What is the message given by responder's bid?

1st _____   2nd _____

Suppose you have the following hand:

♠ 10 6
♥ A J 8 4 2
♦ K 9 5
♣ A 4 2

What would you rebid in the first auction? _____

What would you rebid in the second auction? _____

Exercise Eight — The Finesse

How many tricks can be developed with each of the following suit combinations if the opponents' cards are as favorably placed as possible?

DUMMY:	1) K 7 2	2) 5 2	3) K Q 3	4) A 6 3
DECLARER:	9 4 3	A Q 3	7 4 2	Q 8 2

_____   _____   _____   _____

How would you play each combination? _____

Exercise Seven *Answers* — Responder Jumps

- Responder shows 10 or 11 total points in the first auction and 13 to 15 HCP in the second auction.
- The first response is invitational; the second is forcing.
- Pass in the first auction; bid 3NT in the second.

Exercise Eight *Answers* — The Finesse

1) 1   2) 2   3) 2   4) 2

- In each case, lead toward the card you hope will take a trick.

Exercise Nine — A Finesse against the Ace

(E-Z Deal Cards: #5, Deal 1 — Dealer, North)

Turn up all of the cards on the first pre-dealt deal. Put each hand dummy style at the edge of the table in front of each player.

The Bidding

North is the dealer. Who would open the bidding? What would the opening bid be?

Look at responder's hand. Can responder support opener's suit? Can responder bid a new suit? What would responder bid? What is the bidding message given by responder's bid? Does opener have to bid again? What would opener rebid? What would the contract be? Who would be the declarer?

```
Dealer:        ♠ A 7 3
North          ♥ A 6 2
               ♦ A Q 7 5
               ♣ 5 4 3

♠ 9 5 4                    ♠ K Q J 10
♥ K Q J 10      N          ♥ 8 7 5
♦ 9 8 2       W   E        ♦ 10 6 3
♣ Q 10 8        S          ♣ A J 9

               ♠ 8 6 2
               ♥ 9 4 3
               ♦ K J 4
               ♣ K 7 6 2
```

The Play

Who would make the opening lead? What would the opening lead be?

How many tricks must declarer take to fulfill the contract? How many sure tricks does declarer have? Which suit provides declarer with the opportunity to develop the additional tricks needed to make the contract? Which suit should declarer play after winning the first trick? Why? What has to happen in order for declarer to make the contract?

Bid and play the deal. Did declarer make the contract?

Exercise Nine *Answers* — A Finesse against the Ace

The Bidding

- North opens the bidding with 1♦.
- Responder can't support opener's minor suit and can't bid a new suit, so responder would reply 1NT.
- Responder's bid is invitational; opener doesn't have to bid again.
- Opener would pass.
- The contract would be 1NT. South would be the declarer.

The Play

- West makes the opening lead.
- The opening lead would be the ♥K.
- Declarer needs seven tricks to make the contract.
- Declarer has six sure tricks.
- The club suit provides the best opportunity for an extra trick.
- After taking the lead, the declarer should lead toward the ♣K.
- East must hold the ♣A or clubs must break 3–3.
- Declarer should make the contract.

Exercise Ten — Drawing Trumps with the Help of a Finesse

(E-Z Deal Cards: #5, Deal 2 — Dealer, East)

Turn up all of the cards on the second pre-dealt deal and arrange them as in the previous exercise.

The Bidding

East is the dealer. Who would open the bidding? What would the opening bid be?

Look at responder's hand. Can responder support opener's suit? What is the value of responder's hand? What would responder bid? What is the bidding message given by responder's bid? Does opener have to bid again? What would opener's rebid be?

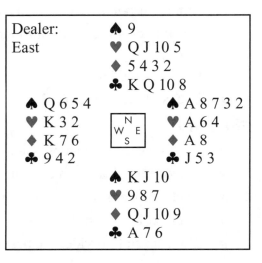

Dealer: East

♠ 9
♥ Q J 10 5
♦ 5 4 3 2
♣ K Q 10 8

♠ Q 6 5 4　　　　♠ A 8 7 3 2
♥ K 3 2　　　　　♥ A 6 4
♦ K 7 6　　　　　♦ A 8
♣ 9 4 2　　　　　♣ J 5 3

♠ K J 10
♥ 9 8 7
♦ Q J 10 9
♣ A 7 6

What would the contract be? Who would be the declarer?

The Play

Who would make the opening lead? What would the opening lead be?

How many tricks must declarer take to fulfill the contract? How many sure tricks does declarer have? Which suit provides declarer with the opportunity to develop the additional tricks needed to make the contract? Which suit should declarer play after winning the first trick? Which card in the suit should declarer play first? Why?

Bid and play the deal. Did declarer make the contract?

Exercise Ten *Answers* — Drawing Trumps with the Help of a Finesse

The Bidding

- East opens the bidding with 1 ♠.
- Responder can support opener's suit. The hand is worth 8 total points, so responder bids 2 ♠.
- The bid is invitational and opener doesn't have to bid.
- Opener would pass.
- The contract would be 2 ♠.
- East is the declarer.

The Play

- South makes the opening lead.
- South leads the ♦ Q.
- Declarer needs eight tricks to make the contract.
- Declarer has five sure tricks.
- The spade suit provides the best chance to take additional tricks.
- After winning the first trick, declarer should play the ♠ A and then a low spade toward the queen — the card declarer hopes will take a trick.
- Declarer should make the contract.

Exercise Eleven — Another Finesse against the King

(E-Z Deal Cards: #5, Deal 3 — Dealer, South)

Turn up all of the cards on the third pre-dealt deal and arrange them as in the previous exercise.

The Bidding

South is the dealer. Who would open the bidding? What would the opening bid be?

Look at responder's hand. What is the value of responder's hand? What would responder bid? What is the bidding message given by responder's bid? Does opener have to bid again? What is the value of opener's hand after hearing responder's bid? What would opener re-bid?

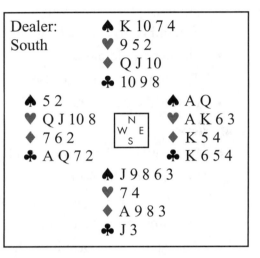

Dealer: ♠ K 10 7 4
South   ♥ 9 5 2
             ♦ Q J 10
             ♣ 10 9 8

♠ 5 2   ♠ A Q
♥ Q J 10 8   ♥ A K 6 3
♦ 7 6 2   ♦ K 5 4
♣ A Q 7 2   ♣ K 6 5 4

           ♠ J 9 8 6 3
           ♥ 7 4
           ♦ A 9 8 3
           ♣ J 3

What would the contract be? Who would be the declarer?

The Play

Who would make the opening lead? What would the opening lead be?

How many tricks must declarer take to fulfill the contract? How many sure tricks does declarer have? Why is declarer unlikely to win a trick with the ♦ K? Which other suit provides declarer with the opportunity to develop the additional trick needed to make the contract? Which suit should declarer play after winning the first trick? How should declarer plan to play the spade suit?

Bid and play the deal. Did declarer make the contract?

Exercise Eleven *Answers* — Another Finesse against the King

The Bidding

- East opens the bidding with 1♣.
- Responder has 9 total points and bids 1♥.
- Since West is already a passed hand, West's bid is invitational. It invites East to bid again with a very good hand. If West had not been a passed hand, this bid would be forcing for one round.
- Opener's hand is now worth 20 total points.
- Opener would rebid 4♥.
- The contract would be 4♥.
- West is the declarer.

The Play

- North makes the opening lead.
- North leads the ♦Q.
- Declarer needs 10 tricks to fulfill the contract.
- Declarer has eight sure tricks.
- Declarer is unlikely to win a trick with the ♦K because it is trapped between North's ♦Q J 10 and South's ♦A.
- The spade suit provides the opportunity to get an extra trick. Also, the club suit should provide an extra trick as long as the opponents clubs are divided 3–2.
- After declarer gets the lead, declarer plays the trump suit, drawing the opponents' trump cards. Then declarer leads a spade toward dummy's ♠A Q, planning to finesse dummy's ♠Q. Declarer then plays clubs.
- Declarer should make the contract.

Exercise Twelve — The Repeated Finesse

(E-Z Deal Cards: #5, Deal 4 — Dealer, West)

Turn up all of the cards on the fourth pre-dealt deal and arrange them as in the previous exercise.

The Bidding

West is the dealer. Who would open the bidding? What would the opening bid be?

Look at responder's hand. What is the value of responder's hand? Can responder support opener's suit? Can responder bid a new suit? What would responder bid? What is the bidding message given by responder's bid? Does opener have to bid again? What would opener rebid?

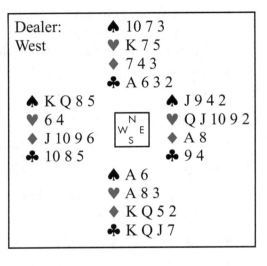

Dealer:
West

♠ 10 7 3
♥ K 7 5
♦ 7 4 3
♣ A 6 3 2

♠ K Q 8 5 　　　　 ♠ J 9 4 2
♥ 6 4 　　　　　　 ♥ Q J 10 9 2
♦ J 10 9 6 　　　　♦ A 8
♣ 10 8 5 　　　　　♣ 9 4

♠ A 6
♥ A 8 3
♦ K Q 5 2
♣ K Q J 7

What would the contract be? Who would be the declarer?

The Play

Who would make the opening lead? What would the opening lead be?

How many tricks must declarer take to fulfill the contract? How many sure tricks does declarer have? Which suit provides declarer with the opportunity to develop the additional tricks needed to make the contract? In which hand should declarer win the first trick? Why? Which suit should declarer play after winning the first trick? If declarer wins the second trick, which suit will declarer play next? Why?

Bid and play the deal. Did declarer make the contract?

Exercise Twelve *Answers* — The Repeated Finesse

The Bidding

- South opens the bidding with 1 ♦.
- Responder has 7 HCP. Since responder can't bid a new suit at the one level, responder bids 1NT.
- This is an invitational bid — opener doesn't have to bid again.
- Since opener's hand is strong, opener jumps to game in notrump (3NT).
- The contract is 3NT.
- North is the declarer.

The Play

- East makes the opening lead.
- East leads the ♥ Q.
- Declarer needs nine tricks.
- Declarer has seven sure tricks.
- The diamonds provide the best opportunity to develop additional tricks.
- Declarer should win the first trick in hand with the king in order to lead toward the ♦ K Q.
- If declarer wins the first diamond trick with a high diamond, declarer should lead a low club to the ace. Declarer plays another diamond toward the remaining high diamond in dummy.
- Declarer should make the contract.

CHAPTER 6
Rebids By Responder

Responder's General Approach to the Second Bid

Responder's Decision with 6 to 9 Total Points

Responder's Decision with 10 or 11 Total Points

Responder's Decision with 12 or More Total Points

Guidelines for Play

Summary

The Finer Points

Exercises

Sample Deals

RESPONDER'S GENERAL APPROACH TO THE SECOND BID

Let's consider what has happened by the time responder is ready to make a second bid, *responder's rebid*. Opener started the description by opening the bidding. Responder made an initial bid asking opener to further describe the hand. Opener then made a rebid that further described the strength and shape of the hand. For example, the auction might have started like this:

OPENER	RESPONDER
1♥	1♠
1NT	

Responder now has heard two bids from opener and is ready to consider the level and strain of the contract. This situation is similar to responder's approach when responding to a 1NT opening bid (Chapter 3). Responder usually has a very accurate description of opener's hand. For example, in the above auction, responder knows that opener has a minimum-strength balanced hand with five hearts and fewer than four spades. Let's consider another example.

Your partner opens the bidding with one of a suit. You respond with a new-suit bid, promising at least 6 total points and at least four cards in the suit named. Your partner rebids in another new suit, and it is your turn to rebid. How do you make your decision?

West	North	East	South
	1♣	Pass	1♥
Pass	1♠	Pass	?

The subject of responder's rebids is not a simple one. This is because there are many ways the bidding can go before responder has a chance to take a second bid. Sometimes the opener will be limited, but sometimes not. In the bidding above, for example, opener could have either a minimum (13–15) or a medium (16–18) hand.

One of the luxuries that responder has when choosing a rebid is that pass is usually an option. Almost all of opener's rebids (including the new-suit rebid above) are non-forcing.

> Responder is usually allowed to pass at
> responder's turn to rebid, but should try to keep
> the bidding going if a game contract is still
> possible.

In other words, the responder should pass at the second turn only if responder knows that a game contract is impossible (and if responder thinks the strain of opener's rebid suggests a reasonable contract).

Responder Categorizes the Strength

Responder decides which of three categories describes the point-count value of responder's hand:

Minimum Hand	6 to 9 total points
Medium Hand	10 or 11 total points
Maximum Hand	12 or more total points

As responder, you consider the point range that opener has described and combine it with your own point count to decide whether the partnership belongs in a partscore or game contract.

Responder Categorizes the Distribution

As responder, you also consider the information that opener has given about distribution when opener made the opening bid and a rebid. You look at your own distribution to determine whether there are any Golden Fits. If you are planning to put the partnership in a game contract, you determine whether there is a Golden Fit in a major suit. Otherwise, you steer the partnership into 3NT. If you are planning to put the partnership in a partscore contract, you look for any available Golden Fit. Otherwise, you place the contract in a notrump partscore.

Responder's Use of the Bidding Messages

Since responder is the captain, responder's bidding messages are important to the opener.

Sign-off Bid: Responder may have enough information after hearing opener's rebid to decide on both the level and strain and to place the contract. Opener is expected to pass when responder makes a sign-off bid, since opener's hand has already been described.

Invitational Bid: Responder still may not have enough information to determine whether the partnership belongs in partscore or game. If that is the case, responder will make an invitational bid. This bid asks opener to pass if opener's hand is at the bottom of the range that has already been shown or to bid on if at the top of the range.

Forcing Bid: Responder may know the partnership belongs in game but still needs more information from opener to determine the appropriate strain. In this case, responder will make a forcing bid asking for a further description of opener's distribution.

The Role of the Responder

As responder, you are the captain. You put the pieces of the puzzle together and come up with a solution. Opener's strength usually has been described within 3 points, and you know the exact strength of your own hand. In addition, you know the partnership needs 25 or more combined total points to be in a Golden Game. With fewer than 25 combined total points, the partnership should settle for a partscore contract.

You also know that a Golden Fit generally plays one trick better than notrump and that the partnership is trying to uncover an eight-card or longer combined trump suit. If there are 25 combined total points but the only Golden Fit is in a minor suit, the contract probably should be 3NT.

> ### As responder, you put it all together and decide:
> - What level?   Game or partscore?
> - What strain?   Golden Fit or notrump?

Keep It Simple

It is impossible to reach the best contract on every deal. There will be times when you end up playing in notrump when a trump contract would have played better. Sometimes, you may play in a partscore when you can make game. Responder makes the best decision using the information available. Responder tries to answer the questions "What level?" and "What strain?" and usually ends up placing the partnership in a satisfactory, if not perfect, contract.

RESPONDER'S DECISION WITH 6 TO 9 TOTAL POINTS

With 6 to 9 total points, responder's first bid will have been one of the following: a raise of opener's suit to the two level, a bid of a new suit at the one level, 1NT. Opener chooses a descriptive rebid that puts opener's hand into the minimum (13 to 15 total points), medium (16 to 18 total points) or maximum (19 to 21 total points) category.

If opener shows a minimum hand, the partnership will have only enough combined strength for a partscore. If opener has a medium hand, the partnership possibly has enough combined strength for game. If opener has a maximum hand, the partnership definitely has enough combined strength for game.

Let's see how responder chooses a rebid in each of these cases.

Opener Has a Minimum Hand

When responder has between 6 and 9 total points and opener shows a minimum-strength hand, responder knows the partnership belongs in a partscore. Opener can have at most 15 total points. Therefore, the partnership will always have fewer than 25 combined total points and responder wants to sign off in the best partscore. This can be accomplished in one of three ways:

- By passing.
- By bidding 1NT if the auction is still at the one level.
- By rebidding at the two level in a suit already mentioned by the partnership.

Suppose the auction starts this way:

OPENER	RESPONDER
1 ♦	1 ♠
1NT	

Opener shows a minimum-strength balanced hand by rebidding 1NT at the cheapest available level. Here is how responder handles the rebid when responder also has a minimum hand (6 to 9 total points).

♠ K J 6 3
♥ 10 4 2
♦ Q 4 3
♣ K 4 2

With only 9 HCP, responder knows the partnership belongs in a partscore. There might be a Golden Fit in diamonds, but opener may have only a four-card suit. Responder can't be sure. Responder would pass.

♠ K Q J 9 7 3
♥ 6 3
♦ 3 2
♣ 10 7 2

Since opener shows a balanced hand, responder knows there is a Golden Fit in spades. With only 8 total points, responder wants the partnership to play in a partscore and rebids 2 ♠. This is a sign-off bid, telling opener to pass.

♠ A 9 7 5
♥ 4
♦ Q 8 6 4 2
♣ 9 3 2

With 7 total points, responder knows the partnership belongs in a partscore. Responder also knows that there is a Golden Fit in diamonds. Responder signs off by bidding 2 ♦, a suit already mentioned by the partnership.

Suppose the auction starts as follows:

OPENER	RESPONDER
1 ♦	1 ♥
2 ♥	

Opener shows a minimum hand with four-card support for responder's suit.

♠ K 9 3
♥ K 10 9 7 2
♦ 4 2
♣ 8 6 4

With 7 total points, responder knows the partnership belongs in a partscore. The partnership has already found a Golden Fit, so responder should pass.

♠ J 3
♥ Q 8 7 5
♦ A 10 8 5 2
♣ 10 3

Responder knows there is a Golden Fit in hearts and, with only 8 total points, knows the partnership should play in a partscore. Even though responder knows there is also a Golden Fit in diamonds, there is no reason to disturb the major-suit contract. Responder passes.

Suppose the auction starts as follows:

OPENER	RESPONDER
1♣	1♥
1♠	

Opener could have a minimum- or medium-strength hand. It is safer for responder to assume opener has a minimum hand and choose a rebid accordingly.

♠ K J 2
♥ J 10 7 3
♦ K J 5
♣ 10 7 2

Responder has 9 HCP. No Golden Fit has been uncovered. With a minimum hand, responder stops in partscore and rebids 1NT. This is a sign-off bid.

♠ K 8 6 3
♥ Q 9 5 2
♦ J 4 3
♣ 8 2

Responder initially values this hand at 6 points. When opener bids 1♣, responder looks for a Golden Fit by bidding 1♥ (*up the line*). When opener rebids 1♠, responder knows there is a Golden Fit in a major suit. Responder now values the hand using dummy points. This brings the total to 7 points — 6 HCP plus 1 point for the doubleton club. The hand is still in the minimum category, and responder knows the partnership belongs in a partscore. Responder would pass.

♠ 4 2
♥ K 10 6 5
♦ 9 3
♣ A 9 7 6 2

Even knowing there is a Golden Fit in clubs when opener starts the bidding with 1♣, responder's first bid is 1♥. Responder is looking for a Golden Fit in a major suit. Opener's rebid has told responder that there is no Golden Fit in a major suit. Responder now signs off in 2♣, putting the partnership in a partscore in its Golden Fit.

Suppose the auction starts as follows:

OPENER	RESPONDER
1 ♦	1 ♠
2 ♣	

Opener could have a minimum- or medium-strength hand, but responder should assume it is minimum. Opener is also showing an unbalanced hand. With a balanced hand and no support for responder's suit, opener would have rebid 1NT.

♠ A 9 6 4　　　With 7 HCP, responder wants to stop in partscore in
♥ 9 8 3　　　　a Golden Fit. There is no spade fit because opener
♦ K 5 2　　　　did not raise responder's suit. Since opener has an
♣ 8 6 4　　　　unbalanced hand with diamonds that are equal in
　　　　　　　　length or longer than clubs, the most likely Golden
Fit is in diamonds, opener's original suit, rather than in clubs. Responder
bids 2 ♦, signing off in the likely Golden Fit.

♠ K 10 7 6 3　　Responder prefers opener's second suit. With only
♥ 8 5　　　　　7 points — 5 HCP plus 1 point each for the two
♦ 10 6　　　　　doubletons — responder would pass.
♣ Q 10 8 2

♠ Q J 9 7 6 3　　Responder doesn't like either of opener's suits and
♥ J 7 5 3　　　　rebids 2 ♠ to sign off in a suit already bid by the
♦ 3　　　　　　　partnership. Bidding a new suit at the two level or
♣ Q 4　　　　　　bidding 2NT is not one of responder's options with
　　　　　　　　　a minimum hand of 6 to 9 total points.

Opener Has a Medium Hand

When responder has 6 to 9 total points and opener shows a medium hand, the partnership may belong in a partscore or game, depending on whether responder is at the bottom or top of the range. If responder has 6 or 7 total points, the partnership belongs in a partscore since opener's maximum is 18 total points. Unless opener has exactly 18 total points and responder has exactly 7 total points (a possibility that will be ignored for simplicity's sake), the partnership will have fewer than 25 combined total points. Therefore, responder wants to sign off in the best partscore.

Responder does this in one of two ways:

> - By passing.
> - By bidding a suit already mentioned by the partnership at the cheapest available level.

If responder has 8 or 9 total points, the partnership belongs in a game contract, since opener's minimum is 16 total points. The partnership will have at least 25 combined total points. For simplicity's sake, the possibility of 8 total points by responder and 16 total points by opener will be ignored since the opener is twice as likely to have 17 or 18 total points. Responder, therefore, wants to ensure that the partnership gets to game. Responder does this in one of two ways:

> - By bidding one of the Golden Games.
> - By bidding a new suit (forcing) to get a further description of opener's hand.

In each of the following cases, responder has a minimum-strength hand (6 to 9 total points) and opener is showing a medium-strength hand.

Suppose the auction starts as follows:

OPENER	RESPONDER
1♥	1♠
3♥	

By jumping in the original suit, opener is showing a medium-strength, unbalanced hand with six hearts.

♠ K 9 6 5 3   Responder has a hand worth 7 total points — 6
♥ 5 2   HCP plus 1 point for the five-card suit. Responder
♦ Q J 6   knows, therefore, that the partnership doesn't have
♣ 7 4 2   enough combined strength for game. Responder
               would pass.

♠ A 10 4 3   Responder, with 9 HCP, knows the partnership
♥ Q 5   belongs in game since opener has at least 16 total
♦ K 8 6   points. Opener also shows an unbalanced hand with
♣ 10 9 6 3   at least a six-card heart suit. Responder bids 4♥,
             placing the partnership in game in its Golden Fit.

♠ K J 8 7   With 9 HCP, responder knows that the partnership
♥ 4   belongs at the game level. With no apparent Golden
♦ K 10 9 3   Fit in a major suit (opener may have only a six-card
♣ Q 10 7 5   heart suit), responder chooses 3NT.

Suppose the auction starts this way:

OPENER	RESPONDER
1♦	1♠
2♥	

Opener shows an unbalanced hand of at least medium strength by
rebidding at the two level in a higher-ranking suit than the original suit
(known as a reverse). Opener could also have a maximum-strength hand,
so responder should not pass.

♠ Q 10 8 7 3   With support for opener's major suit, responder
♥ J 9 5 4   values the hand using dummy points — 5 HCP
♦ 6 5   plus 1 point for each of the doubletons — a total
♣ Q 2   of 7 points. Responder bids 3♥. By bidding at the
               cheapest available level in a suit already mentioned
               by the partnership, responder shows a hand of 6 or
7 points. With a medium hand, opener passes. With a maximum hand,
opener bids game.

♠ A J 7 3   With 7 HCP, responder would like to stop in a
♥ 6 5   partscore. Responder can't pass, however, since the
♦ Q 9 5 4   partnership would not be playing in a Golden Fit.
♣ 7 3 2   Instead, responder returns to opener's original suit
             by bidding 3♦, putting the partnership in a suitable
             trump fit.

♠ K J 10 9 7 5
♥ 4 3
♦ 9 6
♣ Q 6 2

Responder wants to stop in a partscore but doesn't like either of opener's suits. Responder would rebid the spade suit at the cheapest available level, 2♠. This tells opener that responder wants to sign off in a partscore.

♠ K Q 8 7
♥ 8 6 2
♦ 7 4
♣ K J 10 4

With 9 HCP, responder knows the partnership belongs in game. Since responder hasn't found a Golden Fit in a major suit, responder bids 3NT, putting the partnership in one of the Golden Games.

Opener Has a Maximum Hand

When responder has 6 to 9 total points and opener shows a maximum-strength hand, the partnership always belongs in game. Therefore, responder wants to make sure the partnership gets to a suitable game contract. Responder does this in one of three ways:

- By passing if the partnership is already at the game level.
- By bidding one of the Golden Games.
- By bidding a new suit (forcing) to get a further description of opener's hand.

Suppose the auction starts as follows:

OPENER	RESPONDER
1♥	1NT
4♥	

♠ Q 9 5
♥ 10 8
♦ A J 7 5 3
♣ J 6 3

Responder has a hand worth 9 total points — 8 HCP plus 1 point for the five-card suit. Opener's jump to game after responder's 1NT bid shows a maximum hand of 19 to 21 total points. Since the partnership is already in a game contract, responder would pass.

Suppose the auction starts this way with opener showing a balanced hand and 18 or 19 HCP with the rebid:

OPENER	RESPONDER
1♦	1♠
2NT	

♠ Q J 6 3
♥ A 10 4
♦ 7 5 2
♣ 9 6 3

Responder has 7 HCP. Opener's jump to 2NT shows a balanced 18-19 HCP hand. Responder knows the partnership belongs in game and has no available Golden Fit in a major suit. Bid 3NT.

♠ A J 10 8 7 6
♥ 7
♦ Q 8 2
♣ 10 4 2

Responder has 7 HCP plus 2 points for the six-card suit. Since opener is describing a balanced hand, responder knows opener has at least two spades. There must be a Golden Fit. Since the partnership belongs in game, responder bids 4♠, a sign-off bid.

♠ K Q 9 7 5
♥ J 10
♦ 10 3 2
♣ J 9 7

Responder has 8 total points — 7 HCP plus 1 point for the five-card suit. Responder knows there is enough combined strength for game, but is not sure if there is a Golden Fit in spades. Responder bids 3♠ to request opener to bid 4♠ with three-card support or 3NT with only two spades. 3♠ is a forcing bid. Responder has at least 6 total points, and opener has shown a maximum-strength hand.

Put It All Together

With a minimum-strength hand, 6 to 9 total points, responder decides the final contract by combining the value of responder's hand with the value opener showed when rebidding.

Responder's Rebid

Opener's Range	Responder's Range	Final Level	Responder's Option
13 to 15 (Minimum)	6 to 9	Partscore	• Pass. • 1NT • Two-level bid of a suit already mentioned by the partnership
16 to 18 (Medium)	6 or 7	Partscore	• Pass. • Cheapest bid of a suit already mentioned by the partnership
	8 or 9	Game	• Bid a Golden Game. • Bid a new suit.
19 to 21 (Maximum)	6 to 9	Game	• Pass. • Bid a Golden Game. • Bid a new suit.

Let's see how you would handle the following examples.

OPENER	RESPONDER
1♥	1NT
2♥	

♠ K 10 3
♥ 4 3
♦ J 10 6 5 3
♣ Q 7 4

Opener is showing a minimum-strength unbalanced hand. With 7 points, you know the partnership belongs in a partscore. Pass.

	OPENER	RESPONDER
	1♦	1♠
	3♠	

♠ Q J 9 7 4
♥ K 8 2
♦ 5
♣ J 10 6 5

Opener's jump raise shows a medium hand of 16 to 18 total points. With 8 total points, there is enough combined strength for game if opener has 17 or 18 total points. Go for the game and bid 4 ♠.

♠ 10 9 7 4
♥ 6 4
♦ A 8 6 3
♣ A J 9

You have 9 HCP, enough for game opposite opener's medium-strength hand. Carry on to game in your Golden Fit. Bid 4♠.

	OPENER	RESPONDER
	1♥	1♠
	3♣	

♠ K J 6 2
♥ 5 2
♦ Q 10 4 3
♣ J 9 2

Opener is showing a maximum-strength unbalanced hand by jumping in the second suit (jump shift). Even though you have only 7 HCP, there is enough combined strength for game. With no known Golden Fit in a major suit, bid 3NT.

	OPENER	RESPONDER
	1♠	2♠
	3♠	

♠ K 9 4
♥ 9 8
♦ 10 9 7 5 2
♣ Q 10 6

Opener's raise to the three level shows a medium-strength hand. With only 6 points — 5 HCP plus 1 point for the doubleton heart — pass.

♠ J 9 6 3
♥ K 5
♦ A 7 6 2
♣ 9 6 4

Your hand is worth 9 total points — 8 HCP plus 1 point for the doubleton heart. There should be enough combined strength for game, so carry on to 4♠.

RESPONDER'S DECISION WITH 10 OR 11 TOTAL POINTS

With 10 or 11 total points, responder's first bid will have been a raise of opener's suit to the three level (invitational) or a new suit at the one level or two level (forcing). If responder raises opener's suit to the three level, opener will pass with 13 total points or bid game with more.

If responder bids a new suit, opener will choose a descriptive rebid that classifies opener's hand as minimum (13 to 15 total points), medium (16 to 18 total points) or maximum (19 to 21 total points). When opener has a medium or maximum hand, there will always be enough combined strength for game. Even if opener has a minimum hand, the partnership possibly has enough combined strength for game. Let's look at how responder chooses a rebid in each of these cases.

Opener Has a Minimum-Strength Hand

When responder has 10 or 11 total points and opener shows a minimum hand of 13 to 15 total points, the partnership may belong in either a partscore or game. The final contract depends on whether opener is at the bottom or top of the minimum range. If opener has 13 total points, the partnership belongs in a partscore. Unless opener has exactly 14 total points and responder has exactly 11 total points (a possibility that will be ignored for simplicity's sake), the partnership will have fewer than 25 combined total points. If opener has 15 total points, the partnership belongs in game since the partnership will have at least 25 combined total points.

Thus, to determine the proper contract, responder needs to get more information from opener. Responder can do this by making an invitational bid — moving toward a game without actually bidding it. Opener can pass the invitational bid if at the bottom of the range, 13 total points, but bid on to game if at the top of the range, 14 or 15 total points.

Responder makes an invitational bid in one of two ways:

- By bidding 2NT.
- By rebidding at the three level a suit already mentioned by the partnership.

Note that these rebids are distinct from those that responder would make with 6 to 9 total points when opener shows a minimum hand (pass, 1NT, rebid at the two level of a suit already mentioned). In this way, opener will know responder is making an invitational bid rather than a sign-off bid.

In each of the following cases, responder has a medium hand (10 or 11 total points) and opener shows a minimum hand.

Suppose the auction starts as follows:

OPENER	RESPONDER
1♦	1♠
1NT	

♠ K 10 9 5
♥ Q J 4
♦ J 3
♣ A 10 6 2

Opener shows a minimum-strength balanced hand with the rebid of 1NT. Responder has 11 HCP. The partnership should be in a partscore if opener is at the bottom of the range, or in game if opener is at the top of the range. Since there does not appear to be a Golden Fit, responder invites game by bidding 2NT. Opener will pass if at the bottom of the range but carry on to 3NT if at the top.

♠ A Q 10 9 7 6
♥ 5
♦ 10 7 2
♣ K 8 3

Responder has 11 total points — 9 HCP plus 2 points for the six-card suit. Opener shows a balanced hand, so responder knows there is a Golden Fit in spades. To make an invitational rebid, responder rebids the suit at the three level, 3♠. Since responder would have bid only 2♠ with 6 to 9 total points, opener will know this is an invitational bid, not a sign-off bid.

♠ A 9 6 4 2
♥ 5 3
♦ A J 7 5 2
♣ 6

Responder has 11 total points — 9 HCP plus 1 point for each of the five-card suits. Responder invites game by bidding 3♦, a suit already bid by the partnership. Responder doesn't bid 2♦, since that would be a sign-off bid showing a hand in the 6 to 9 total-point range.

Now suppose the auction starts this way:

OPENER	RESPONDER
1 ♥	2 ♣
2 ♥	

♠ A J 10
♥ 4 2
♦ K 10 5
♣ Q 10 9 6 3

Responder has a balanced hand without support for opener's major suit with 10 HCP and 1 point for the long club. Although there is the possibility opener has six hearts, your hand looks like notrump, so bid an invitational 2NT.

♠ J 10 2
♥ 3
♦ K 10 5
♣ A J 10 9 5 4

With 11 points, 9 HCP plus 2 points for the six-card suit and an unbalanced hand with no fit for opener's suit, responder rebids 3 ♣.

Opener Has a Medium Hand

If responder has 10 or 11 total points and opener shows a medium hand of 16 to 18 total points, the partnership has at least 26 combined total points and belongs in a game contract. Therefore, responder wants to ensure that the partnership gets to game.

Responder does this in one of two ways:

> • By bidding one of the Golden Games.
>
> • By bidding a new suit (forcing) to get a further description of opener's hand.

OPENER	RESPONDER
1 ♣	1 ♠
3 ♣	

Opener shows an unbalanced hand of medium strength (16 to 18 total points). Let's look at how responder handles the following hands, all in the medium range (10 or 11 total points).

♠ K J 10 5   Responder has 11 HCP and knows there is no Golden
♥ Q J 7   Fit in a major suit, although there is a Golden Fit in
♦ A 9 3   clubs. Responder puts the partnership in the Golden
♣ 7 6 3   Game of 3NT.

♠ A Q J 9 7 6 3   Responder has an unbalanced hand with 11 total
♥ J 10 3   points. When opener shows a medium hand, re-
♦ 5   sponder knows the partnership belongs in game. It
♣ 4 2   looks as if the most probable Golden Game is 4♠.
                 This will be a Golden Fit unless opener has no spades.

♠ K J 10 7 3   Responder has 11 total points but is not sure of the
♥ 5 4   best strain for the contract. In this case, responder
♦ A J 9 6 2   bids a new suit, 3♦, to get opener to make a further
♣ 10   descriptive bid. After hearing opener's next bid, re-
                 sponder should know whether the partnership should
be in a Golden Game in spades or notrump.

Opener Has a Maximum Hand

If responder has 10 or 11 total points and opener shows a maximum-
strength hand of 19 to 21 total points, the partnership has at least 29
combined total points and belongs at least in game.

Responder ensures that the partnership gets to a game contract in
one of two ways:

> • By bidding one of the Golden Games.
> • By bidding a new suit to get a further de-
>   scription of opener's hand.

Suppose the auction starts off as follows:

OPENER	RESPONDER
1♥	1♠
2NT	

Opener shows a balanced hand with 18 or 19 HCP. Let's see how
responder handles the following hands, all in the medium range (10 or
11 total points).

♠ J 10 9 5
♥ Q 6
♦ A J 5 3
♣ K 8 2

With 11 HCP and no sign of a Golden Fit in a major suit, responder would put the partnership in the Golden Game of 3NT.

♠ Q 10 9 7 4 2
♥ 3
♦ A 10 3
♣ Q 6 2

Opener has shown a balanced hand. Responder knows there is a Golden Fit in spades and can take the partnership directly to the Golden Game, 4♠.

♠ A J 10 8 2
♥ 9 4
♦ K J 3
♣ J 6 2

With only a five-card spade suit, responder is not certain whether there is a Golden Fit in spades. Responder rebids 3♠ to get a further description of opener's hand. Opener will bid 4♠ with three-card support or 3NT without three-card support for the spade suit.

Put It All Together

With a medium hand of 10 or 11 total points, responder combines the value of the hand with the value shown by opener's rebid to decide the contract. (See Summary for Chapter 6.)

Responder's Rebid

Opener's Range	Responder's Range	Final Level	Responder's Option
13 to 15 (Minimum)	10 or 11	Partscore or game	• Bid 2NT. • Make a three-level call in a suit already bid by the partner-ship.
16 to 18 (Medium)	10 or 11	Game	• Bid a Golden Game. • Bid a new suit.
19 to 21 (Maximum)	10 or 11	Game	• Bid a Golden Game. • Pass in game. • Bid a new suit.

Let's see how you would handle the following examples.

OPENER	RESPONDER
1 ♣	1 ♠
2 ♠	

♠ K 10 9 7 3 2   Opener shows a minimum-strength hand with spade
♥ 5 3   support. You have 9 HCP plus 2 points for the six-
♦ Q 5   card suit. Make an invitational raise to 3 ♠.
♣ A 9 4

OPENER	RESPONDER
1♦	1♠
2♥	

♠ A J 10 8
♥ J 8 2
♦ 10 4
♣ K Q 9 6

Opener shows a medium-strength hand by bidding a second suit at the two level which is higher-ranking than the original suit. With 11 HCP and no Golden Fit in a major suit, bid 3NT.

♠ Q 9 8 6 3
♥ Q 10 7 4
♦ 5
♣ K J 3

With four-card support for opener's second suit, you can value your hand using dummy points — 8 HCP plus 3 points for the singleton. Opposite opener's medium-strength hand, this is enough to put the partnership in game, 4♥.

OPENER	RESPONDER
1♥	2♣
4♥	

♠ 10 8 6
♥ K 3
♦ Q 7 2
♣ K Q 9 7 5

Opener shows a maximum hand. Since the partnership is already in a game contract, responder may pass.

RESPONDER'S DECISION WITH 12 OR MORE TOTAL POINTS

With 12 or more total points, responder will initially bid a new suit or jump to 2NT over opener's bid of one in a suit.

When responder has 12 or more total points, there are enough combined points for game even if opener has a minimum-strength hand. There are some other considerations. In addition to the bonus for bidding and making a game contract, there is an additional bonus for bidding and making a slam (a six-level or seven-level contract). A brief discussion of slam bidding is included in the Appendix. For now, it is sufficient to know the partnership needs about 33 combined points to undertake a slam contract. When opener shows a medium-strength hand, there is some possibility for a slam contract. When opener shows a maximum-strength hand, there is a strong possibility for a slam contract.

Opener Has a Minimum-Strength Hand

If responder has 12 or more total points and opener shows a minimum-strength hand of 13 to 15 total points, the partnership has at least 25 combined total points and belongs in a game contract.

Responder ensures that the partnership gets to game in one of two ways:

> • By bidding one of the Golden Games.
>
> • By bidding a new suit at the three level to get a further description of opener's hand.

Suppose the auction starts as follows:

OPENER	RESPONDER
1 ♦	1 ♠
1NT	

Opener shows a minimum-strength balanced hand. Let's look at how responder handles the following hands.

♠ A J 9 4
♥ J 10
♦ K 9 6 3
♣ A 4 2

Responder has 13 HCP and knows there is no Golden Fit in a major suit. Responder is certain the partnership belongs in a game contract and takes the partnership directly to game, 3NT.

♠ 10 9 7 6 5 2
♥ A 8
♦ 6 4
♣ A K J

Responder has 12 HCP plus 2 points for the six-card suit, a total of 14 points. Responder knows there is a Golden Fit in spades since opener has shown a balanced hand. Responder rebids 4 ♠.

♠ A Q 8 6 3 Responder has 16 points — 15 HCP plus 1 point for
♥ K Q 9 2 the five-card suit. Responder knows the partnership
♦ 5   belongs in game but is not sure of the strain. Needing
♣ A 3 2   further information from opener, responder bids a
new suit at the three level, 3 ♥. Opener now has an
opportunity to further describe the hand. The partnership may belong in
spades, hearts or notrump.

Opener Has a Medium-Strength Hand

If responder has 12 or more total points and opener shows a medium-strength hand of 16 to 18 total points, the partnership has 28 or more combined total points and belongs in at least a game contract.

Since the partnership needs about 33 points for a slam contract, there is also the possibility of a slam when responder has 15 or more total points. To keep things simple, we won't consider the possibility of slam for the time being.

When responder wants to ensure that the partnership gets to a game contract, responder proceeds in one of two ways:

> - By bidding one of the Golden Games.
> - By bidding a new suit at the three level to get a further description of opener's hand.

Suppose the auction starts as follows:

OPENER	RESPONDER
1 ♥	1 ♠
3 ♥	

Opener shows a medium-strength unbalanced hand. Let's look at how responder handles the following hands.

♠ K Q J 2 Responder has 13 HCP. Since opener has an unbal-
♥ A 10   anced hand and at least six cards in the original suit,
♦ 6 5 3   responder knows there is a Golden Fit in hearts and
♣ Q J 6 5 takes the partnership to game, 4 ♥.

♠ A K Q 6   There doesn't appear to be a Golden Fit in a major
♥ 5   suit. Responder puts the partnership in the Golden
♦ K 10 9 2   Game of 3NT.
♣ J 10 6 3

Suppose the auction starts off this way:

OPENER	RESPONDER
1 ♦	1 ♠
3 ♦	

♠ Q J 10 7   Responder has 14 HCP. Even though there is a fit in
♥ K Q 3   diamonds, responder bids to a Golden Game, 3NT.
♦ 9 8 5 2
♣ A Q

♠ A Q 10 7 6   Responder has 15 points — 13 HCP plus 1 point
♥ A 9 6 3 2   for each of the five-card suits. Responder knows the
♦ 5   partnership belongs in game but is not sure of the
♣ K 5   best strain. To get further information from opener,
                         responder bids a new suit, 3 ♥, and waits to hear
what opener has to say. Responder should receive the information necessary to make a decision.

Opener Has a Maximum-Strength Hand

If responder has 12 or more total points and opener shows a maximum-strength hand of 19 to 21 total points, the partnership may belong
in a slam contract. Slam bidding is beyond the scope of this chapter. It
is discussed briefly in the Appendix and will be discussed in the second
book in this series, *Play of the Hand in the 21st Century*.

Put It All Together

With a maximum hand, 12 or more total points, responder combines the value of the hand with the value shown by opener's rebid to decide on the final contract.

Responder's Rebid

Opener's Range	Responder's Range	Final Level	Responder's Option
13 to 15 (Minimum)	12 or more	Game	• Bid a Golden Game. • Bid a new suit at the three level.
16 to 18 (Medium)	12 or more	Game or slam	• Bid a Golden Game. • Bid a new suit at the three level.
19 to 21 (Maximum)	12 or more	Game or slam	• Bid a slam or game as appropriate.

Let's see how you would handle the following examples.

OPENER	RESPONDER
1♦	1♠
2♦	

♠ A K J 9 7 6 3
♥ —
♦ A 9 7
♣ 6 3 2

Opener shows an unbalanced hand in the minimum range (13 to 15 total points). You have 12 HCP plus 3 points for the seven-card suit. That's enough for game. The best game appears to be 4♠, so that's the bid you would make.

♠ A Q 9 7
♥ K J 3
♦ J 9 5
♣ Q 10 7

With 13 HCP and no Golden Fit in a major suit, you take the partnership to game in notrump, 3NT.

♠ A J 8 6 3
♥ A 5
♦ 2
♣ K J 4 3 2

You know the partnership belongs in game, but the best strain is not clear. Bid a new suit, 3♣, to elicit more information from opener. If opener shows some support for spades, you may play in 4♠. Otherwise bid 3NT.

OPENER	RESPONDER
1♣	1♠
2♥	

♠ A K 9 7 3
♥ A 8 6 4
♦ 10 4
♣ J 5

Opener shows at least a medium-strength hand by bidding a second suit at the two level that is higher-ranking than the original suit. With enough for game and support for opener's hearts, bid the Golden Game, 4♥.

♠ Q J 7 6
♥ Q 8 2
♦ K Q 3
♣ Q J 3

With 13 HCP and no Golden Fit in a major suit, rebid 3NT.

GUIDELINES FOR PLAY

The various techniques for developing tricks that have been discussed in previous chapters (promotion, length, finesse) apply to both notrump and trump contracts. In a trump contract, however, when analyzing the alternatives, declarer discovers there are additional ways to develop extra tricks. One way is to take advantage of the trumps in the dummy.

Ruffing in Dummy

NORTH (Dummy)	SOUTH (Declarer)
♠ 4	♠ A 3 2
♥ 9 8 7	♥ A K Q J 10
♦ 7 6 5 4	♦ A 2
♣ 8 7 6 5 4	♣ A 3 2

Suppose South plays in a contract with hearts as the trump suit. South has eight sure tricks — five heart tricks and the three aces in the other suits. If South takes all of the sure tricks, South will be left with five cards, none of which will win a trick. Such cards are called losers.

One of the advantages of playing in a trump contract is that you can occasionally use your trumps to win a trick you would otherwise lose. In the above hands, before playing all of the trumps, South could play the ♠A, then lead a low spade and play one of dummy's trumps. This is called ruffing a loser in dummy. The advantage of this play is that South ends up with an additional trick. In fact, South could ruff both of the losing spades in dummy and end up with two additional tricks, a total of 10.

Ruffing in Declarer's Hand

Ruffing losers in dummy is a useful way to take extra tricks. You should look for this possibility in a trump contract whenever there is a short suit (void, singleton, doubleton) in dummy. Ruffing in your own hand when you are declarer usually doesn't gain a trick.

Suppose we change the hands slightly:

NORTH (Dummy)	SOUTH (Declarer)
♠ A 3 2	♠ 4
♥ 9 8 7	♥ A K Q J 10
♦ 7 6 5 4	♦ A 2
♣ A 3 2	♣ 8 7 6 5 4

South again starts with eight sure tricks. When South plays the ♠4 to dummy's ace and then leads a low spade from dummy and ruffs, there are still only eight tricks. Instead, South should plan on establishing the club suit if extra tricks are needed.

The general guideline to get extra tricks is to ruff your losers in the dummy, not in your hand. Save the trumps in your hand for drawing the opponents' trumps and for stopping the opponents from taking tricks in other suits.

SUMMARY

When you make your rebid as responder, you put your hand into one of these categories according to the point-count value (using dummy points if planning to support opener's major suit):

Minimum Hand   6 to 9 total points

Medium Hand   10 or 11 total points

Maximum Hand   12 or more total points

By combining this information with the strength and distribution shown by opener's rebid, you try to decide the level and strain of the contract. When you have enough information, you sign off in the appropriate contract. If you need more information, you make an invitational or forcing bid using the following guidelines:

Responder's Rebid

Opener's Range	Responder's Range	Final Level	Responder's Option
13 to 15 (Minimum)	6 to 9	Partscore	• Pass. • Bid 1NT. • Bid at the two level a suit already mentioned by the partnership.
	10 or 11	Partscore or game	• Bid 2NT. • Bid at the three level a suit already mentioned by the partnership.
	12 or more	Game	• Bid a Golden Game. • Bid a new suit at the three level.
16 to 18 (Medium)	6 or 7	Partscore	• Pass. • Bid at the lowest level a suit already mentioned by the partnership.
	8 or 9	Game	• Bid a Golden Game. • Bid a new suit.
	10 or 11	Game	• Bid a Golden Game. • Bid a new suit.
	12 or more	Game or slam	• Bid a Golden Game or slam if appropriate.
19 to 21 (Maximum)	6 to 9	Game	• Pass. • Bid a Golden Game. • Bid a new suit.
	10 or 11	Game	• Pass. • Bid a Golden Game. • Bid a new suit.
	12 or more	Game or slam	• Bid a Golden Game or slam if appropriate.

THE FINER POINTS

Responder Bids a New Suit

After hearing opener's rebid, the responder can usually determine the appropriate level and strain. There are times, however, when responder needs further information from opener in order to make a decision. Responder does this by making a forcing bid.

Responder's bid of a new suit at the cheapest level is always forcing, (*i.e.,* opener must bid again), unless opener specifically has rebid 1NT. In that case, a bid of a new suit is not forcing if it is lower-ranking than responder's original suit. For example:

OPENER	RESPONDER
1♦	1♥
1NT	2♣

Since responder's second suit, clubs, is lower ranking than the first suit, hearts, opener could pass when preferring clubs to hearts. To make a forcing bid, responder must jump to the three level, 3♣. The summary of responder's options reflects this by noting that responder can bid a new suit at the three level with 12 or more total points when opener's hand is in the minimum range.

Strictly speaking, responder does not have to bid a new suit at the three level to make a forcing bid if the new suit is higher-ranking than responder's original suit.

For example:

OPENER	RESPONDER
1♦	1♥
1NT	2♠

Since spades rank higher than hearts, responder's rebid is forcing. Responder does not have to jump to 3♠, which would use up a lot of room on the Bidding Scale. The illustrated auction shows an example of a responder's reverse for which 12 or more total points are required.

There are auctions in which even an old suit bid by responder is forcing. When the partnership has shown enough combined strength for game, any bid below the game level is forcing. For example:

OPENER	RESPONDER
1♦	1♥
3♣	3♥

Opener shows a maximum-strength hand and responder must have at least 6 total points, so the partnership has enough combined strength for game. Based on this logic, responder's 3♥ rebid is forcing.

After Opener's Reverse

In the previous chapter, we learned that when opener bids a second suit at the two level that is higher ranking than the original suit (a reverse), the reverse bid can show either a medium- or a maximum-strength hand. For example:

OPENER	RESPONDER
1♦	1♠
2♥	

Since hearts are higher-ranking than diamonds, opener's rebid of 2♥ shows at least a medium-strength hand of 16 to 18 total points. Since a jump shift to 3♥ would use up a lot of room on the Bidding Scale, the rebid could also be used when opener has a maximum-strength hand of 19 to 21 points.

Responder should assume that opener has a medium hand, but because opener may have a maximum-strength hand, responder can't pass even with 6 or 7 total points. Responder must bid again to allow opener to further describe opener's strength. With 6 or 7 total points, responder can bid an old suit at the cheapest available level (2♠, 3♦ or 3♥ in the above example) or bid 2NT. With a medium-strength hand, opener can pass; with a maximum-strength hand, opener will carry on to game.

Exercise One — Responder's Rebid Decides What Level

Partner opens the bidding 1♦ and you respond 1♥. What are three rebids opener could make to specifically show a minimum-strength hand?

_____   _____   _____

What strength would a rebid of 1♠ or 2♣ by opener show?

_____

A 1NT rebid by opener shows a balanced hand with 13 or 14 HCP. What is the minimum number of points responder can hold to decide the partnership should play in game? _____

With what range of points is responder uncertain whether the partnership should be in game or partscore? _____

What is the maximum number of points responder can hold to decide the partnership should play in a partscore? _____

Exercise Two — Responder's Rebid when Opener Shows
                              a Minimum Hand

Suppose the bidding is:

OPENER	RESPONDER
1♥	1♠
2♠	

Add the high-card points and the distribution points of the following hands. Classify each hand as a minimum (6 to 9 total points), medium (10 or 11 total points) or maximum (12 or more total points). At what level should the contract be played (partscore, possible game or game). In what strain should the contract be played? What is your rebid?

1) ♠ 9 8 7 6	2) ♠ Q 10 9 4 2	3) ♠ Q J 7 4 2
♥ A 5	♥ 9 8	♥ K 3
♦ Q 7 4 3 2	♦ A K 6	♦ A J 4
♣ 9 3	♣ J 4 3	♣ Q J 3
HCP:_____	HCP:_____	HCP:_____
Distr. Pts.:_____	Distr. Pts.:_____	Distr. Pts.:_____
Total Pts.: _____	Total Pts.: _____	Total Pts.:_____
Range:_____	Range: _____	Range: _____
Level: _____	Level: _____	Level: _____
Strain: _____	Strain: _____	Strain:_____
Rebid: _____	Rebid:_____	Rebid:_____

Exercise One Answers — Responder's Rebid Decides What Level

- 1NT, 2 ♦, 2 ♥.

- 1 ♠ would show either a minimum- or a medium-strength hand. 2 ♣ would show at least 12 total points and an unbalanced hand.

- Responder needs at least 12 total points to be sure the partnership should be in game.

- With 10 or 11 total points, responder is uncertain whether the partnership should be in game or partscore.

- If responder has 9 total points (or fewer), the decision should be to play in partscore.

Exercise Two Answers — Responder's Rebid when Opener Shows a Minimum Hand

1)	2)	3)
6 HCP	10 HCP	14 HCP
1 distr. pt.	1 distr. pt.	1 distr. pt.
7 total pts.	11 total pts.	15 total pts.
Minimum	Medium	Maximum
Partscore	Possible game	Game
Spades	Spades	Spades
Pass	3 ♠	4 ♠

Exercise Three — Responder's Rebid when Opener Bids a
                      Second Suit

Suppose the bidding is: OPENER   RESPONDER
                                 1♣   1♥
                                 1♠

Add the high-card points and the distribution (or dummy) points of
the following hands. Classify each hand as minimum (6 to 9 total points),
medium (10 or 11 total points) or maximum (12 or more total points).
At what level should the contract be played (partscore, possible game
or game) and in what strain should the contract be played. What is your
rebid?

1) ♠ Q 3 2	2) ♠ J 5 2	3) ♠ 10 8 3
♥ A 10 9 4	♥ A Q 8 3	♥ K Q 9 4
♦ Q J 6	♦ K J 6	♦ A J 4
♣ 7 5 2	♣ 10 8 6	♣ K Q 8

HCP:_____	HCP:_____	HCP:_____
Distr. Pts.:_____	Distr. Pts.:_____	Distr. Pts.:_____
Total Pts.: _____	Total Pts.: _____	Total Pts.: _____
Range:_____	Range: _____	Range: _____
Level: _____	Level: _____	Level: _____
Strain: _____	Strain:_____	Strain:_____
Rebid: _____	Rebid:_____	Rebid:_____

Exercise Three *Answers* — Responder's Rebid when Opener
Bids a Second Suit

1) 9 HCP
0 distr. pts.
9 total pts.
Minimum
Partscore
Notrump
1NT

2) 11 HCP
0 distr. pts.
11 total pts.
Medium
Possible game
Notrump
2NT

3) 15 HCP
0 distr. pts.
15 total pts.
Maximum
Game
Notrump
3NT

Exercise Three (cont.) — Responder's Rebid when Opener Bids a Second Suit

4) ♠ J 7
   ♥ K J 10 8 6 3
   ♦ 9 2
   ♣ 7 5 2

5) ♠ A 8
   ♥ K Q 10 9 7 4
   ♦ 8 6 2
   ♣ 9 5

6) ♠ K J 8 2
   ♥ A K 8 3
   ♦ 5 2
   ♣ K 7 3

HCP:_____

Distr. Pts.:_____

Total Pts.: _____

Range:_____

Level: _____

Strain: _____

Rebid: _____

HCP:_____

Distr. Pts.:_____

Total Pts.: _____

Range: _____

Level: _____

Strain:_____

Rebid:_____

HCP:_____

Distr. Pts.:_____

Total Pts.: _____

Range: _____

Level: _____

Strain:_____

Rebid:_____

7) ♠ 6 2
   ♥ Q J 7 5
   ♦ 4 3
   ♣ K 10 9 4 2

8) ♠ 8 2
   ♥ K 9 6 2
   ♦ 7 4
   ♣ A Q 9 7 4

9) ♠ Q 10 7 2
   ♥ A 9 7 4 2
   ♦ K 2
   ♣ 10 9

HCP:_____

Distr. Pts.:_____

Total Pts.: _____

Range:_____

Level: _____

Strain: _____

Rebid: _____

HCP:_____

Distr. Pts.:_____

Total Pts.: _____

Range: _____

Level: _____

Strain:_____

Rebid:_____

HCP:_____

Distr. Pts.:_____

Total Pts.: _____

Range: _____

Level: _____

Strain:_____

Rebid:_____

Exercise Three (cont.) *Answers* — Responder's Rebid when Opener Bids a Second Suit

4) 5 HCP
   2 distr. pts.
   7 total pts.
   Minimum
   Partscore
   Hearts
   2 ♥

5) 9 HCP
   2 distr. pts.
   11 total pts.
   Medium
   Possible game
   Hearts
   3 ♥

6) 14 HCP
   1 dummy pt.
   15 total pts.
   Maximum
   Game
   Spades
   4 ♠

7) 6 HCP
   2 dummy pts.
   8 total pts.
   Minimum
   Partscore
   Clubs
   2 ♣

8) 9 HCP
   2 dummy pts.
   11 total pts.
   Medium
   Possible game
   Clubs or notrump
   3 ♣

9) 9 HCP
   2 dummy pts.
   11 total pts.
   Medium
   Possible game
   Spades
   3 ♠

Exercise Four — Responder's Rebid when Opener Shows a
Medium Hand

Suppose the bidding is:

OPENER	RESPONDER
1 ♥	1 ♠
3 ♥	

What is the range of opener's hand?_____

Value your hand as responder. Then decide at what level the contract
should be played and in what strain the contract should be played. What
is your rebid?

1) ♠ K 10 7 4 3	2) ♠ A J 8 2	3) ♠ A 10 7 3
♥ 9 2	♥ 7	♥ K 10
♦ Q J 6 2	♦ K 10 4 3	♦ 7 4 3
♣ 10 4	♣ Q 9 8 6	♣ Q 9 6 2

Total Pts.: _____   Total Pts.: _____   Total Pts.: _____

Level: _____   Level: _____   Level: _____

Strain: _____   Strain: _____   Strain: _____

Rebid: _____   Rebid: _____   Rebid: _____

Exercise Four *Answers* — Responder's Rebid when Opener Shows a Medium Hand

- Opener's hand has 16 to 18 total points (medium range).

1) 7 total points
   Partscore
   Hearts
   Pass

2) 10 total points
   Game
   Notrump
   3NT

3) 9 total points
   Game
   Hearts
   4 ♥

Exercise Five — Responder's Rebid when Opener Shows a Maximum Hand

Suppose the bidding is:

OPENER	RESPONDER
1 ♦	1 ♥
2NT	

What is the range of opener's hand?_____

Value your hand as responder. Then decide at what level the contract should be played and in what strain the contract should be played. What is your rebid?

1) ♠ 9 4
   ♥ K 10 8 4
   ♦ Q J 9 3
   ♣ 10 7 2

2) ♠ 8
   ♥ Q J 10 8 3 2
   ♦ A 6 5
   ♣ 9 4 2

3) ♠ K 5 2
   ♥ A J 9 4 3
   ♦ J 10 8
   ♣ 4 3

Total Pts.: _____   Total Pts.: _____   Total Pts.: _____

Level: _____   Level: _____   Level: _____

Strain: _____   Strain:_____   Strain:_____

Rebid: _____   Rebid:_____   Rebid:_____

Exercise Six — Ruffing Losers

Construct the following hands for North and South:

NORTH (Dummy)	SOUTH (Declarer)
♠ 8 6 4 2	♠ A K Q J 10 9
♥ 5 3	♥ A K 6
♦ J 7 3	♦ 9 4 2
♣ A 9 4 2	♣ 5

Suppose South plays in a contract of 4 ♠. How many sure tricks does South have?_____

How can South take an additional trick? _____

Could South get an additional trick by leading a club to dummy's ace and then leading a club and ruffing it? _____

What conclusion can you draw from this? _____

_____

Exercise Five *Answers* — Responder's Rebid when Opener
Shows a Maximum Hand

- Opener has 19 to 21 total points (maximum range). However, the
  jump shift into notrump by opener specifically guarantees 18 or
  19 HCP.

1)	6 total points	2)	9 total points	3)	10 total points
	Game		Game		Game
	Notrump		Hearts		Possibly hearts
	3NT		4♥		3♥

Exercise Six *Answers* — Ruffing Losers

- South has nine tricks.
- An additional trick could be developed by ruffing the third heart
  in dummy.
- There would not be an additional trick since you have counted
  six spade winners already.
- The conclusion is that you get an extra trick by ruffing in the short
  hand (dummy) rather than in the hand that is long in trumps.

Exercise Seven — Developing a Trick by Ruffing in Dummy

(E-Z Deal Cards: #6, Deal 1 — Dealer, North)

Turn up all of the cards on the first pre-dealt deal. Put each hand dummy style at the edge of the table in front of each player.

The Bidding

North is the dealer. Who would open the bidding? What would the opening bid be?

Look at responder's hand. Responder's job is to try to find a Golden Fit in a major suit if there is one. Can responder bid a new suit? What would responder bid?

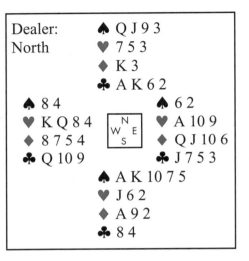

```
Dealer:        ♠ Q J 9 3
North          ♥ 7 5 3
               ♦ K 3
               ♣ A K 6 2
    ♠ 8 4              ♠ 6 2
    ♥ K Q 8 4    N     ♥ A 10 9
    ♦ 8 7 5 4  W   E   ♦ Q J 10 6
    ♣ Q 10 9     S     ♣ J 7 5 3
               ♠ A K 10 7 5
               ♥ J 6 2
               ♦ A 9 2
               ♣ 8 4
```

What is the bidding message given by responder's bid? Does opener have to bid again? What is the range of opener's hand? What would opener rebid?

What is the range of responder's hand? At what level does responder want to play the contract? In what strain does responder want to play the contract? What would responder rebid?

What would the contract be? Who would be the declarer?

The Play

Who would make the opening lead? What would the opening lead be?

How many tricks must declarer take to fulfill the contract? How many sure tricks does declarer have? Which suit provides declarer with an opportunity to develop the additional trick needed to make the contract? What must declarer do to develop the additional trick?

Bid and play the deal. Did declarer make the contract?

Exercise Seven *Answers* — Developing a Trick by Ruffing in Dummy

The Bidding

- North opens the bidding with 1♣.
- Responder can bid a new suit at the one level, 1♠.
- Responder's bid is forcing and opener has to bid again. Since opener's hand is in the minimum range, opener rebids 2♠.
- Responder's hand is maximum. Responder wants to ensure that the partnership plays in game.
- Responder would rebid 4♠.
- 4♠ is the contract and South is the declarer.

The Play

- West makes the opening lead.
- The opening lead would be the ♥K.
- Declarer needs 10 tricks to make the contract.
- Declarer has nine sure tricks.
- The diamond suit provides the opportunity to develop an additional trick because the third round can be ruffed in the dummy.
- Declarer has to leave a trump in the dummy to ruff the third diamond.
- Declarer should make the contract.

Exercise Eight — Getting Ready to Ruff in Dummy

(E-Z Deal Cards: #6, Deal 2 — Dealer, East)

Turn up all of the cards on the second pre-dealt deal and arrange them as in the previous exercise.

The Bidding

East is the dealer. Who would open the bidding? What would the opening bid be?

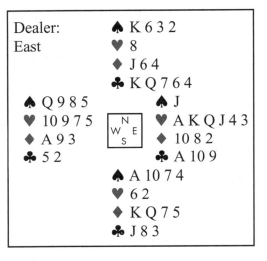

Dealer: East

♠ K 6 3 2
♥ 8
♦ J 6 4
♣ K Q 7 6 4

♠ Q 9 8 5   ♠ J
♥ 10 9 7 5   ♥ A K Q J 4 3
♦ A 9 3   ♦ 10 8 2
♣ 5 2   ♣ A 10 9

♠ A 10 7 4
♥ 6 2
♦ K Q 7 5
♣ J 8 3

Look at responder's hand. Can responder support opener's suit? What is the value of responder's hand? What would responder bid?

What is the bidding message given by responder's bid? Does opener have to bid again? What is the range of opener's hand? What would opener rebid?

What is the range of responder's hand? At what level does responder want to play the contract? In what strain does responder want to play the contract? What would responder rebid?

What would the contract be? Who would be the declarer?

The Play

Who would make the opening lead? What would the opening lead be?

How many tricks must declarer take to fulfill the contract? How many sure tricks does declarer have? Which suit provides declarer with an opportunity to develop the additional trick needed to make the contract? What must declarer do to develop the additional trick?

Bid and play the deal. Did declarer make the contract?

Exercise Eight *Answers* — Getting Ready to Ruff in Dummy

The Bidding

- East opens the bidding with 1 ♥.
- Responder can support opener's suit and has 7 points, including 1 dummy point.
- Responder bids 2 ♥.
- Responder's bid is invitational, and opener doesn't have to bid again.
- Opener's hand is medium, so opener bids 3 ♥.
- Responder's hand is minimum. Responder wants to play in partscore in hearts.
- Responder passes the 3 ♥ bid.
- The contract is 3 ♥.
- East is the declarer.

The Play

- South makes the opening lead.
- South leads the ♦ K.
- East needs nine tricks to fulfill the contract.
- Declarer has eight sure tricks.
- The clubs provide an opportunity for an extra trick if declarer plays the clubs twice so that there are none in the dummy. Declarer has to leave at least one heart in the dummy to ruff the third round of clubs.

Exercise Nine — Delaying Drawing Trumps

(E-Z Deal Cards: #6, Deal 3 — Dealer, South)

Turn up all of the cards on the third pre-dealt deal and arrange them as in the previous exercise.

The Bidding

South is the dealer. Who would open the bidding? What would the opening bid be?

Look at responder's hand. What would responder bid? What is the bidding message given by responder's bid? Does opener have to bid again? What is the range of opener's hand? What would opener rebid?

What is the range of re-sponder's hand? At what level

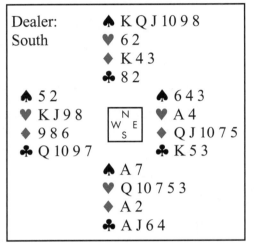

Dealer: ♠ K Q J 10 9 8
South   ♥ 6 2
         ♦ K 4 3
         ♣ 8 2

♠ 5 2   ♠ 6 4 3
♥ K J 9 8   ♥ A 4
♦ 9 8 6   ♦ Q J 10 7 5
♣ Q 10 9 7   ♣ K 5 3

         ♠ A 7
         ♥ Q 10 7 5 3
         ♦ A 2
         ♣ A J 6 4

does responder want to play the contract? In what strain does responder want to play the contract? What would responder rebid?

What would opener bid next? Why? What would the contract be? Who would be the declarer?

The Play

Who would make the opening lead? What would the opening lead be?

How many tricks must declarer take to fulfill the contract? How many sure tricks does declarer have? Which suit provides declarer with an opportunity to develop the additional trick needed to make the contract? Can declarer draw trumps right away? If not, why not?

Bid and play the deal. Did declarer make the contract?

Exercise Nine *Answers* — Delaying Drawing Trumps

The Bidding

- South opens the bidding with 1♥.

- Responder can't support the hearts but can bid a new suit — 1♠.

- Responder's bid is forcing, and opener has to bid again.

- Opener's hand is medium. Since the hand is unbalanced, opener rebids a lower-ranking new suit — 2♣. This can show a minimum or medium hand.

- Responder's hand is medium.

- Responder might want to play in a game in spades.

- Responder rebids 3♠.

- Opener bids 4♠, because opener knows responder has at least six spades and 10 or 11 total points.

- The contract is 4♠ and North is the declarer.

The Play

- East makes the opening lead.

- The opening lead is the ♦Q.

- Declarer needs to take 10 tricks.

- Declarer has nine sure tricks.

- The diamonds provide the opportunity for an extra trick.

- Declarer can't draw all of the trumps right away because one spade must be kept in the dummy to ruff the third round of diamonds.

- Declarer should make the contract.

Exercise Ten — Delaying Drawing Trumps

(E-Z Deal Cards: #6, Deal 4 — Dealer, West)

Turn up all of the cards on the fourth pre-dealt deal and arrange them as in the previous exercise.

The Bidding

West is the dealer. Who would open the bidding? What would the opening bid be?

Look at responder's hand. What would responder bid?

What is the range of opener's hand? Is opener's hand balanced or unbalanced? What would opener rebid?

What is the range of responder's hand? Does the partnership have a Golden Fit in a major suit? What would responder rebid? Who would be the declarer?

Dealer: West

```
                 ♠ Q J 10 9
                 ♥ J 9 2
                 ♦ 9 7 3
                 ♣ 9 8 5
   ♠ A 7 3                    ♠ 8 5 2
   ♥ K 6          N           ♥ A 7 5 3
   ♦ K Q 10 8   W   E         ♦ A 6 4 2
   ♣ A Q J 2      S           ♣ 7 4
                 ♠ K 6 4
                 ♥ Q 10 8 4
                 ♦ J 5
                 ♣ K 10 6 3
```

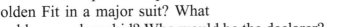

The Play

Who would make the opening lead? What would the opening lead be?

How many tricks must declarer take to fulfill the contract? How many sure tricks does declarer have? How can declarer develop additional tricks in the club suit? What does declarer have to hope for? From which hand should declarer lead clubs? Why? Which other suit should provide an additional trick?

Bid and play the deal. Did declarer make the contract?

Exercise Ten *Answers* — Delaying Drawing Trumps

The Bidding

- West opens the bidding with 1 ♦.
- Responder bids 1 ♥.
- Opener's hand is in the maximum range and is balanced.
- Opener rebids 2NT.
- Responder's hand is minimum.
- The partnership doesn't have a Golden Fit in a major suit, only in diamonds. Responder bids 3NT.
- West would be the declarer.

The Play

- North makes the opening lead.
- The opening lead is the ♠Q.
- Declarer needs nine tricks to make the contract.
- Declarer has seven sure tricks.
- Declarer can hope to develop an extra club trick either by playing the ace and queen so that the jack is good or by trying the finesse — leading toward the ♣A Q J combination and hoping that South has the ♣K. The diamond suit should provide four tricks as long as the diamonds divide relatively evenly.

CHAPTER 7
Overcalls and Bids by the Advancer

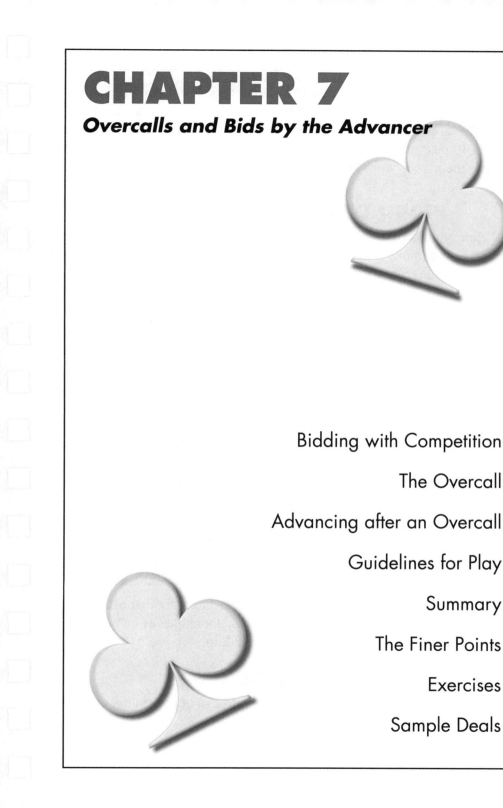

Bidding with Competition

The Overcall

Advancing after an Overcall

Guidelines for Play

Summary

The Finer Points

Exercises

Sample Deals

In the first six chapters, you have reached your contract without any bidding by the opponents. Now it is time to consider what happens when both sides are competing for the contract. We use the term competitive bidding to describe sequences in which both partnerships are bidding, because the partnerships are competing for the final contract.

BIDDING WITH COMPETITION

When your side opens the bidding, you hope to be able to find a Golden Game in either spades, hearts or notrump. When you can't, you hope to play the contract in a partscore in either a Golden Fit or notrump. You and your partner want to exchange information in an orderly fashion without interruption from the opponents.

When an opponent opens the bidding, the likelihood of your side reaching a Golden Game is greatly reduced. Your opponent's opening bid announces at least 13 total points. There are only 40 high-card points in total in the deck. Even if opener has a minimum hand, that leaves approximately 27 points unaccounted for. (This is only an approximation, since players include distributional points in the total count.) You and your partner need most of the outstanding points in order to reach a game contract. This is not impossible, but it means that reaching game is usually not the most important consideration when deciding to take competitive action.

In addition, you probably won't be able to exchange information without interference from the opponents. You are now in a competitive bidding situation. This means that various levels on the Bidding Scale will be taken up by the opponents' opening bid and subsequent auction.

How does this affect the way the partnership thinks about the bidding? Let's look at some of the advantages and disadvantages of entering the auction when an opponent has opened the bidding.

Advantages of Competitive Bidding

There are several advantages to bidding after an opponent has opened the bidding:

- Your partnership may have enough combined strength to make a partscore or even a game. You should start describing your hand as soon as possible.

- If your side doesn't have the strength to make a contract, you still may be able to interfere with the opponents' exchange of information and make it difficult for them to arrive at their best contract.

- If the opponents do play the contract, the information from your bidding may help your side defend the contract better, including getting a good opening lead.

Disadvantages of Competitive Bidding

There are risks to be considered when your side gets involved in the auction after an opponent opens the bidding:

- If you are bidding to interfere with the opponents but don't have enough strength in your combined hands, you might end up playing a contract you can't make.

- At the same time you are giving your partner information about your hand, you are also giving information to the opponents that might help them during the auction and/or play.

Nothing is perfect! You need to balance the advantages and disadvantages when considering a competitive call.

Maybe it sounds like a good idea to enter the auction with the sole purpose of interfering with the opponents' bidding. One player could try to outbid the opponents just to prevent them from playing a contract. However, there are two additional factors to take into account — vulnerability and the penalty double.

Vulnerability

On each deal, your side is said to be either *vulnerable* or *nonvulnerable*. Vulnerability relates to the scoring bonus you get for bidding and making a game or slam contract or the scoring penalty for not making your contract. If you are vulnerable, the bonuses and penalties are higher.

How vulnerability is decided depends on the form of scoring. In duplicate bridge, the vulnerability is predetermined for any given deal. Sometimes both sides are nonvulnerable, sometimes both sides are vulnerable and sometimes one side is vulnerable while the other side is not. In duplicate bridge, your side is vulnerable on approximately half the deals. In rubber bridge, a side is nonvulnerable until it bids and makes its first game. At that time the side becomes vulnerable. There are more details in the Appendix. For now, it is sufficient to know that a side is either nonvulnerable or vulnerable at the start of any deal.

Vulnerability affects the scoring in the following manner:

- The bonus for making a vulnerable game contract is larger than the bonus for making a nonvulnerable game contract (see Appendix).

- The penalty for going down in a nonvulnerable contract is 50 points per trick, whereas the penalty for going down in a vulnerable contract is 100 points per trick.

- The bonus for making a small slam or a grand slam contract is larger when vulnerable (see Appendix).

For example, suppose you are in a contract of 4♠. From Chapter 1, you may recall that your trick score for making this contract is 120 points (30 points for each trick in a major suit). If you make the contract in duplicate play or *Chicago-style* rubber bridge, you receive a game bonus in addition to your trick score. If you are nonvulnerable, you get a total of 420 points (120 + 300) for making 4♠. If you are vulnerable, you get 620 points (120 + 500).

If you are defeated in your contract by three tricks (you take only seven tricks instead of 10), however, you lose a penalty of 150 points (3 x 50) if you are nonvulnerable or 300 points (3 x 100) if you are vulnerable.

It is dangerous to bid too high when you are vulnerable. The vulnerability puts a constraint on your competitive actions and must be kept in mind when considering whether or not to interfere with the opponents' auction.

The Penalty Double

There is something else that prevents a player from bidding too much without risking a severe penalty — the *penalty double*. If your opponents bid to a contract that you don't think they can make, you can say "Double" when it is your turn to call. If the contract is doubled and declarer is defeated, the penalty is increased. However, declarer receives an additional bonus if the contract is not defeated.

Here are a few pointers about making a penalty double:

- You can double only your opponents' contract. If you don't think your partner can make the contract, keep it to yourself!

- You can double only when it is your turn to call.

- A double does not end the auction — the other players still have an opportunity to call. If three passes follow the double, then the final contract is said to be doubled. If there is another bid, the auction continues and the double is no longer in effect.

The effects of the penalty double and the vulnerability combine to determine the size of the penalty as follows:

- The penalty for going down in a doubled contract when nonvulnerable is 100 points for the first undertrick, 200 points for the second and third undertricks and 300 points each for subsequent undertricks.

- The penalty for going down in a doubled contract when vulnerable is 200 points for the first undertrick and 300 points each for subsequent undertricks.

For example, if you are doubled in a contract of 4♠ and defeated by three tricks, the penalty is 500 points (100 + 200 + 200) if you are nonvulnerable, and the penalty is 800 points (200 + 300 + 300) if you are vulnerable. The effects of vulnerability and the penalty double can limit the amount of bidding you can afford to do in competition.

When discussing the penalty double, however, remember that the declarer may not necessarily go down. If you are doubled for penalty in a contract and make it, your side will get bonus points. You can even be doubled into game! 2♠ doubled and making is a game worth 470 points nonvulnerable and 670 points vulnerable (see Appendix).

You have been opening the bidding and responding for six chapters without knowing about vulnerability or the penalty double. How do these factors affect what you have learned to this point? All the bids discussed so far are made regardless of the vulnerability or fear of being doubled. It is when everyone gets into the auction (especially when you are bidding merely to interfere with the opponents) that you must keep your eye on the vulnerability and consider whether an opponent might double you.

The potential of having your bids doubled for penalty adds an exciting aspect to the bidding and has the potential to affect the way you declare a hand.

THE OVERCALL

The simplest form of competitive action when the opponents start the bidding is a bid at the cheapest available level. This is called an *overcall* because you are making a "call" over the opponent's bid.

Here are some examples of overcalls:

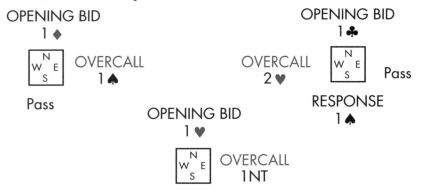

An overcall may be made at the one level, the two level or even higher. It may be made in a suit or in notrump. Let's look at some of the requirements for making an overcall.

How Long a Suit Do You Need to Overcall?

When you make an overcall in a suit, you should have at least a five-card suit. This applies whether you are overcalling in a major suit or a minor suit. Try to have a strong six-card suit to overcall at the two level or higher.

One reason for requiring a five-card suit is to minimize the risk of entering the auction when an opponent has opened the bidding. If you are left to play in your suit, you would like to have plenty of trumps. In addition, the longer your suit is, the less likely the opponents are to make a penalty double.

There is another reason for requiring a five-card or longer suit. Your partner will usually lead your suit if the opponents play the contract. You want the suit to be a source of tricks for your side, not the opponents'.

Let's look at some examples. Suppose the opponent on your right has opened the bidding 1 ♦ .

♠ A 6
♥ A Q J 10 8
♦ 9 5
♣ K 6 4 2

With a strong five-card heart suit, overcall 1 ♥ . Even if you are left to play there, hearts should make a satisfactory trump suit. If the opponents play the contract, you would like partner to lead a heart.

♠ A 8 2
♥ 5 3
♦ 7 4
♣ A K Q 9 7 4

With a good six-card club suit, you want to enter the bidding both to compete and to tell partner something about your hand. Because of the opening bid, you will have to overcall 2 ♣ .

♠ A J 10 7 5
♥ A Q 9 6 3
♦ 7
♣ J 10

You have a choice of suits to overcall. Use the same guidelines as when opening the bidding — bid the higher-ranking suit first, 1 ♠ . You may have an opportunity to show the heart suit later if the auction continues and the level doesn't get too high.

You would have opened the bidding with all of the above hands. Does this mean that you need the same strength to overcall as you do to open the bidding? Let's take a look at the strength requirements.

The Strength for a One-Level Overcall in a Suit

Consider the following hand:

♠ K Q J 10 5
♥ K 7 2
♦ 5 2
♣ 8 4 3

You have 9 HCP plus 1 point for the five-card suit. With only 10 points, you are not strong enough to open the bidding. Your partner would assume that you had at least 13 total points, and you might well get the partnership too high on the Bidding Scale during the auction.

Suppose, however, you are West. South, on your right, is the dealer and opens the bidding 1 ♦ . Your side is nonvulnerable and the opponents are vulnerable. Can a case be made for overcalling 1 ♠?

Let's look at a possible layout for the entire deal:

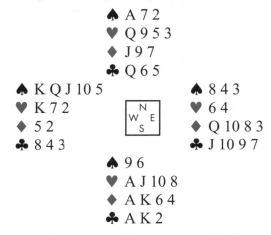

First, consider what happens if North and South are left to bid with no interference from your side. South has a balanced hand with 19 HCP, too strong to open the bidding 1NT. South would start the auction with 1 ♦ . Holding 9 HCP, North would respond 1 ♥ . South, with a maximum hand and four-card support for responder's suit, would jump to game. The contract would be 4 ♥ and it should be successful. North should lose only one spade trick, one heart trick and one diamond trick.

For making the contract, North and South will get a trick score of 120 points (4 x 30) plus a bonus of 500 points for a vulnerable game — a total of 620 points.

Let's see what happens if West interferes with the orderly exchange of information between North and South. South opens the bidding with 1 ♦ . This time, West overcalls 1 ♠. Now North has a problem. With only 9 HCP, not enough to bid a new suit at the two level, North can't bid 2 ♥ . Instead, with 6 to 9 total points, North probably would compromise by responding 1NT. With only 3 points, East would pass. South, with a maximum balanced hand, might jump to 3NT. Notice how the overcall could result in North and South missing their Golden Fit.

Because of the overcall, East would lead partner's suit, spades. After winning the trick, North would have to establish heart tricks to make the contract. West will win a trick with the ♥ K, and since the contract is notrump, West will take all of the sure spade tricks. With four spade tricks and one heart trick, East and West will defeat the contract.

This shows how an overcall can be effective. It might make it difficult for the opponents to get to the best contract, and it might help the defense make a good opening lead.

What risk does West run by overcalling? Left to play in 1♠, West would most likely take five tricks, suffering a penalty of 100 points (50 points per trick when nonvulnerable). Even if the opponents doubled the overcall, the penalty would be only 300 points. In both cases, West would be better off by overcalling rather than by keeping quiet and giving the opponents an easy route to 620 points.

The other risk is that partner would assume West has a stronger hand. On this hand, it doesn't matter, and that will often be the case in a competitive auction. However, some danger exists as we shall see shortly. Partner will have to take this into consideration when advancing a one-level overcall.

In general, an overcall in a suit at the one level can be made on a hand with less than the value of an opening bid, provided the overcaller has a good suit. An overcall should be based on either a good hand or a long strong suit (or both). There is no reason to overcall if your hand is minimum and contains a weak suit.

The Strength for a Two-Level Overcall in a Suit

It is not always a good idea to overcall on a hand with less strength than an opening bid. Suppose you pick up the following hand:

♠ 8 4 3   You have 9 HCP plus 1 point for the five-card suit.
♥ K Q J 10 5   This hand is very similar to the one in the previous
♦ K 7 2   section. You're West, but this time the opening bid
♣ 5 2   on your right is 1♠. To show your heart suit, you
                   would have to overcall at the two level. Also, this
time your side is vulnerable and the opponents are nonvulnerable. Can a case be made for overcalling 2♥?

Here is a possible layout for the entire deal:

```
                 ♠ 2
                 ♥ A 9 8 7
                 ♦ A 9 6
                 ♣ A J 9 6 4
   ♠ 8 4 3                      ♠ J 10 9 7
   ♥ K Q J 10 5     ┌─────┐     ♥ 6 4
   ♦ K 7 2          │  N  │     ♦ 8 4 3
   ♣ 5 2            │ W E │     ♣ Q 10 8 3
                    │  S  │
                    └─────┘
                 ♠ A K Q 6 5
                 ♥ 3 2
                 ♦ Q J 10 5
                 ♣ K 7
```

First, let's see what happens if North and South are left to bid with no interference. South, holding an unbalanced hand with a five-card major, opens 1♠. With 14 total points, enough to bid a new suit at the two level, North responds 2♣. South rebids 2♦ to show a second suit, and North, knowing there was enough combined strength for game and no likely Golden Fit in a major suit, puts the partnership in 3NT. This contract should be successful. North has at least three spade tricks, one heart trick, three diamond tricks (actually four, since E–W's diamonds split 3–3) and two club tricks. Even if East leads a heart (unlikely since West didn't overcall), North makes the contract with the help of a finesse for the ♦ K.

North and South will get a trick score of 100 (130) points plus a bonus of 300 points for a nonvulnerable game, a total of 400 (430) points.

Now, let's see what happens if West tries to interfere with the exchange of information between North and South by overcalling. Again South starts the bidding with 1♠. This time West overcalls 2♥. North is in a good position to double for penalty. North knows that with the 13 or more points that South holds, the combined partnership strength should keep West from making the contract.

If left to play in a doubled contract of 2♥, West will not fare well. With good defense, West can be held to only four heart tricks and will end up being defeated by four tricks. Since West is vulnerable, the penalty will be 1,100 points (200 + 300 + 300 + 300). This is a heavy price to pay, since the opponents would score only 400 (430) points if West had not interfered.

The strength and shape of the hand is virtually identical to that in the previous section. The difference comes from the change in vulnerability and bidding level. When considering whether to overcall, you must be careful to watch both the vulnerability and the level at which you must overcall. It is all right to overcall with a good five-card suit at the one level with slightly less than opening-bid strength when you are nonvulnerable. If you are vulnerable or have to bid at the two level, however, you need more strength. Overcalls at the two level (or higher) suggest a hand that is strong enough to open the bidding.

1NT Overcall

An overcall of 1NT is similar to a 1NT opening bid. You need a balanced hand with 15 to 18 HCP, but there is one additional consideration. An opening bid in a suit provides information about the shape of opener's hand that will help opener's partner get off to a good opening lead for their side. Because of this, if you overcall with 1NT, you generally should have some strength and/or length in the suit bid by your opponent.

Let's look at two examples. Suppose your right-hand opponent has opened the bidding 1 ♥.

♠ K 3	With a balanced hand with 17 HCP, you may overcall
♥ A Q 8	1NT. You have some strength in the opponent's suit,
♦ K Q J 8	so you don't mind if they lead a heart.
♣ Q 10 6 2	

♠ A Q 3	You have a balanced hand with 16 HCP . You would
♥ 6 2	open the bidding 1NT if you had the chance. Rather
♦ K Q J 8 7	than overcall 1NT with a small doubleton in the
♣ A 10 3	opponent's suit, however, you would do better to
	overcall in your five-card suit, 2 ♦.

When the Opponents Bid Your Suit

Suppose you pick up the following hand:

♠ A Q J 10 5   You intend to open the bidding 1 ♠, but the opponent

♥ 10 7 2   on your right bids 1 ♠. It makes no sense for you to

♦ A 9 3   overcall 2 ♠. There is no advantage in competing

♣ Q 6   with your opponent in the same suit. You will not

find much spade support in your partner's hand if your opponent has enough spades to bid the suit.

Should you try for a penalty double? It's too soon for that. Furthermore, a double by you in the second position is not for penalty it is for takeout. (See Chapter 8.) You would warn the opponents that spades isn't their suit, and they might bid to a better spot. Also, you may not be able to defeat them at such a low level. As we will see in the next chapter, you seldom double a partscore for penalty when your partner has not bid.

With a hand like this, pass — even though you have an opening bid. You do not have to compete if your hand is unsuitable. Besides, the opponents currently are considering playing with your best suit as trump. Silence is golden!

Put It All Together

When an opponent opens the bidding, consider whether to overcall using the following guidelines:

> ### Requirements for an Overcall in a Suit
>
> • A five-card or longer suit. Try to have a six-card suit to overcall at the two level.
>
> • 8–16 HCP (10–17 total points). Overcalls at the two level suggest a hand that is strong enough to have opened the bidding.
>
> ### Requirements for a 1NT Overcall
>
> • 15–18 HCP
>
> • Balanced hand
>
> • Some strength in the opponent's suit

Let's look at some examples. Your side is nonvulnerable and the opponent on your right opens the bidding 1 ♦. What would you do with the following hands?

♠ J 9 7 5 3
♥ K 8 5
♦ Q 6 3
♣ K 8

You have only 9 HCP, and you don't have a good five-card suit. Pass.

♠ A K J 10 7
♥ K 8 3
♦ 7 2
♣ 10 8 5

Overcall 1 ♠. You have a good suit.

♠ K Q 3
♥ 7 3
♦ A 2
♣ A J 10 8 7 3

To overcall clubs, you must bid at the two level. With a six-card suit and 14 HCP, overcall 2 ♣. With good strength and a good suit, now is the time to act. You may not get an opportunity later in the auction.

♠ A Q 10
♥ 9 6 2
♦ K Q 10
♣ K Q J 6

With a balanced hand, 17 HCP and some strength in the opponent's suit, you have the perfect hand to overcall 1NT. This will describe your hand to partner, who can take it from there.

♠ A 7 3
♥ J 5
♦ K J 10 8 4
♣ A 9 4

Your opponent has bid your suit. Pass and see how the auction develops.

ADVANCING AFTER AN OVERCALL

When you respond to partner's overcall, you are called the advancer. You are obviously a responder to the overcaller, but to avoid confusion during competitive auctions, it will be clearer if you think of the responder to the overcaller as the advancer. When you are the advancer, you can do all the same things that you can to when partner opens the bidding. You can pass, raise partner's suit, show a new suit of your own or bid notrump. There is one additional thing that you can do. You can make a cuebid. A cuebid is the bid of a suit first mentioned by the opponents. The cuebid is really the only truly forcing call that the advancer can make in our bidding system, and it promises a limit raise or better in the overcaller's suit. The cuebid asks the overcaller about the quality of the overcall:

Opener	Overcaller	Responder	Advancer (You)
(1 ♦)	1 ♠	(Pass)	2 ♦
(Pass)	?		

2 ♠ = minimum overcall
Other = extra strength (11 or 12 HCPs minimum)

However, if the advancer knows there is game even with the overcaller just having a minimum bid, the advancer should bid game directly and not worry about using the cuebid.

Since an overcall in a suit promises at least a five-card suit, the advancer needs only three-card support to raise. The most important thing to say about bidding as the advancer is that you want to take the bidding to the level that will be the best for your side, considering that your final contract may be doubled for penalty. If you have support for your partner, it is important to show it right away in case you run into interference from your opponents. You should keep in mind that your partner as the overcaller may not have an opening hand if the overcall is made at the one level.

To decide how to advance the bidding when your partner has overcalled, it would be nice if we could use the same responses as when our partner opens the bidding. However, since we may be advancing the bid when our partner does not have an opening hand, we have to be more cautious with our bids. The main reason we respond with a 6-point hand when partner opens is that partner could have 19 to 21 HCPs and we might belong in game — so we must bid. When partner overcalls, this is not the case, since the maximum total points partner could have is 17.

Therefore, before considering an advance to partner's overcall, try to have at least 8 or 9 total points. If you have only 6 points, even with a fit for partner, you may end up too high on the bidding ladder. But don't worry, you may have a chance to bid again.

Opener	Overcaller	Responder	Advancer (You)
(1♣)	1♥	(Pass)	Pass
(2♣)	Pass	(Pass)	2♥
(Pass)	Pass	(Pass)	

The overcaller will hear in this auction that you have a fit but not many points.

Suppose the opponent on your left bids 1♣ and your partner overcalls 1♠. What would you bid with the following hands? Remember to value your hand using dummy points when raising partner's major.

♠ J 10 9
♥ 6
♦ K 8 7 6 4
♣ J 7 4 3

With three-card support for partner's suit, your hand is worth 8 points — 5 HCP plus 3 points for the singleton heart. Raise to 2♠.

♠ Q J 7 2
♥ K Q 3
♦ K 8 7 5
♣ 10 9

With 11 HCP plus 1 point for the doubleton club, you have slightly better than a limit raise. Bid 2♣, which is a cuebid. If partner bids 2♠, you may pass knowing you have not missed game. If the opponents compete, you should be willing to compete to 3♠.

If partner makes a different call, game is likely, so you can bid 4♠.

♠ J 10 9 8
♥ —
♦ A 8 5 3
♣ K J 8 7 3

You have 9 HCP plus 5 points for the heart void for a total of 14. Raise partner all the way to game, 4♠. (If partner had opened the bidding 1♠, you would have responded 2♣, forcing.) Remember partner's overcall is based on either a good hand or a long strong suit.

Suppose the opponent on your left bids 1♣ and your partner overcalls 1♦. How would you compete with the following hands?

♠ A 9 3
♥ 6 2
♦ K 10 7 4
♣ J 7 4 3

With four-card support for partner's suit and 8 HCP plus 1 point for the doubleton heart, raise to 2♦.

♠ K 2
♥ K 7 3
♦ A Q 7 5
♣ 9 7 5 2

With 12 HCP plus 1 point for the doubleton spade and four-card support for partner's suit, make a 2♣ cuebid. Remember if there is game, we want to try for 3NT.

♠ Q J 8
♥ K 9 3
♦ A Q 5
♣ K J 10 7

You have support for partner's suit and are strong enough to raise to game. With some strength in the opponent's suit, choose the Golden Game of 3NT rather than 5♦.

♠ A K 10 8
♥ 9 5 2
♦ Q J 4
♣ K J 2

Although you have support for partner, you would rather play in notrump if your partner has some hearts. Cuebid 2♣. If partner bids 2♦, you may pass, since partner shows a minimum. But if partner bids hearts, you can bid 3NT.

The Advancer Bids a New Suit

The advancer can't always support partner's overcall — sometimes the advancer bids a new suit. Whether this bid of a new suit is forcing depends on your agreement with partner. To make it easier for newer players, we will assume that you and your partner have agreed that a new-suit bid is forcing (see The Finer Points on page 254). Now, you can bid after partner's overcall in the same manner as responding to an opening bid when you do not have support for partner's suit.

One thing to remember, however, is that we don't want to get into a bidding competition with our own partner. If there is no combined eight-card fit in our hands and we don't have the points needed for game, the sooner we sign off in the bidding, the better we will be — and hopefully not be doubled for penalty.

One further point. Partner has shown a five-card or longer suit. Generally, you should advance the bidding only in a five-card or longer suit. (See the next section for what to do if you can't bid a new suit.) We will see in the next chapter that partner has a different method of competing if partner is interested in hearing about your four-card suits.

Suppose the bidding is opened 1♦ and your partner overcalls 1♥. Let's see what you would do with the following hands.

♠ K J 10 7 3 ♥ J 8 ♦ 9 4 2 ♣ A J 7	You do not have support for partner's suit, but you do have 11 total points. That's more than enough to bid. Bid a new suit, 1 ♠, and wait to hear partner's rebid before deciding what to do.
♠ J 9 7 6 3 ♥ 5 ♦ 10 9 6 3 ♣ Q 4 2	Even though you don't care for partner's suit, you don't have enough strength to bid a new suit at the one level. Pass.
♠ A K 6 ♥ 6 3 ♦ 10 9 4 ♣ A K Q 9 4	You have enough points to go to game, but you don't know where the contract should be played. Bid 2 ♣, just as you would if partner had opened the bidding, to get a further description of partner's hand.

The Advancer Bids Notrump

If the advancer can't raise the overcall and can't bid a new suit, perhaps the advancer can bid notrump. The advancer needs some strength in the opponent's suit to do this. If the advancer suggests notrump as a place to play, the advancer should have a few extra points more than if this wasn't a competitive auction. Remember, we need to take tricks based on high cards since we cannot ruff the opponent's high cards. It would be nice if we could stick with the same notrump response ranges for both opening bids and overcalls, but it just doesn't work in some cases.

The following are the recommended ranges for the advancer:

1NT — 8–11 HCP	
2NT — 12–15 HCP	(Remember, partner can have as little as 8 HCP for an overcall on the one level. This range helps to ensure you don't get too high on the bidding ladder.)
3NT — 16+ HCP	

Let's see how this works.

The opponent on your left opens 1 ♥ and your partner overcalls
1 ♠.

♠ 9 8
♥ K J 3
♦ A J 10 8 7
♣ 10 9 3

With 9 HCP, bid 1NT, showing a hand in the 8 to 11 HCP range with some strength in the opponent's suit.

♠ J 3
♥ K Q 10 2
♦ A 9 3
♣ Q 10 8 3

With this good balanced hand of 12 HCP and some strength in the opponent's suit, jump to 2NT. If partner had opened the bidding, this would show 13 to 15 HCP.

♠ Q 3
♥ A Q J
♦ K Q 8 5
♣ Q 10 7 4

With a balanced hand of 16 HCP, no support for partner's suit and some strength in the opponent's suit, jump right to 3NT.

Advancing after a Two-Level Overcall

When your partner overcalls at the two level, you know that partner has at least a five-card suit and the strength of an opening bid. Some of the bidding room, however, has been taken up by the opponents' bidding. You are in the position of bidding after an opening one-bid starting at the two level. You no longer have the luxury of showing a hand in the 6 to 9 total point range by raising partner to the two level, bidding a new suit at the one level or bidding 1NT.

Remember, we still are playing that a cuebid is forcing and shows the equivalent of a limit raise or better and that new suits by the advancer are forcing (see The Finer Points). So, again, bid while keeping in mind that we want to show support as soon as possible.

Let's see how this works. The opponent on your left bids 1 ♠ and your partner overcalls 2 ♥.

♠ Q 9 7
♥ 9 7
♦ 10 9 4 3
♣ K J 5 2

You have 6 HCP. If partner had opened the bidding 1 ♥, you would have responded 1NT, showing a hand in the 6 to 9 total point range. There is no room to do this over partner's overcall. Pass.

♠ Q 9
♥ K 8 3
♦ K J 7 4
♣ J 10 7 3

You have support for partner's suit and 11 total points — 10 HCP plus 1 point for the doubleton. Cuebid 2♠, promising at least a limit raise which is what you have.

♠ A 8 2
♥ Q 10 7 4
♦ K Q 9 3 2
♣ J

With 12 HCP plus 3 points for the singleton club, raise partner directly to 4♥.

Advancing after an Overcall of 1NT

A 1NT overcall shows a balanced hand with 15 to 18 HCP — a slightly wider range than a 1NT opening bid along with some strength in the opener's suit. The advancer's guidelines are the same as when partner opens 1NT (Chapter 3). The advancer, as captain, usually knows enough to sign off in the appropriate contract.

Let's look at a few examples. The opponent on your left bids 1♣ and your partner overcalls 1NT.

♠ J 10 9 7 6 3
♥ 9 5
♦ Q 8 2
♣ 6 3

With only 5 total points, you know the partnership belongs in a partscore. Since partner has a balanced hand, there is a Golden Fit in spades. Sign off in 2♠.

♠ K 10 4
♥ 10 8 4
♦ K Q J 7 4
♣ 9 6

With 9 HCP plus 1 point for the five-card suit, you know there is enough combined strength for game. With no Golden Fit in a major suit, bid 3NT.

♠ 10 8 4
♥ J 6
♦ K 9 6 3
♣ J 10 7 3

With 5 HCP, you know the partnership belongs in a partscore. Since your hand is balanced, pass.

Put It All Together

The opponent on your left opens 1 ♣ and your partner overcalls 1 ♥. What would you bid with each of the following hands?

♠ Q J 10 8 7 ♥ 3 2 ♦ K 4 ♣ A 8 7 4	You have 10 HCP plus 1 point for the five-card suit for a total of 11 points. Since you can't support partner's suit, bid your own suit at the one level, 1 ♠. Partner may have 16 HCP, so you want to keep the bidding open since there is a possibility of game.
♠ J 8 2 ♥ 10 5 ♦ K 10 7 6 3 ♣ K Q 4	You have 9 HCP. You can't support partner's suit, and you don't have a suit you can bid at the one level. Bid 1NT, since you have a stopper in the opponents' suit.
♠ A 4 ♥ K 10 3 ♦ K 9 8 6 4 ♣ 7 5 2	You have support for partner's suit and 10 HCP plus 1 point for the doubleton. Cuebid 2 ♣ to show your limit raise.

Rebids by the overcaller should be based upon what the advancer has to say, whether there is a possibility for game or whether you just want to be competitive. If the advancer has not shown strength with a cuebid, proceed with caution. Remember, if you go too high on the bidding scale, you may be doubled for penalty.

GUIDELINES FOR PLAY

When playing in a trump contract, it is generally a good idea to draw the opponents' trumps before taking your sure tricks in other suits. This is to prevent the opponents from ruffing one of your sure tricks. There are times, however, when you have to delay drawing trumps because you have more pressing concerns.

Discarding Losers

Consider the following hands:

NORTH (Dummy)
♠ 6 5 4 3
♥ J 7 4 3
♦ Q 7
♣ A K Q

SOUTH (Declarer)
♠ K Q J 10 9 8 7
♥ A 6
♦ 5 3
♣ 7 4

Suppose you are in a contract of 4♠ and your opponent leads the ♥ K. You need 10 tricks and you start by counting your sure tricks. You have four — the ♥ A and the ♣ A K Q. You would plan to promote six additional tricks in the spade suit by driving out the opponents' ace.

Normally, it would be a good idea to lead spades as soon as possible. You want to "take your losses early." But look what happens if you win the ♥ A and play the ♠ K right away. The opponents can win the ace and take their ♥ Q and two diamond tricks to defeat your contract. What went wrong?

In addition to counting your winners, you have to be aware of the potential tricks you might lose if the opponents gain the lead. In the above deal, you have four potential losers once your ♥ A is gone — one spade, one heart and two diamonds.

What can you do about this? You have to look for a way to eliminate one of your losers before giving up a trick to the opponents. You can do this by playing the ♣ A K Q and discarding one of your losers (the ♥ 6, ♦ 5 or the ♦ 3). You are running the risk that an opponent will be able to ruff one of your club tricks, but you have no choice. You must eliminate one of your losers before giving up the lead.

Once you have discarded one of your losers on dummy's ♣ Q, it is safe to drive out the opponents' ♠ A. They will be able to take only two other tricks before you regain the lead, draw the remaining trump (if any) and take the rest of the tricks.

In a trump contract, you should always count the losers in your hand (not the losers in the dummy) if you may have to give up the lead before taking all of the tricks you need. If you have too many losers, you must look for a way to eliminate one or more of them. One method, as we saw in the last chapter, is to ruff losers in the dummy. If this is not possible, you can try discarding losers on extra winners in the dummy. Such considerations help you decide whether you should draw trumps right away or delay drawing trumps because you have more important things to do first.

SUMMARY

When an opponent opens the bidding, you may compete by overcalling if your hand meets the requirements.

Requirements for an Overcall in a Suit

- A five-card or longer suit (for both majors and minors). Try to have a six-card suit to overcall at the two level.
- 8–16 HCP (or 10 to 17 total points). Overcalls at the two level suggest a hand that could have opened the bidding.

Requirements for a 1NT Overcall

- 15 to 18 HCP.
- Balanced hand.
- Some strength in the opponent's suit.

Advancing after an Overcall in a Suit

If your partner overcalls in a suit, you may pass, raise, bid a new suit or bid notrump.

Your decision to do any of these things should be based on eight-card suit fits with partner or a good suit of your own coupled with high cards. Remember, the only truly forcing bid by the advancer in our system is a cuebid, which promises a limit raise (10–11 total points) or better. Suit raises are based on showing the eight-card (or better) fit and should not be better than a limit raise (start with the cuebid here) unless you can go directly to game in the overcalled suit.

Although the material has given you some examples of how to use new suits as forcing, you and your partner should decide if you want new suits to be forcing (see The Finer Points).

With a minimum hand (8–9 total points):

- Show support for partner with a raise
- Bid a new suit at the one level with no support and a good five-card suit of your own.

With a limit raise or better hand (10–11+ total points)
- Bid a new suit even at the two level with no support for partner's overcall and a good five-card suit of your own.
- Make a cuebid to describe a limit-raise hand with support for partner's overcall and then:
  1. Stop below game in the appropriate partscore if partner shows less than an opening hand with the rebid.
  2. Bid game if partner shows more than the minimum overcall by bidding another suit.
- Bid game if you have enough total points opposite a minimum overcall.

A notrump advance shows no fit for partner (most likely two-card support) and no suit of your own, but it does show strength in the opponent's suit.

> Respond 1NT with 8–11 HCP.
> Respond 2NT with 12–15 HCP.
> Respond 3NT with 16+ HCP.

Advancing after a 1NT Overcall

If your partner overcalls 1NT, you bid as if partner opened the bidding 1NT.

With 0 to 7 total points
- Bid 2♦, 2♥ or 2♠ with a five-card or longer suit (2♣ is reserved for the Stayman convention.)
- Otherwise, pass.

With 8 or 9 total points
- Bid 2NT (2♣ may be used to uncover an eight-card major-suit fit).

With 10 to 15 total points
- Bid 4♥ or 4♠ with a six-card or longer suit.
- Bid 3♥ or 3♠ with a five-card suit.
- Otherwise, bid 3NT (2♣ may be used to uncover an eight-card major-suit fit).

THE FINER POINTS

New Suit Forcing

This text states that not all players treat a new suit by the advancer as forcing. In fact, the Standard American Yellow Card, which is what many new partnerships use as their guideline to bidding agreements, does not list a new suit by the advancer as forcing. Recognize that there are a number of bidding areas where players have the option of doing one thing or another — there is no right or wrong way. This is one such area.

The Cuebid Response

Whenever you bid a suit that an opponent has already bid, you are making a cuebid. Cuebids are used in competitive bidding sequences to tell partner that your hand is strong. In this chapter, we learned that a cuebid of the opponent's suit is equivalent to a limit raise or better. For the newer player, we suggested that the advancer bid game directly if the advancer knows it is there. You should recognize that established partnerships can use cuebids in a more complicated fashion. Even so, they would always promise a limit raise or better hand. However, the word cuebid has another meaning in bridge terms. It is also a control-showing bid used to investigate the possibilities of slam. You will learn more about control-showing cuebids in the Play textbook.

Jump Overcalls

Not all competitive auctions occur in a one-over-one sequence. Take a look at these overcalls:

West	North	East	South
	1♣	2♥	

Or

West	North	East	South
1♠	3♦		

These bids are a part of a class of bids known as preempts. Preempts take up bidding space making it hard for the opponents to find their best contract. Hands that preempt have strong trick-taking potential in their own suit, but have fewer total points than an opening hand. Preempts are based on six-, seven- or eight-card suits. You will learn more about preempts in the Play textbook.

Exercise One — More on Scoring

When you are considering bidding in competition, scoring becomes important. Fill in the following chart. Notice the difference it makes to the score whether or not you are vulnerable or doubled. You are in 3 ♥ and are defeated two tricks.

	Nonvulnerable	Vulnerable
Undoubled	_____	_____
Doubled	_____	_____

Exercise Two — The Overcall

The opponent on your right opens the bidding 1 ♦. What would you bid with each of the following hands?

1) ♠ A Q 8 7 4
♥ 7 6
♦ J 10 8
♣ A K 3

2) ♠ 7 4 2
♥ A J
♦ A 8
♣ K Q 10 9 7 5

3) ♠ A 3 2
♥ K Q 8
♦ K J 10 2
♣ K J 2

_____ _____ _____

Exercise One *Answers* — More on Scoring

	Nonvulnerable	Vulnerable
Undoubled	100 points	200 points
Doubled	300 points	500 points

Exercise Two *Answers* — The Overcall

1) 1♠   2) 2♣   3) 1NT

Exercise Three — The Strength and Shape for an Overcall

1) Consider the following hand.

♠ A 7 2
♥ K Q J 9 3
♦ J 5 4
♣ 9 2

If you were the dealer, what would you bid? _____

If the opponent on your right opened the bidding 1♣, would you consider overcalling 1♥? _____What would you hope to accomplish? _____

Would it matter if the opponent on your right opened 1♠? _____
Would it make a difference if you were vulnerable? _____

2) Consider the following hand.

♠ Q 4
♥ K 8 7 3
♦ A J 2
♣ K 9 6 2

If you were the opening bidder, what would you bid? _____

If the opponent on your right opened the bidding 1♣, would you overcall 1♥? _____ If not, why not? _____
What would you do? _____

Exercise Four — Whether to Overcall

The opponent on your right opens the bidding 1♥. Your side is non-vulnerable. What would you do with each of the following hands?

1) ♠ A Q J 10 8   2) ♠ K 8 4 2   3) ♠ 10 3
   ♥ 7 3   ♥ 8 7 3   ♥ 3
   ♦ A 9 5   ♦ 5   ♦ A Q J 7 3
   ♣ 10 4 2   ♣ A K Q 10 6   ♣ A K 9 4 2

   _____   _____   _____

4) ♠ A Q J   5) ♠ K 4   6) ♠ 6 3
   ♥ K 9 7 3   ♥ K Q 10   ♥ A K J 8 4
   ♦ J 8   ♦ A J 9 3   ♦ A J 8
   ♣ Q 8 6 3   ♣ K J 10 8   ♣ 10 7 3

   _____   _____   _____

Exercise Three *Answers* — The Strength and Shape for an Overcall

1) • Pass
   • Yes. You would interfere with the opponents' bidding, compete for the contract, tell partner something about your hand and perhaps push the opponents too high.
   • Yes. If the opponent opened 1 ♠, you would have to overcall 2 ♥ rather than 1 ♥. This is more dangerous, since you would need eight tricks rather than seven to make the contract.
   • It would be more costly if you didn't make your contract if you were vulnerable. Therefore, it is more dangerous to overcall when you are vulnerable.

2) • Open 1 ♣.
   • You would not overcall 1 ♥ because the suit is not long enough. You would have to pass.

Exercise Four *Answers* — Whether to Overcall

1) 1 ♠	2) 2 ♣	3) 2 ♦
4) Pass	5) 1NT	6) Pass

Exercise Five — Advancing after a One-Level Overcall

Your left-hand opponent opens 1♣ and your partner overcalls 1♠.
What would you bid with the following hands?

1) ♠ A 8 7　　　2) ♠ J 6 3 2　　　3) ♠ K 10 7 5 3
   ♥ 10 9　　　　　♥ 9　　　　　　　♥ —
   ♦ K 7 6 3　　　♦ K Q 8 7　　　♦ A J 8 2
   ♣ J 7 5 2　　　♣ Q 8 7 6　　　♣ Q 10 7 3

_____　_____　_____

Your left-hand opponent opens 1♣ and your partner overcalls 1♥.
What would you bid with the following hands?

4) ♠ 9 7 3 2　　　5) ♠ A Q J 8 5　　　6) ♠ Q 10 8
   ♥ Q 2　　　　　♥ 10 4　　　　　　♥ 7 6
   ♦ K 8 6 5　　　♦ K 8 3　　　　　♦ K 10 6 3
   ♣ 7 5 3　　　　♣ J 4 2　　　　　♣ K J 10 7

_____　_____　_____

Exercise Six — Advancing after a Two-Level Overcall

Your left-hand opponent opens 1♠ and your partner overcalls 2♥.
What do you bid with the following hands?

1) ♠ K 10 7 3　　　2) ♠ A 8　　　　3) ♠ J 3
   ♥ J 4　　　　　　♥ K J 5　　　　♥ A 10 7 2
   ♦ Q J 6 2　　　　♦ Q 10 6 2　　　♦ A K J 8
   ♣ 7 4 2　　　　　♣ J 5 4 2　　　♣ 10 4 2

_____　_____　_____

Exercise Five *Answers* — Advancing after a One-Level Overcall

When partner overcalls, the advancer wants to get to the right contract as quickly as possible because both sides are in the auction. If you have support for the overcaller's suit, you bid at the appropriate level or cuebid — the more you have, the more you bid. You don't mention a new suit first with 13 or more points, as you would in response to an opening bid.

1) 2♠	2) 2♣	3) 4♠
4) Pass	5) 1♠	6) 1NT

Because partner could have less than an opening bid to make an overcall at the one level, the advancer must be more cautious than when responding to an opening bid. Without support for partner's suit, the advancer should have at least 8 points to make a bid.

Exercise Six *Answers* — Advancing after a Two-Level Overcall

1) Pass   2) 2♠   3) 4♥

Exercise Seven — Advancing after a 1NT Overcall

When partner overcalls 1NT, you can bid in the same manner as when partner opens the bidding 1NT. You are the captain. It is your role to decide at what level and in what strain to play the contract.

Your left-hand opponent opens 1♦ and your partner overcalls 1NT. What would you bid with the following hands?

1) ♠ 4
   ♥ 9 7 6 5 3 2
   ♦ Q J 7
   ♣ 6 4 2

2) ♠ K J 3
   ♥ Q 9 6
   ♦ A J 3
   ♣ 7 5 4 2

3) ♠ 8 7 5 3
   ♥ K 9 6 2
   ♦ 10 8 3
   ♣ 7 5

_____   _____   _____

Exercise Eight — Discarding Losers

Construct the following hands for North and South:

NORTH (Dummy)
♠ A K 6
♥ J 5 4 3
♦ A 8 3
♣ J 5 4

WEST   EAST
♦ K

SOUTH
♠ 3
♥ Q 10 9 8 7 6
♦ 7 6 5
♣ A K Q

Suppose you (South) are in a contract of 4♥ and the opening lead is the ♦ K. How many tricks will you have to lose when developing the trump suit? _____

How many tricks could you potentially lose in the diamond suit? ____
Should you start playing the trump suit right away? _____

If not, why not?_____

Exercise Seven *Answers* — Advancing after a 1NT Overcall

    1) 2♥   2) 3NT   3) Pass

Exercise Eight *Answers* — Discarding Losers

- You have to lose two tricks in the trump suit.
- There are two potential losers in diamonds.
- You can't draw trumps right away because the opponents would take two diamond tricks and two trump tricks. Instead, you must first discard one of your diamond losers on the extra spade winner in the dummy.

Exercise Nine — Overcalling

(E-Z Deal Cards: #7, Deal 1 — Dealer, North)

Turn up all of the cards on the first pre-dealt deal. Put each hand dummy-style at the edge of the table in front of each player.

The Bidding

North is the dealer. Who would open the bidding? What would the opening bid be? What would East bid? What is this bid called?

What would South do in response to partner's opening bid? Has East's bid affected South's response?

What would West bid in response to East's overcall? What does North do now? Does North

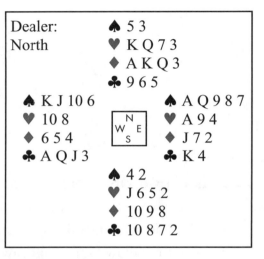

```
Dealer:          ♠ 5 3
North            ♥ K Q 7 3
                 ♦ A K Q 3
                 ♣ 9 6 5
    ♠ K J 10 6          ♠ A Q 9 8 7
    ♥ 10 8       N      ♥ A 9 4
    ♦ 6 5 4    W   E    ♦ J 7 2
    ♣ A Q J 3    S      ♣ K 4
                 ♠ 4 2
                 ♥ J 6 5 2
                 ♦ 10 9 8
                 ♣ 10 8 7 2
```

have an opportunity to finish describing the hand?

What message is given by West's bid? What rebid would East make?

What would the contract be? Who would be the declarer?

The Play

Who would make the opening lead? Which suit would be led? Why?

How many tricks must declarer take to fulfill the contract? How many sure tricks does declarer have? Which suit should declarer play first after winning a trick? Why? What will happen to the two low hearts in declarer's hand?

Bid and play the deal. Did declarer make the contract?

Exercise Nine *Answers* — Overcalling

The Bidding

- North opens the bidding with 1♦.
- East bids 1♠. This is an overcall.
- South passes. East's bid did not affect South's response.
- West, with 12 total points, bids 2♦, a cuebid.
- North, with a minimum-strength hand, passes.
- West's response is invitational or better in support of spades.
- East bids game, since East has 15 total points and West has shown at least 11 total points.
- The contract is 4♠ and East is the declarer.

The Play

- South makes the opening lead of the ♦10, partner's bid suit.
- Declarer needs 10 tricks.
- Declarer has 10 sure tricks.
- Declarer draws the trumps first since declarer doesn't have to give up the lead to do this.
- The two low hearts in declarer's hand will be discarded on the clubs in the dummy.
- Declarer should make the contract.

Exercise Ten — Delaying Drawing Trumps

(E-Z Deal Cards: #7, Deal 2 — Dealer, East)

Turn up all of the cards on the second pre-dealt deal and arrange them as in the previous exercise.

The Bidding

East is the dealer. Who would open the bidding? What would the opening bid be?

What would South bid?

What would West do in response to partner's opening bid? Has South's bid affected West's response?

What would North bid following South's overcall? Would North make the same bid if South had opened the bidding at the one level?

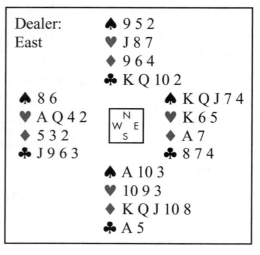

```
Dealer:        ♠ 9 5 2
East           ♥ J 8 7
               ♦ 9 6 4
               ♣ K Q 10 2
  ♠ 8 6                      ♠ K Q J 7 4
  ♥ A Q 4 2        N         ♥ K 6 5
  ♦ 5 3 2      W     E       ♦ A 7
  ♣ J 9 6 3        S         ♣ 8 7 4
               ♠ A 10 3
               ♥ 10 9 3
               ♦ K Q J 10 8
               ♣ A 5
```

What does East do now? Why does East not have to make a rebid?

What would the contract be? Who would be the declarer?

The Play

Who would make the opening lead? Which suit would be led? Why?

How many tricks must declarer take to fulfill the contract? How many sure tricks does declarer have? Which suit should declarer play first after winning the first trick? Why must declarer sometimes delay drawing trumps?

Bid and play the deal. Did declarer make the contract?

Exercise Ten *Answers* — Delaying Drawing Trumps

The Bidding

- East opens the bidding with 1 ♠.
- South overcalls 2 ♦.
- West passes, because West can no longer bid 1NT.
- North passes. If South had opened 1 ♦, North would have responded 1NT.
- East passes, since East has a minimum-strength opening bid.
- The contract is 2 ♦ and South is the declarer.

The Play

- West leads the ♠ 8, the suit partner bid.
- Declarer needs eight tricks and has four sure tricks. However, declarer has six losers — two in spades, three in hearts and one in diamonds.
- Declarer should play clubs first, discarding one of the losers on the extra club winner in dummy. Declarer sometimes must delay drawing trumps because there are too many quick losers if a trump trick has to be lost.
- Declarer can expect to make the contract.

Exercise Eleven — Another Fast Discard

(E-Z Deal Cards: #7, Deal 3 — Dealer, South)

Turn up all of the cards on the third pre-dealt deal and arrange them as in the previous exercise.

The Bidding

South is the dealer. Who would open the bidding? What would the opening bid be?

What would West bid?

What would North do in response to partner's opening bid?

What is the value of East's hand after West's overcall? What would East bid? Would East make the same bid if West had opened the bidding?

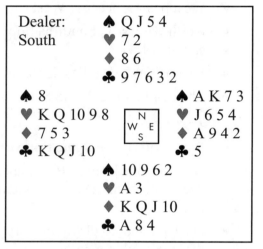

```
Dealer:        ♠ Q J 5 4
South          ♥ 7 2
               ♦ 8 6
               ♣ 9 7 6 3 2
♠ 8                              ♠ A K 7 3
♥ K Q 10 9 8      N              ♥ J 6 5 4
♦ 7 5 3        W     E           ♦ A 9 4 2
♣ K Q J 10        S              ♣ 5
               ♠ 10 9 6 2
               ♥ A 3
               ♦ K Q J 10
               ♣ A 8 4
```

What would the contract be? Who would be the declarer?

The Play

Who would make the opening lead? Which suit would be led? Why?

How many tricks must declarer take to fulfill the contract? How many sure tricks does declarer have? How can declarer avoid losing two diamond tricks? Which suit should declarer play first after winning the first trick? Why? What will declarer do next?

Bid and play the deal. Did declarer make the contract?

Exercise Eleven *Answers* — Another Fast Discard

The Bidding

- South opens the bidding with 1♦.
- West overcalls 1♥.
- North passes.
- East has 12 HCP plus 3 distribution points — 15 points in total.
- East begins with a cuebid of 2♦ followed by 4♥, if partner has not already bid it.
- If West had opened the bidding, East would bid a new suit, 1♠, forcing, since East is too strong to bid 3♥.
- The contract is 4♥.
- West is the declarer.

The Play

- North leads the ♦8, top of a doubleton in partner's suit.
- West needs 10 tricks and has three sure tricks. However, West also has four losers — one in hearts, two in diamonds and one in clubs.
- Declarer can avoid losing one diamond trick by discarding a diamond on the extra spade winner in dummy.
- After winning the first trick, declarer plays the spades in order to discard one diamond loser right away. Declarer can then draw trumps.
- Declarer should make the contract.

Exercise Twelve — The 1NT Overcall

(E-Z Deal Cards: #7, Deal 4 — Dealer, West)

Turn up all of the cards on the fourth pre-dealt deal, and arrange them as in the previous exercise.

The Bidding

West is the dealer. Who would open the bidding? What would the opening bid be?

What would North bid?

What would East do in response to partner's opening bid?

What is the value of South's hand? Does South know whether the partnership belongs in game or partscore?

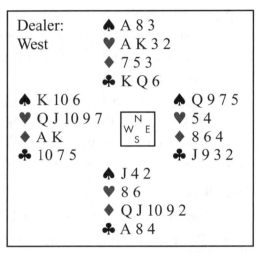

```
Dealer:        ♠ A 8 3
West           ♥ A K 3 2
               ♦ 7 5 3
               ♣ K Q 6
♠ K 10 6            ♠ Q 9 7 5
♥ Q J 10 9 7       ♥ 5 4
♦ A K              ♦ 8 6 4
♣ 10 7 5           ♣ J 9 3 2
               ♠ J 4 2
               ♥ 8 6
               ♦ Q J 10 9 2
               ♣ A 8 4
```

What strain should the partnership play in? What would South bid?

What would West do next?

What is the message given by South's bid? What would North rebid? Why?

What would the contract be? Who would be the declarer?

The Play

Who would make the opening lead? Which suit would be led? Why?

How many tricks must declarer take to fulfill the contract? How many sure tricks does declarer have? Which suit can declarer use to develop additional tricks? Why shouldn't declarer take the sure tricks in the other suits first?

Bid and play the deal. Did declarer make the contract?

Exercise Twelve *Answers* — The 1NT Overcall

The Bidding

- West opens the bidding with 1♥.
- North overcalls 1NT.
- East passes.
- South has 9 points. South doesn't know whether the partnership belongs in game or partscore. The strain should be notrump.
- South would bid 2NT, showing 8 or 9 points.
- West passes.
- South made an invitational bid. North makes a judgment call and passes with 16 points, holding no intermediate cards (tens or nines) and no five-card suit.
- The contract is 2NT.
- North is the declarer.

The Play

- East leads the ♥5, top of a doubleton in the suit partner has bid.
- Declarer has six sure tricks and needs eight tricks to make the contract.
- Declarer can develop extra tricks in diamonds by playing them right away. If declarer plays the sure tricks in other suits first, it will be too late to develop the diamond winners. The opponents will get the lead, and they will have enough winners in the other suits to defeat the contract.
- Declarer should make the contract. Declarer will take only eight tricks if West (correctly) continues leading hearts after winning the first diamond trick.

CHAPTER 8
Takeout Doubles and Advances

The Takeout Double

Advancing after a Takeout Double

The Advancer Considers Notrump

Rebids by the Takeout Doubler

Guidelines for Play

Summary

The Finer Points

Exercises

Sample Deals

THE TAKEOUT DOUBLE

In the last chapter, we saw how a double used for penalty affects the scoring. If you double the opponents' contract and they don't make it, the penalty is increased. If they do make the contract, the number of points the opponents collect is increased.

There is another use for the double. It can be used as a request for partner to bid. This type of double is called a *takeout double.* Like the penalty double, it is used in competitive bidding situations.

Doubling for Takeout

Suppose your opponent opens the bidding 1 ♥ and you have the following hand:

♠ K Q 9 8   You would like to bid something to show your part-
♥ 3   ner that you have enough strength to compete. To
♦ A 10 7 6   overcall, however, you need a five-card suit. With
♣ K Q 4 2   this type of hand, you aren't sure which suit your
side should compete in. You'd like to know partner's best suit, since you have support for clubs, diamonds and spades. The takeout double is a call that accomplishes this. It announces a hand with the strength of an opening bid that has support for each of the unbid suits. The takeout double asks partner a question — "What is your best suit, partner?"

Penalty or Takeout?

If there are two kinds of doubles, the penalty double and the takeout double, how does your partner know which one you mean? You can't say, "I'd like to make a penalty double of 1 ♥" or "I'd like to make a takeout double of 1 ♥." The only word you are allowed to use is *double.*

Here are three guidelines to help you determine if a double is for takeout. In order for a double to be a takeout double:

1. Neither the doubler nor the doubler's partner have previously made a bid (previous passes are okay).

2. The opposing partnership has bid either one or two suits (notrump is not a suit).

3. It is either the doubler's first or second turn to bid.

Here are some examples:

NORTH	EAST	SOUTH	WEST
1♥	Double		

Since the double is of a partscore, and since neither East nor West has bid, it is a takeout double.

NORTH	EAST	SOUTH	WEST
1♥	Pass	2♥	Pass
4♥	Double		

Since the double is of a game contract, it is a penalty double.

NORTH	EAST	SOUTH	WEST
1♥	Pass	2♣	Double

Since the double is of a partscore, and since neither East nor West has bid, it is a takeout double.

NORTH	EAST	SOUTH	WEST
Pass	1NT	Double	

South's double is for penalty since the opponents have not bid any suits.

Distributional Requirements for the Takeout Double

When you make a takeout double, you are asking your partner to pick the suit partner likes best. You must have support for the suit partner chooses. Ideally, when you make a takeout double, you will have at least four cards in each of the unbid suits.

Let's look at our previous example.

Your opponent opened the bidding 1 ♥ and you held:

♠ K Q 9 8   You were ready to accept whichever suit your partner
♥ 3   picked.
♦ A 10 7 6
♣ K Q 4 2

In a competitive situation, however, things aren't always ideal. Every time you want to make a takeout double, you won't hold a singleton and three four-card suits.

Suppose your opponent starts the bidding with 1 ♥ and you hold:

♠ K Q 9 8   You have four-card support for spades and diamonds
♥ 3 2   but only three-card support for clubs. A takeout
♦ A 10 7 6   double is the best available call. You hope that partner
♣ K Q 4   will not choose clubs, but if that happens, perhaps
                partner will have five of them and you will play in
                a Golden Fit.

Not all hands are suitable for a takeout double. Suppose your opponent starts the bidding with 1 ♥ and you have this hand:

♠ 3   This hand looks similar to the earlier example.
♥ K Q 9 8   However, you don't have support for spades, one
♦ A 10 7 6   of the unbid suits. If you ask for partner's best suit,
♣ K Q 4 2   partner may choose spades and you would be in a
                bad contract. With this type of hand, you have to pass
                and await developments.

Let's look at some other examples. Suppose your opponent opens the bidding with 1 ♣.

♠ A 8 5 4   Make a takeout double. If partner picks hearts or
♥ A 9 7 2   spades, you have four-card support. If partner picks
♦ A 6 3   diamonds, partner will have to be satisfied with three-
♣ Q 5   card support. At the very least, you are competing
                with this hand.

♠ A J 4
♥ A Q 7 2
♦ A Q 3
♣ 9 6 2

You have four-card support for hearts but only three-card support for spades and diamonds. Your extra strength, however, should compensate. Making a takeout double is preferable to bidding 1NT with no strength in the opponent's suit.

♠ A 4
♥ K 9 3
♦ Q 7 4 2
♣ K J 7 3

You have four-card support for only one of the unbid suits, and you have no extra strength to compensate. Pass, since the hand is not suitable for either an overcall or a takeout double.

The Strength of the Takeout Double

Making a takeout double is like opening the bidding for your side. You should have the strength of an opening bid — at least 13 points. However, there is an interesting way of valuing your hand for the takeout double. Count dummy points! You are asking your partner to pick the suit for the contract, so you will be the dummy. Because you can value your hand in this fashion, hands that would be too weak to open the bidding when counting HCP and length may become strong enough for a takeout double.

Suppose the bidding is opened 1 ♥ by the opponent on your right.

♠ K Q 7 6
♥ 8
♦ K 10 4 3
♣ Q 9 7 4

You have only 10 HCP, but you can add 3 points for the singleton heart. This gives you 13 total points — enough to make a takeout double.

♠ A 10 8 5
♥ 10 6
♦ Q 9 4
♣ A Q 6 2

You have 12 HCP plus 1 point for the doubleton heart. Again, this gives you enough to make a takeout double.

♠ Q 6 5 3
♥ —
♦ A K 8 2
♣ J 10 7 6 3

You would not open the bidding with this hand. When an opponent opens 1 ♥, however, your hand can be valued with dummy points to give you 10 HCP plus 5 points for the heart void. Double!

Takeout doubles may also be used to show a hand with 18 or more total points (too strong to overcall.) The takeout doubler might not have support for all the unbid suits in this case.

The Bidding Message of the Takeout Double

The takeout double sends a special message in the bidding. The takeout double primarily asks partner to pick one of the unbid suits. Partner should never pass without great length or great strength in the opponent's suit. Remember, the doubler is asking partner to bid.

Put It All Together

When an opponent opens the bidding, you may make a takeout double of a partscore contract if your partner has not bid and if your hand satisfies the basic requirements.

> ### Requirements for a Takeout Double
>
> • A takeout double promises at least three-card support for all unbid suits with 13 or more total points,
>
> OR
>
> • Any hand with 18 or more total points (that is, a hand too strong to overcall).

The perfect distribution for a takeout double is 4–4–4–1 with the singleton in the opponent's suit. The more HCP the doubler has, the more the doubler's distribution is allowed to stray from 4–4–4–1.

Let's look at some example hands. The opponent on your right opens the bidding with 1 ♦.

♠ J 10 9 7   With 10 HCP and 3 points for the singleton diamond,
♥ Q 6 4 2   double. You have four-card support for all of the
♦ 7   unbid suits.
♣ A K 8 6

♠ K Q J 8 6
♥ K 9 3
♦ 4
♣ A 10 6 4

Although you have some support for all of the unbid suits, this hand is more suited to an overcall of 1 ♠. With only three-card support for hearts, you want to emphasize the good five-card spade suit.

♠ Q 8 6
♥ A 4
♦ K Q 7 3
♣ J 9 4 2

Pass. You have neither the required strength nor the distribution to overcall or make a takeout double.

♠ K 8 6 4
♥ A Q 3 2
♦ —
♣ Q 10 8 6 2

Your hand is not strong enough to overcall clubs at the two level. Counting 5 dummy points for the void in diamonds, however, you have enough to double. This is the best way to compete with this hand.

♠ A
♥ K Q J 10 3 2
♦ 5
♣ K Q J 5 4

This hand is too good for a simple overcall. Make a takeout double and then bid hearts. Partner will know you have 18+ total points.

ADVANCING AFTER A TAKEOUT DOUBLE

The Advancer Considers the Bidding Message

When you respond to partner's takeout double, you are called the advancer. In competitive auctions, it is easier to remember that the partner of the takeout doubler (or overcaller) is called the advancer.

After a takeout double, which is primarily forcing, the advancer must bid even if the hand contains no points. Look at what would happen if the advancer were to pass:

NORTH	EAST	SOUTH	WEST
			(advancer)
1 ♠	Double	Pass	Pass

North would be pleased to pass since East has announced shortness in spades. It will be very difficult for East–West to prevent North from taking seven tricks and making the contract. Therefore, even when holding a weak hand, West has to consider the consequences of not bidding.

If South bids after the double, however, West may pass.

NORTH	EAST	SOUTH	WEST (advancer)
1 ♠	Double	2 ♠	Pass

In this situation, it is acceptable for West to pass, because North–South would be in a contract of 2 ♠, undoubled. South's bid erases the double by East. In addition, if East wants to bid, there will be an opportunity to do so.

The Advancer Classifies the Strength of the Hand

There are three ranges for the advancer when replying to the takeout double. These ranges are somewhat similar to those we use when advancing an overcall or responding to an opening bid.

Minimum hand	0 to 8 total points
Medium hand	9 to 11 total points
Maximum hand	12 or more total points

The Advancer Considers the Distribution

When partner makes a takeout double, the bid describes a hand with support for the unbid suits. The advancer wants to pick the suit that is best for the partnership. The advancer's first choice is to bid a major suit, since the partnership wants to find a Golden Fit in a major suit. Because the partnership is in a competitive situation, it also wants to get to the best contract as quickly as possible.

The Advancer's Decision with 0 to 8 Total Points

With 0 to 8 total points, the advancer wants to make a bid as cheaply as possible. The advancer can frequently bid at the one level since a takeout double doesn't use up any room on the Bidding Scale.

As the advancer, your first choice is a four-card or longer major suit. Your second choice is a four-card or longer minor suit. Your last choice is notrump. Because partner's takeout double denies strength in the suit bid by the opponents, bid notrump only when you have considerable strength in the opponent's suit. We will consider notrump advances in a separate section.

Suppose the opponent on your left opens the bidding with 1♣ and your partner doubles. Assuming the next opponent passes, let's see how you handle the bidding on the following hands.

♠ 8 7 4 ♥ J 9 6 5 2 ♦ 9 6 2 ♣ 4 3	You have a very weak hand, only 1 HCP plus 1 point for the five-card suit. You are obliged to bid, however, because partner has doubled. Choose your best suit, hearts, and bid at the cheapest level, 1♥.
♠ Q 7 4 3 ♥ K J 9 ♦ J 9 7 5 4 ♣ 3	You have a choice of bidding your five-card diamond suit or your four-card spade suit. In a competitive auction, the partnership is interested in finding a major-suit fit as quickly as possible. Bid 1♠ even though you have more diamonds than spades.
♠ A 7 6 4 2 ♥ 9 8 ♦ 8 7 6 4 ♣ K 3	Bid 1♠. You're at the top of your range and will bid again if the opponents continue to compete for the contract. If they bid 2♣, you should rebid 2♠.
♠ J 10 ♥ 3 2 ♦ Q 10 5 ♣ K Q J 10 9 2	You never should pass partner's takeout double without great length and strength in the opponent's suit. Remember, partner is asking you to bid. This is the type of hand you need to pass. You are essentially converting the takeout double to a penalty double.

The Advancer's Decision with 9 to 11 Total Points

When the advancer has 9 to 11 total points, the partnership may be headed toward a game contract, since the takeout doubler shows a hand worth at least 13 points. The advancer needs to know if the doubler has any extra strength. To find out, the advancer invites game by jumping one level.

A jump in response to a takeout double is invitational asking partner to clarify the hand.

Let's see how the advancer bids with a medium-range hand of 9 to 11 total points. Assume the opponent on your left opens the bidding with 1 ♥ and your partner doubles.

♠ 10 9 7 4
♥ Q 8 6
♦ K Q J 8
♣ K 3

With 11 HCP, the advancer wants to invite opener to bid on to game. Although the diamond suit looks better than the spade suit, the advancer still prefers to bid the major suit. It is more likely that the partnership can make a game contract in spades than in diamonds. To show a medium hand, jump to 2 ♠.

♠ Q 6 3
♥ 8 2
♦ A 10 9 7 5
♣ A 6 3

The advancer has 10 HCP plus 1 point for the five-card suit. To show a medium-range hand, the advancer jumps to 3 ♦. Note that the advancer has to bid at the three level with a diamond suit and can stay at the two level with a spade suit.

♠ K Q 10 2
♥ 10 4 2
♦ A 6 5
♣ Q 9 3

With 11 HCP, the advancer has a perfect 2 ♠ response with this hand.

The Advancer's Decision with 12 or More Total Points

With 12 or more total points, the advancer knows that the contract should be played at the game level, since partner also has at least 13 total points. The advancer wants to choose one of the Golden Games, so the contract will be 4 ♠, 4 ♥ or 3NT, whenever possible. Again, we will consider notrump advances separately. The advancer's decision is straightforward on most hands because the doubler has shown interest in the unbid major suit or suits and usually has four-card support.

When the advancer has 12 or more total points, there are many bids that could be made to invite the doubler to give more information about the hand. For now, however, the bidding is made simpler by having the advancer immediately place the partnership in the best game.

Let's look at some examples. The bidding is opened with 1♠ by the opponent on your left, partner doubles and your opponent on the right passes.

♠ 7 2
♥ A 9 7 5 2
♦ A K 3
♣ J 5 2

With 12 HCP plus 1 point for the five-card suit, the advancer has enough for game. Because partner has shown support for the unbid suits with a takeout double, the advancer knows there is a Golden Fit in hearts and can jump directly to game, 4♥.

♠ K 3
♥ A K 8 4
♦ A 9 2
♣ J 10 7 3

The advancer has enough for game. The most likely game is 4♥. It is possible that partner has only three-card support for hearts. Lacking more sophisticated bidding methods, a direct jump to 4♥ is the most reasonable bid.

In this example, partner makes a takeout double of a 1♦ opening bid and your opponent on the right passes.

♠ A Q 6 4
♥ K J 7 2
♦ A K 3
♣ 6 5

This is difficult. You want to know which major suit partner prefers. In order to find out, employ the cuebid response, 2♦. When partner bids a major, raise to game.

THE ADVANCER CONSIDERS NOTRUMP

When the advancer considers notrump, the ranges are slightly different from those the advancer uses when bidding in a suit. While this is slightly more information for you to remember, it is more accurate. Remember, playing in notrump requires high-card points to be effective and the advancer must take this into consideration in determining the proper bid. Don't forget that Golden Games require 25 total points. With the 25 total points, you can take 10 tricks in spades or hearts, but probably only nine tricks in notrump — hence, the necessity for more high-card points on a per trick basis in notrump.

The 1NT response to a takeout double is a forward-going bid suggesting 8–10 HCP and at least one stopper in the opponent's suit. Jump to 2NT with a similar hand and 11–12 HCP. Jump to 3NT with 13 or more HCP.

Assume the opponent on your left opens 1 ♥ your partner makes a takeout double and the next hand passes.

♠ 9 7 3   Bid 1NT not 2 ♦. This hand is balanced with much
♥ K Q J   of its strength in the opponent's suit. The heart cards
♦ Q 10 6 3   represent a double stopper and the hand looks like it
♣ J 4 3   will play better in notrump.

♠ 7 6 4   Bid 2NT. This 12 HCP hand is too strong for a
♥ A Q 10   1NT bid. Partner is invited to go to 3NT with extra
♦ Q 10 8 5   HCPs.
♣ A 8 7

♠ Q 6   With 14 HCP and no four-card spade suit, the proper
♥ A Q 9   Golden Game is notrump. So, bid 3NT even though
♦ J 10 8 2   you probably have a Golden Fit in a minor suit.
♣ A J 10 2

REBIDS BY THE TAKEOUT DOUBLER

The rebid by the takeout doubler is similar to the rebid by an opening bidder (Chapter 5). The doubler classifies the hand into one of three categories:

Minimum hand	13 to 15 total points
Medium hand	16 to 18 total points
Maximum hand	19 to 21 total points

Doubler's Decision with a Minimum Hand, 13 to 15 Total Points

After a double, the advancer shows a minimum hand, from 0 to 8 total points, by bidding at the cheapest level. The takeout doubler should pass partner's minimum bid and leave the partnership in a partscore.

If the advancer shows a medium hand, 9 to 11 total points, doubler should take another look at the strength of the hand. If doubler is at the bottom of the range, 13 or 14 points, pass is the right call. If doubler is at the top, 15 total points, doubler may invite to game.

If the advancer bids a game to show a maximum hand, 12 or more total points, the decision has already been made. The doubler passes.

Doubler's Decision with a Medium Hand, 16 to 18 Total Points

When the advancer shows a minimum hand of 0 to 8 total points, the doubler moves up the Bidding Scale one level to show a medium hand of 16 to 18 total points. The advancer will now know that the takeout doubler has a medium-strength hand and will decide on the final contract.

If the advancer shows a medium hand of 9 to 11 total points, the partnership must have enough combined strength for game. The takeout doubler can now bid a game.

The advancer won't hold a maximum hand of 12 or more total points very often when the takeout doubler has 17 or 18 total points. However, the partnership should be happy in a game contract when this is the case.

Doubler's Decision with a Maximum Hand, 19 to 21 Total Points

If the advancer shows a minimum hand of 0 to 8 total points, the takeout doubler jumps a level of bidding to show extra strength. This bid won't always get the partnership to a game contract because the advancer could have a hand with very few points. (The advancer will tend to have fewer points when the takeout doubler holds a maximum hand). Alerted to the strength of the takeout doubler's hand, the advancer can bid accordingly.

If the advancer shows a medium hand of 9 to 11 total points, the takeout doubler will carry on to game.

It would be extremely unusual for the advancer to have a maximum hand of 12 total points when the takeout doubler has a maximum hand. If this occurs, the partnership will bid to a slam contract.

Put It All Together

Suppose your right-hand opponent opens 1 ♥. You make a takeout double, and your partner bids 1 ♠ to show a minimum hand (0 to 8 total points). What do you rebid with the following hands?

♠ 10 9 7 4 ♥ 10 ♦ A J 8 6 ♣ A Q 6 4	You have a minimum-strength hand — 11 HCP plus 3 points for the singleton heart. The advancer has no more than 8 total points and may not have any points at all. Pass. If the opponents bid again, you will leave any further bidding up to partner.
♠ Q 10 8 3 ♥ — ♦ A Q 7 6 2 ♣ A 9 5 3	You have 12 HCP plus 5 points for the void in hearts, a total of 17 points. With a medium-strength hand, there is some possibility of game if the advancer has the top of the range. Raise to 2 ♠ to tell the advancer you have 16 to 18 total points.
♠ A 9 8 4 ♥ — ♦ A K 7 6 2 ♣ A 9 5 3	You have 20 total points, a maximum-strength hand. Jump to 3 ♠ to tell the advancer you have a hand in the 19 to 21-point range. The advancer will then decide if the partnership has 25 total points for game.

GUIDELINES FOR PLAY

To improve your play when you are declarer, you should always make a plan. The most important decisions usually come early in the deal. Later, it may be too late! As soon as the dummy comes down, you should take the time to plan the play. By making a plan, you can review what went right and what went wrong after the deal has been played. By going over your plan and the results of your play, you can improve your game.

Making a Plan

To make a plan, declarer goes through four basic steps:

1. **P**ause to consider your objective
2. **L**ook at your winners and losers
3. **A**nalyze your alternatives
4. **N**ow put it all together

1. *Pause to consider your objective.* Determine the number of tricks needed to make the contract.

2. *Look at your winners and losers.* See how close you are to your objective. Count the number of sure tricks you have.

3. *Analyze your alternatives.* Determine the resources you have available. Look at each suit to see how you can develop additional tricks.

4. *Now put it all together.* Decide how to proceed. Review the various alternatives you discovered in the previous step.

The first two steps were discussed in Chapter 2. From these steps, you know how many additional tricks you must develop to make the contract. If you don't need any more tricks, you can take your tricks and run. The third step encompasses the various techniques discussed in Chapters 3 through 7:

- Promoting high cards
- Developing tricks in long suits
- Finessing (leading toward the high card)
- Ruffing losers in the dummy
- Discarding losers

Often you will discover more than one possibility. In the fourth step, you must choose from among your options or perhaps plan to combine them. In doing this, you must be careful to watch your entries, decide whether to draw trumps right away and so on.

While playing, watch to see how your plan is working. As you get more experienced, you will learn to formulate better plans and uncover additional possibilities.

Let's look at an example of making a plan.

NORTH (Dummy)   SOUTH (Declarer)
♠ A 10 5   ♠ 8 6 3
♥ 7 6 3   ♥ A K 8
♦ K 9 6 2   ♦ A 8 7 3
♣ 7 4 2   ♣ A Q 5

Suppose you are in a contract of 1NT, and the opening lead is the ♥ J. You start by determining your objective: you need to win seven tricks. Next you count your sure tricks: the ♠A, the ♥A K, the ♦A K and the ♣A — a total of six. You need to develop one more trick to make your contract.

What are the possibilities? There are no extra tricks possible in spades or hearts. You have eight diamonds in the combined hands. It might be possible to develop an extra trick in this suit if the opponents' cards are split 3–2. In clubs, you could take a finesse, hoping East has the king.

Now, you must *Put it all together.* Should you plan to play the diamond suit or the club suit first? In fact, you can combine your options: play the ♦ A and the ♦ K first to see if both opponents follow suit. If they do, the missing diamonds must be split 3–2, and you can lead the suit again to develop a diamond trick. If the missing diamonds are not divided 3–2, you can try the club finesse instead.

You formulate your plan, and then you put it into action. If you're defeated, you'll know why — you were unlucky! The diamonds broke 4–1, and West had the ♣K. The play of each deal suddenly turns into an adventure!

SUMMARY

One way to compete in the auction is by making a takeout double.

You can tell when a double is for takeout by using the following as a guideline:

Guidelines for Recognizing a Takeout Double

- Neither the doubler nor the doubler's partner have previously made a bid (previous passes are okay).
- The opposing partnership has bid either one or two suits (notrump is not a suit).
- It is either the doubler's first or second turn to bid.

To make a takeout double, you need a hand that satisfies the following criteria:

Requirements for a Takeout Double

- 13 or more total points, and
- Support for the unbid suits.

or

- A hand with 18+ points that is too strong for an overcall.

Advances by Takeout Doubler's Partner

With a minimum hand (0 to 8 total points):

- Bid a four-card or longer major suit at the cheapest level.
- Bid a four-card or longer minor suit at the cheapest level.
- Pass is not an option unless you have great length and strength in the opponent's suit.

With a medium hand (9 to 11 total points):

- Jump in a four-card or longer major suit.
- Jump in a four-card or longer minor suit.

With a maximum hand (12 or more total points):

- Jump to game in a four-card or longer major suit.
- Cuebid the opponent's suit to ask doubler for assistance in finding the best game contract.

Notrump Advances
- 1NT response shows 8–10 HCP and at least one stopper in the opponent's suit.
- 2NT response shows 11–12 HCP and at least one stopper in the opponent's suit.
- 3NT shows 13 or more HCP with at least one stopper in the opponent's suit.

Rebids by the Takeout Doubler
With a minimum hand (13 to 15 total points):
- Pass if partner bids at the cheapest level.
- Pass with 13 or 14 points if partner jumps a level. Invite a Golden Game with 15 total points if partner jumps a level.

With a medium hand (16 to 18 total points):
- Raise one level if partner bids at the cheapest level.
- Bid a Golden Game if partner jumps a level.

With a maximum hand (19 to 21 total points):
- Jump raise if partner bids at the cheapest level.
- Bid a Golden Game if partner jumps a level.

THE FINER POINTS

A More In-depth Look at the Takeout Double

The text explains the classic use of the takeout double. It shows a hand of opening bid strength with support for the unbid suits. In the last chapter, it was mentioned that some players like to put an upper limit of 17 total points on the overcall. The takeout double also is used to show a hand too strong to make a simple overcall. With such a hand, you start by doubling. Partner will assume you have made a normal takeout double and bid accordingly. Now, you bid your suit. If partner happens to choose your suit, you can raise.

This is in accordance with the discussion on rebids by the takeout doubler. After partner makes a minimum response, the takeout doubler bids again holding a medium- or maximum-strength hand. If the takeout doubler bids a new suit, the advancer can interpret this to show at least 18 total points — a hand too strong to overcall — and generally a one-suited hand.

You must be careful not to abuse the takeout double. If you make a takeout double of 1♦ with only a long heart suit, your partner might jump to 4♠, expecting you to have support. That is why you need a strong hand of 18 or more total points to double without support for all of the unbid suits. The more points you have, the less likely that partner will have enough to jump — which would make it difficult for you to show your suit. Also, the extra strength should compensate for the lack of support if partner does jump to a high-level contract.

A More In-depth Look at the Cuebid Response

As discussed at the end of the previous chapter, a partnership will usually not want to play in a suit that has been opened by the opponents. A bid of the opponent's suit, called a cuebid, can be assigned a special meaning. If your partner makes a takeout double, you can use a bid of the opponent's suit to ask for further information from partner. You could make this bid if you have a hand of 12 or more total points. You know you want to play in a game contract, but you don't know in which strain.

For example, suppose the opponent on your left opens the bidding 1 ♦. Your partner doubles and you hold the following hand:

♠ A 9 7 5　　　　With 14 points, you know there is enough com-
♥ A 9 7 5　　　　bined strength for game. Which contract should you
♦ Q 3　　　　　　choose? Should you jump to 4 ♥ or 4 ♠? Whichever
♣ A 8 2　　　　　one you choose, partner may have only three-card
　　　　　　　　　support while having four-card support in the other
major. It is even possible that your side belongs in 3NT or 5 ♣.

You can solve the problem by bidding 2 ♦, the opponent's suit. This is a forcing bid, asking partner for a further description. If partner bids hearts, you jump to 4 ♥. If partner bids spades, you jump to 4 ♠. If partner bids notrump, you raise to 3NT.

The cuebid is useful for advancing to a takeout double or an overcall, but it is not essential when first starting out.

Takeout Doubles at Higher Levels

In the last chapter, we said that not all competitive actions occur in a one-over-one sequence. The higher the level that the takeout double is made, the more strength it requires. Take a look at these examples.

NORTH	EAST	SOUTH	WEST
3 ♥	Double		

This action takes substantially more HCP than a takeout double of 1 ♥. After all, the advancer may have to bid with no points.

NORTH	EAST	SOUTH	WEST
1 ♠	Pass	2 ♠	Double

West's double is for takeout. West must have a pretty strong hand to force partner to bid at the three level.

Exercise One — Takeout or Penalty?

In the following auctions, is West's double for takeout or penalty?

	NORTH	EAST	SOUTH	WEST	
1)	Pass	Pass	1♦	**Double**	_____

	NORTH	EAST	SOUTH	WEST	
2)	1♣	Pass	1♥	**Double**	_____

	NORTH	EAST	SOUTH	WEST	
3)	Pass	Pass	1NT	**Double**	_____

	NORTH	EAST	SOUTH	WEST	
4)	Pass	Pass	1♥	Pass	
	2♥	Pass	4♥	**Double**	_____

Exercise Two — The Takeout Double

The opponent on your right opens 1♥. Using dummy points to determine the value of your hand, decide whether you would make a takeout double with the following hands.

1) ♠ J 8 4 3
♥ 10 9
♦ K Q 7
♣ A Q 10 2

2) ♠ A Q 4 3
♥ 8
♦ A 7 3 2
♣ J 4 3 2

3) ♠ K 9 6 3
♥ —
♦ K 9 8 7 2
♣ A 8 7 3

HCP: _____   HCP: _____   HCP:_____

Dummy
points: _____   Dummy
points: _____   Dummy
points:_____

Total
points: _____   Total
points: _____   Total
points:_____

Exercise One *Answers* — Takeout or Penalty?

    1) Takeout   2) Takeout   3) Penalty   4) Penalty

Exercise Two *Answers* — The Takeout Double

1)	12 HCP	1 dummy point	13 total points	Double
2)	11 HCP	3 dummy points	14 total points	Double
3)	10 HCP	5 dummy points	15 total points	Double

Exercise Three — Choosing the Competitive Action

To enter the auction after an opponent has opened the bidding, you can overcall or double. What would you do with each of the following hands if the opponent on your right opens 1♣?

1) ♠ A J 10 6 3
   ♥ 4 3
   ♦ K 9 3
   ♣ K Q 6

2) ♠ A J 5 3
   ♥ Q 10 8 6
   ♦ K J 4 2
   ♣ 9

3) ♠ Q J 10
   ♥ A J 4 3
   ♦ K 10 2
   ♣ A K 6

_____

_____

_____

4) ♠ A 3
   ♥ A Q 8 6 3
   ♦ K J 9 5 2
   ♣ 4

5) ♠ A 8
   ♥ A K J 10 9 3
   ♦ A Q 3
   ♣ 8 5

6) ♠ Q 7 5
   ♥ A J
   ♦ Q 9 7 4
   ♣ K Q 8 3

_____

_____

_____

Exercise Four — Advancing a Takeout Double with 0 to 8 Total Points

Your left-hand opponent opens the bidding 1♠, and your partner doubles. Your right-hand opponent passes. What do you bid with each of the following hands?

1) ♠ 9 8
   ♥ Q 10 5 3
   ♦ K J 7 2
   ♣ 8 7 2

2) ♠ J 10
   ♥ K 3
   ♦ Q J 10 8 4
   ♣ 8 6 5 3

3) ♠ A J 9 3
   ♥ K 10 5
   ♦ J 4 2
   ♣ 10 9 6

_____

_____

_____

Exercise Three *Answers* — Choosing the Competitive Action

1) 1♠   2) Double   3) 1NT

4) 1♥   5) Double, then show   6) Pass
                          your hearts later

Exercise Four *Answers* — Advancing a Takeout Double with
0 to 8 Total Points

1) 2♥   2) 2♦   3) 1NT

Exercise Five — Advancing a Takeout Double with 9 to 11 Total Points

Your left-hand opponent bids 1 ♥ and your partner doubles. Your right-hand opponent passes. What do you bid with each of the following hands?

1) ♠ J 10 7 6 3
 ♥ 9 4 2
 ♦ A Q 6
 ♣ K 3

2) ♠ Q 10 3
 ♥ K J 10 8
 ♦ A 9 2
 ♣ J 7 3

3) ♠ A 8 2
 ♥ 10 9
 ♦ K Q J 10 8
 ♣ 8 6 2

_____   _____   _____

Exercise Six — Advancing a Takeout Double with 12 or More Total Points

Your left-hand opponent bids 1 ♦ and your partner doubles. Your right-hand opponent passes. What do you bid with each of the following hands?

1) ♠ 8 6
 ♥ A K 8 4 2
 ♦ A 9 3
 ♣ J 5 4

2) ♠ A 6 3
 ♥ K 4 2
 ♦ Q J 9 8
 ♣ A 10 3

3) ♠ Q 10 7 6 4 3
 ♥ 9
 ♦ J 8
 ♣ A K J 6

_____   _____   _____

4) ♠ A Q 6 4
 ♥ K J 7 2
 ♦ A 10 3
 ♣ 6 5

_____

Exercise Five *Answers* — Advancing a Takeout Double with 9 to 11 Total Points

1) 2♠   2) 2NT   3) 3♦

Exercise Six *Answers* — Advancing a Takeout Double with 12 or More Total Points

1) 4♥   2) 3NT   3) 4♠

4) Bid 2♦ , since you are unsure which game contract is best.

Exercise Seven — Rebids by the Takeout Doubler

Your right-hand opponent bids 1 ♥ and you double. Your partner bids
1 ♠. What do you rebid with each of the following hands?

1) ♠ 9 8 6 2   2) ♠ K Q J 6   3) ♠ A 9 6 2
   ♥ 3 2   ♥ —   ♥ 4
   ♦ A 10 6   ♦ K Q 9 4   ♦ K 8 7 3
   ♣ A K J 3   ♣ A J 8 6 2   ♣ A K J 2

_____   _____   _____

Exercise Eight — Making a Plan

Construct the following hands for North and South:

NORTH
♠ 10 3
♥ A 7 5
♦ 9 8 6 5 3
♣ 9 5 2

WEST   EAST
♥ Q

SOUTH
♠ A Q 5
♥ K 8 2
♦ A K 4
♣ A K 8 6

South is the declarer at 3NT and West leads the ♥ Q.

How many sure tricks does South have? _____

What are the possibilities of developing additional tricks in each
suit?_____

What would South's plan be? _____

How does this help South determine in which hand to win the first
trick? _____

Exercise Seven *Answers* — Rebids by the Takeout Doubler

   1) Pass   2) 3♠   3) 2♠

Exercise Eight *Answers* — Making a Plan

- South has seven sure tricks.
- South could get one extra trick in spades if East has the king; two extra tricks in diamonds if the missing diamonds are divided 3–2; one extra trick in clubs if the missing clubs are divided 3–3.
- South should try to develop the diamonds, since there is a possibility of two extra tricks.
- South should win the first trick with the ♥K. Dummy's ♥A will be needed later as an entry to the established diamond tricks.

Exercise Nine — The Takeout Double

(E-Z Deal Cards: #8, Deal 1 — Dealer, North)

Turn up all of the cards on the first pre-dealt deal. Put each hand dummy-style at the edge of the table in front of each player.

The Bidding

North is the dealer. Who would open the bidding? What would the opening bid be?

Would East like to compete in the auction? How can East compete? Is there any danger?

What would South's response be to North's opening bid? Is South's response affected by East's bid?

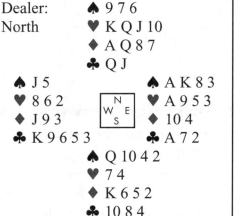

```
Dealer:      ♠ 9 7 6
North        ♥ K Q J 10
             ♦ A Q 8 7
             ♣ Q J
♠ J 5                      ♠ A K 8 3
♥ 8 6 2         N          ♥ A 9 5 3
♦ J 9 3       W   E        ♦ 10 4
♣ K 9 6 5 3     S          ♣ A 7 2
             ♠ Q 10 4 2
             ♥ 7 4
             ♦ K 6 5 2
             ♣ 10 8 4
```

What is the bidding message given by East's call? What would West respond?

What would North bid next? What would East bid? Why? What would the contract be? Who would be the declarer?

The Play

Who would make the opening lead? What would the opening lead be?

How many tricks must declarer take to fulfill the contract? How many sure tricks does declarer have? Declarer should look at each suit to decide what possibilities there are for developing tricks. What does declarer plan to do in the diamond suit? What does declarer plan to do in the trump suit? What should declarer's plan be?

Bid and play the deal. Did declarer make the contract?

Exercise Nine *Answers* — The Takeout Double

The Bidding

- North opens the bidding with 1♦. Some players may choose to open 1NT but, using judgment, 1♦ is a better bid since three points are wasted in the ♣Q J doubleton.

- East can compete by making a takeout double. There is some danger that West will have no points and no suit to bid.

- South passes. South's call is not affected by East's double.

- East's call is forcing, and West has to bid. West bids 2♣.

- North passes.

- East passes with a minimum-strength hand after hearing West make a minimum bid.

- The contract is 2♣ and West is the declarer.

The Play

- North leads the ♥K, top of a sequence.

- Declarer needs eight tricks to make the contract.

- Declarer has five sure tricks.

- Declarer wants to ruff a losing diamond in the dummy.

- Declarer wants to draw the opponents' trumps, hoping they divide 3–2.

- Declarer needs to ruff the losing diamond first before drawing trumps.

- Declarer should take eight tricks.

Exercise Ten — Using Dummy's Trumps

(E-Z Deal Cards: #8, Deal 2 — Dealer, East)

Turn up all of the cards on the second pre-dealt deal and arrange them as in the previous exercise.

The Bidding

East is the dealer. Who would open the bidding? What would the opening bid be?

What would South do?

What would West do in response to partner's opening bid? Has South's call affected West's response?

What would North bid?

What would the contract be? Who would be the declarer?

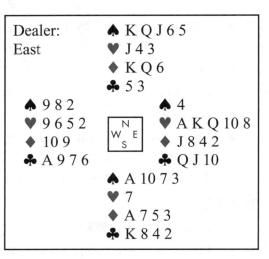

Dealer: ♠ K Q J 6 5
East   ♥ J 4 3
            ♦ K Q 6
            ♣ 5 3

♠ 9 8 2   ♠ 4
♥ 9 6 5 2   ♥ A K Q 10 8
♦ 10 9   ♦ J 8 4 2
♣ A 9 7 6   ♣ Q J 10

            ♠ A 10 7 3
            ♥ 7
            ♦ A 7 5 3
            ♣ K 8 4 2

The Play

Who would make the opening lead? Which suit would be led? Which suit would be led at the second trick?

How many tricks must declarer take to fulfill the contract? How many tricks does declarer have? What possibilities are there in the heart suit? The diamond suit? The club suit? What is declarer's plan? How does declarer's plan affect the play of the trump suit?

Bid and play the deal. Did declarer make the contract?

Exercise Ten *Answers* — Using Dummy's Trumps

The Bidding

- East opens the bidding with 1 ♥.
- South would make a takeout double.
- West passes. West's call is not affected by South's double.
- North bids 4 ♠.
- The contract is 4 ♠ and North is the declarer.

The Play

- East leads the ♥ A. Next, East leads the ♣ Q.
- Declarer needs to take 10 tricks and has eight sure tricks.
- There is a possibility of an extra trick if the missing diamonds are divided 3–3. In clubs, there is the possibility that East has the ace.
- The best chance is to ruff hearts in the dummy.
- Declarer has to leave two trumps in the dummy to do this.
- Declarer must delay drawing the opponents' trumps.
- Declarer makes the contract.

Exercise Eleven — Careful Play in a Side Suit

(E-Z Deal Cards: #8, Deal 3 — Dealer, South)

Turn up all of the cards on the third pre-dealt deal and arrange them as in the previous exercise.

The Bidding

What would South open?

What would West do?

What would North do in response to partner's opening bid?

What is the value of East's hand? What would East bid to show this strength?

What is the bidding message given by East's bid? What would West rebid?

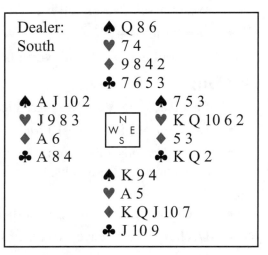

Dealer: ♠ Q 8 6
South   ♥ 7 4
           ♦ 9 8 4 2
           ♣ 7 6 5 3

♠ A J 10 2   ♠ 7 5 3
♥ J 9 8 3   ♥ K Q 10 6 2
♦ A 6   ♦ 5 3
♣ A 8 4   ♣ K Q 2

          ♠ K 9 4
          ♥ A 5
          ♦ K Q J 10 7
          ♣ J 10 9

What would the contract be? Who would be the declarer?

The Play

Who would make the opening lead? What would the opening lead be?

How many tricks must declarer take to fulfill the contract? How many sure tricks does declarer have? How can declarer develop an additional trick in the spade suit? What is declarer's plan?

Bid and play the deal. Did declarer make the contract?

Exercise Eleven *Answers* — Careful Play in a Side Suit

The Bidding

- South opens the bidding with 1 ♦.
- West would make a takeout double.
- North passes.
- East bids 2 ♥ with a hand worth 11 total points.
- East's bid is invitational.
- With 14 HCP plus 1 point for the doubleton diamond, West would bid 3 ♥, inviting game. East, having the maximum 11 total points for the range, will bid 4 ♥.
- The contract is 4 ♥ and East is the declarer.

The Play

- South leads the ♦ K.
- Declarer needs 10 tricks to make the contract.
- Declarer has five sure tricks.
- Declarer establishes four heart tricks by leading trumps and knocking out the ace.
- Declarer can get an extra trick in spades by leading twice toward the A–J–10 combination if South has either the king or the queen or both the king and the queen.
- Declarer's plan is to draw the trumps and then try to get an extra trick in spades.
- Declarer makes the contract.

Exercise Twelve — Careful Play in the Trump Suit

(E-Z Deal Cards: #8, Deal 4 — Dealer, West)

Turn up all of the cards on the fourth pre-dealt deal and arrange them as in the previous exercise.

The Bidding

What would West open?

What would North do?

What would East do in response to partner's opening bid?

What would South bid? What is the point range of South's bid?

What would West do next?

```
Dealer:      ♠ K Q 3 2
West         ♥ 9 5
             ♦ K J 6
             ♣ A K Q J
♠ A 10 8              ♠ J 5
♥ A K Q 6 3          ♥ 10 8 7 2
♦ 10 9 8            ♦ 7 5 4 2
♣ 6 3                ♣ 10 9 5
             ♠ 9 7 6 4
             ♥ J 4
             ♦ A Q 3
             ♣ 8 7 4 2
```

What is the value of North's hand? How does North describe the strength of the hand?

What is the bidding message given by North's rebid? What would South rebid? Why?

What would the contract be? Who would be the declarer?

The Play

Who would make the opening lead? Which suit would be led?

How many tricks must declarer take to fulfill the contract? How many sure tricks does declarer have? How should declarer plan to play the spade suit? What role will declarer's ♦ A and ♦ Q play? What is declarer's plan?

Bid and play the deal. Did declarer make the contract?

Exercise Twelve *Answers* — Careful Play in the Trump Suit

The Bidding

- West opens the bidding with 1 ♥.
- North would make a takeout double.
- East would pass.
- South's hand is in the minimum range, so South would bid 1 ♠.
- West passes.
- North has a maximum-strength hand and describes the hand by jumping the bidding.
- North bids 3 ♠.
- North is making an invitational bid. South will go on to game knowing that North has 19 to 21 points.
- The contract is 4 ♠ and South is the declarer.

The Play

- West leads the ♥ A.
- Declarer needs to take 10 tricks.
- Declarer has seven sure tricks.
- Declarer should plan to lead toward the ♠ K Q.
- Declarer's ♦ A Q will provide the entries to do this.
- Declarer should make the contract.

CHAPTER 9
The Stayman Convention

The Stayman Convention

Responding with Game-Forcing Hands

Responding with Invitational Hands

Responding with Weak Hands

Handling Interference

Summary

Exercises

Sample Deals

THE STAYMAN CONVENTION

In Chapter 3, you learned how to respond when partner opens 1NT. An opening notrump bid narrowly defines opener's strength and distribution. It is usual for the partnership to reach a good contract after this beginning.

In this chapter, we will look at an artificial, or conventional, bid that is very useful when responding to an opening bid of 1NT, the Stayman convention.

The Stayman Convention

When partner opens the bidding with 1NT, responder, as captain, decides the level and strain of the contract. When selecting the strain, responder wants to determine if the combined hands have a Golden Fit — eight or more cards — in a major suit. The Stayman convention allows responder to do that. First of all, a convention is an artificial bid that does not pertain to the strain named — in this case 2♣. The reason we play conventions is that they help us with bidding questions that normal bidding methods cannot answer.

Let's look at your hand:

♠ A Q 7 2
♥ K Q 5 4
♦ 9 8 7 6
♣ 8

Your partner has opened 1NT. What do you know about this hand? You know there are enough points for game. You have 11 HCP and partner's opening 1NT bid shows 15 to 17 HCP.

What don't you know? You don't know whether or not you have a Golden Fit with your partner. If partner has four hearts or four spades, you want to play in game in four of the suit partner has. If partner doesn't hold four cards in either major, you want to play in 3NT. None of the bidding you learned in Chapter 3 will help you find out if partner has a four-card major. The Stayman convention comes to the rescue!

Opener's Rebid

The Stayman convention, invented by George Rapée and publicized in an article written by Sam Stayman, is used to ask if opener has a four-card major suit. In order to use Stayman, responder must have at least one four-card major with at least an invitational hand of 8 or 9 total points. Responder bids 2♣ after opener's 1NT. With a four-card or longer major suit, opener responds in that suit at the two level. If opener has both four-card majors, the heart suit is rebid first, going up the line. Without a four-card major suit, opener rebids 2♦. The 2♣ response and the 2♦ rebid are artificial (conventional) calls that do not imply any information about the club and diamond suits respectively.

Here are some examples of the 1NT opener's rebid when responder bids 2♣:

♠ A 8 7 3   Rebid 2♠ to show the four-card spade suit.
♥ Q J 10
♦ A Q 8
♣ K 8 5

♠ A K   Rebid 2♥ to show the four-card heart suit. Re-
♥ 10 9 7 3   sponder is not interested in how good a suit you have,
♦ K Q 9 2   merely whether you have four of the suit.
♣ A J 10

♠ K 10 2   With no four-card major, rebid 2♦. This says noth-
♥ A K 5   ing about your diamond holding. It's an artificial
♦ 8 2   (conventional) response saying that you don't have
♣ A Q 10 6 3   a four-card major suit. Responder will bid again.

♠ K J 5 2   Rebid 2♥. Rebidding with both majors is similar to
♥ A 10 4 2   bidding four-card suits up the line when responding
♦ A J   to an opening bid of 1♣ or 1♦. If it turns out that
♣ K 10 5   responder isn't interested in hearts, you can show
                  the spade suit at your next opportunity.

To summarize, the opener has only three choices after responder bids 2♣, Stayman:

1) 2♦ shows no four-card major.

2) 2♥ shows a four-card heart suit and maybe four spades.

3) 2♠ shows a four-card spade suit and denies four hearts.

Remember, the 1NT opener can never pass the 2♣ bid!

Let's look at the Stayman convention in action.

RESPONDING WITH GAME-FORCING HANDS

When responder has 10 or more total points

With 10 or more total points, responder knows the partnership belongs in a game contract, since opener has at least 15 HCP. The only thing in question is the strain. If there is a Golden Fit in a major suit, the partnership belongs in 4♥ or 4♠; otherwise, the partnership belongs in 3NT.

Holding one or two four-card major suits, responder can determine the best contract by using the Stayman convention to uncover a Golden Fit. Responder starts by bidding 2♣, asking opener to show a four-card major. If opener rebids 2♠, showing a four-card spade suit, responder can place the contract in 4♠ when responder holds a four-card spade suit. Similarly, if opener rebids 2♥, responder can raise to 4♥. Finally, if opener rebids 2♦, denying four cards in either major, responder can jump to 3NT, knowing there is no Golden Fit in a major suit.

For example, suppose partner opens the bidding 1NT, and you hold this hand:

♠ A Q 7 2
♥ K Q 5 4
♦ 9 8 7 6
♣ 8

You respond 2♣, asking if opener has a four-card major suit. If partner rebids 2♥ or 2♠, you can jump directly to game in that suit knowing you have found a Golden Fit. If opener rebids 2♦, you know there is no Golden Fit in a major suit. You will then bid 3NT.

> Note that when responder rebids 3NT after opener's 2♦ reply to Stayman or raises opener's 2♥ or 2♠ reply to game, responder is making a sign-off bid — the 1NT opener should always pass.

Let's change the hand a bit. Again, partner opens 1NT.

♠ A Q 7	Respond 2♣. Responder doesn't need both majors
♥ K Q 5 4	to use Stayman. If opener rebids 2♥, responder puts
♦ 9 8 7 6	the partnership in 4♥. If opener rebids 2♦, showing
♣ 8 2	no four-card major, or 2♠, showing four spades,
	responder places the contract in 3NT.

Here's another situation. Again, partner opens 1NT.

♠ A Q 7 2	You respond 2♣ to find out if opener has a four-card
♥ K Q 5	major suit, and opener rebids 2♥. You don't know if
♦ 9 8 7 6	opener has a four-card spade suit or not, so you rebid
♣ 8 2	3NT. Now opener must wonder, "Why did responder
	bid 2♣ and then show no interest in my heart suit?"

The answer must be that responder was interested only in spades. After all, you did use the Stayman convention, so you must have at least one four-card major.

If opener corrects to 4♠ in the last example, it would indicate that opener has both majors and is confident that bidding game in spades is the correct bid, putting the partnership in its Golden Fit. Opener is making a sign-off bid and responder should pass, knowing that the correct level and strain for the final contract have been reached.

Look at this next example. How does responder handle a five-card major suit? Responder can make a forcing response of 3♥ or 3♠ to tell opener to bid 4♥ or 4♠ with three-card or longer support, otherwise to bid 3NT.

♠ A 4	Respond 3♥. With a five-card suit and a game-going
♥ K J 7 4 3	hand, you don't need to ask if opener has a four-card
♦ Q 8 2	heart suit; three-card support will be sufficient. Us-
♣ 10 4 2	ing standard methods, responder jumps to 3♥. This
	is a forcing bid, asking opener to choose between

3NT and 4♥. With a doubleton heart, opener will rebid 3NT; with three or more hearts, opener will continue to 4♥. There is no need to use the Stayman convention.

With a six-card major suit, responder knows that a Golden Fit exists, since opener has a balanced hand. Responder can bid game in the appropriate major suit. For example:

♠ A J 9 7 6 5   Respond 4♠. With a six-card major suit, there's no
♥ K 7 6   need for responder to use Stayman. Opener must
♦ 8 6   hold at least two spades. Responder can take the
♣ 8 2   partnership directly to 4♠. This is a sign-off bid,
                  and opener is expected to pass.

In the following example, holding both major suits, the responder starts with the Stayman convention to find out if opener also has a four-card major.

♠ A 10 6 4 2   Respond 2♣. With a four-card major suit and a five-
♥ Q J 10 6   card or longer major suit, responder starts with 2♣.
♦ K 8 5   If opener shows either major, responder can jump to
♣ 9   game in the major. If opener rebids 2♦, responder
                  now jumps to 3♠, a forcing bid asking opener to
choose between 3NT and 4♠. Responder finds out if opener has either a four-card heart suit or three or more spades — the best of all worlds.

What about this situation?

♠ 9 6 2   Respond 3NT. Don't bid 2♣ Stayman since you
♥ 7 4   aren't interested in a major suit.
♦ Q 7 2
♣ A K J 8 6

RESPONDING WITH INVITATIONAL HANDS

When Responder Has 8 or 9 points

With 8 or 9 points, responder is not sure of the right level and wants to invite game. When responder is interested in placing the contract in a major suit, responder can start with 2♣, the Stayman convention, to check for a major-suit fit or to show an invitational hand with a five-card or longer major suit.

Partner opens 1NT, and this is the responder's hand:

♠ A Q 7 2   This 8 HCP hand is only strong enough to invite
♥ Q 5 3   game opposite a 1NT opening bid of 15 to 17 HCP.
♦ 9 8 7 6   If this hand contained no four-card major, it would
♣ 8 7   invite by responding 2NT. With four spades, how-
               ever, it is a good idea to investigate for an eight-card
fit. Stayman does the trick.

If opener denies having a four-card major by rebidding 2♦, this hand should respond by making an invitational 2NT bid. Without Stayman, this is the same call you would normally make. Remember 3NT still could be a great contract if opener holds a maximum 1NT.

If opener shows four hearts by rebidding 2♥, an invitational 2NT bid from you is still the correct rebid. If opener also has a four-card spade suit, opener will then rebid 3♠ with a minimum hand and 4♠ with a maximum hand.

If opener replies 2♠ to your Stayman inquiry, you have found a Golden Fit. Invite to game by raising to 3♠. Partner will pass with a minimum hand, but go on to 4♠ with a maximum hand.

If opener has fewer than four spades, opener will pass 2NT with a minimum hand but go on to 3NT with a maximum. The proper strain and level will always be found.

> Responder's rebids of 2NT and three of opener's
> major after Stayman are invitational bids.

Let's make another slight change to the hand:

♠ A Q 7 2   This time the hand has 9 HCP, just one more than
♥ K 5 3   before. However, if partner rebids spades in response
♦ 9 8 7 6   to the Stayman inquiry, the Golden Fit has been
♣ 8 7   found, and this hand can be revalued using dummy
                   points. This hand is now worth 10 total points, and
                   responder can bid game.

There is one other type of hand for which the Stayman convention can be used:

♠ K J 8 4 3   This hand contains a five-card spade suit and 9 total
♥ 9   points — too much to sign off in 2♠, but not strong
♦ A 8 6   enough to bid 3♠ forcing to game. Responder would
♣ 10 9 6 2   like to invite game while showing the five-card major
                   suit. Stayman allows responder to accomplish this
                   goal.

Start with Stayman. If opener rebids 2♦ or 2♥, continue with 2♠. This suggests an invitational hand with a five-card spade suit. Opener can then either pass, raise to 4♠, rebid 2NT or even rebid 3NT, depending on the strength of the hand as well as the number of spades it possesses. If you have a Golden Fit, you will find it, otherwise you will play in notrump. The final contract will be at the correct level in the correct strain.

> With an invitational hand that contains a
> five-card major, begin with Stayman
> and then rebid your major.

Here are some examples of how responder handles an invitational hand when looking for a major-suit fit following partner's opening 1NT bid:

♠ A 9 6 4   Respond 2♣. If opener rebids 2♥, raise to 3♥.
♥ Q 8 7 6   This is an invitational bid, showing 8 or 9 points.
♦ Q 7 6   Opener can pass or continue to 4♥. If opener re-
♣ 8 5   bids 2♠, invite by raising to 3♠. If opener rebids
                   2♦, denying a four-card major suit, rebid 2NT, an
                   invitational bid.

♠ 10 6
♥ K J 10 5
♦ J 7 6
♣ Q J 8 7

Respond 2♣. With 8 HCP, responder is not sure whether the partnership belongs in partscore or game. If opener has a minimum, 15 HCP, there isn't enough combined strength for game. If opener has a maximum, 17 HCP, there is enough for game. Start by using the Stayman convention. If opener rebids 2♥, showing a four-card heart suit, responder can invite to game by raising to 3♥. With a maximum, opener rebids 4♥; otherwise, opener passes 3♥. If opener rebids 2♦ or 2♠, responder can bid 2NT, again inviting opener to bid game with a maximum or pass with a minimum. The Stayman convention gives responder the best of both worlds — responder can invite opener to bid a game and look for a Golden Fit in a major suit along the way.

♠ A J 8 7
♥ 9 6
♦ 9 8 7
♣ K 10 5 4

Respond 2♣. If opener rebids 2♠, raise to 3♠. If opener rebids 2♦ or 2♥, bid 2NT. Opener could have four spades after a rebid of 2♥, since opener bids four-card majors up the line. If that is the case, opener can now bid 3♠ with a minimum hand or 4♠ with a maximum hand, drawing the inference that you must be interested in spades if you aren't interested in hearts.

♠ A 7 2
♥ K J 5 3
♦ J 9 8 7
♣ 8 7

Respond 2♣. You have 9 HCP. If opener rebids hearts, the Golden Fit has been found, and this hand can be revalued using dummy points. The hand is now worth 10 total points, and responder can bid game, 4♥.

♠ 10 8
♥ 9 7 5
♦ K Q 7 4 3
♣ K 6 5

Respond 2NT to invite opener to bid game with a maximum. Don't bid 2♣, since you aren't interested in a major suit.

♠ K Q 7 4 2
♥ 7 6
♦ 9 4 2
♣ K 8 3

Start with 2♣. You want to invite game and are interested in a major suit. If partner bids 2♠, you can raise to 3♠. If partner bids 2♦ or 2♥, you can bid 2♠. Opener should interpret this as an invitational hand with five or more spades. Also, if you held an invitational hand with 8 or 9 points and only four spades, you would have bid 2NT when you found that opener did not have four spades. Thus, your bidding shows an invitational hand with five or more spades. Opener can pass or bid 2NT with a minimum hand; opener can jump to 4♠ or 3NT with a maximum hand.

RESPONDING WITH WEAK HANDS

When Responder Has 0 to 7 Points

In general, with 0 to 7 points, responder does not have enough bidding room to use the Stayman convention.

♠ J 8 4 3   Pass. Although responder could be lucky using Stay-
♥ Q 10 6 3   man if opener rebids 2♥ or 2♠, it's best to pass and
♦ 5 3   hope opener can take seven tricks in 1NT. If opener
♣ J 9 3   rebids 2♦ over Stayman, responder is badly placed.
                       Passing would leave the partnership in a poor spot,
but any rebid by responder would show at least invitational strength. If responder rebids 2NT, for example, opener might accept by bidding 3NT. The partnership would be too high.

Here is an exception.

♠ J 8 4 3   Respond 2♣. An exception can be made when re-
♥ Q 10 6 3   sponder is short in clubs. Now responder can pass
♦ J 9 5 3   any rebid by opener. If opener rebids 2♥ or 2♠,
♣ 3   the partnership has found a fit and you may pass. If
                       opener rebids 2♦, pass and hope the partnership is
at least in a playable spot.

HANDLING INTERFERENCE

If your partnership decides to use a convention such as Stayman, you need to have agreements so you know what to do when the opponents interfere in the auction. For example, what do you do if an opponent overcalls 2♦ over your partner's 1NT opening bid and you want to ask if partner has a four-card major? Would 3♣ be Stayman? Without firm agreements, the partnership can run into difficulty in such situations.

Standard Methods when RHO Interferes

The standard agreement is to continue to use your conventional responses to 1NT if an opponent doubles, since no bidding room has been used. If an opponent overcalls, however, the partnership has to abandon most conventional responses because there is no longer enough bidding room. The standard agreements after partner opens 1NT and your right-hand opponent overcalls are the following:

- The bid of a suit at the two level is a natural bid, showing five or more cards in the suit bid, and is non-forcing. Opener is allowed to raise with a maximum, since responder could have passed with a very weak hand.

- The bid of a suit at the three level is natural. It shows five or more cards in the suit and is forcing.

- A bid of the opponent's suit — a cuebid — is forcing and acts as a substitute for the Stayman convention. Opener bids a four-card major or rebids notrump with no major suit.

- 2NT is invitational, and 3NT is to play.

- Double is a penalty double.

You are East after the auction has gone:

WEST	NORTH	EAST	SOUTH
1NT	2♥	?	

♠ K J 10 8 3
♥ J 4
♦ 10 8 7 3
♣ Q 5

Bid 2♠. This is a natural, non-forcing response, showing a five-card or longer suit. Opener will treat this as a mildly invitational bid, since you would have passed with a very weak hand.

♠ K 4 2
♥ 3
♦ 10 8 3
♣ A Q J 8 7 5

Bid 3♣. This is a natural bid, showing a five-card or longer club suit. It's a forcing bid, showing the strength the partnership needs to continue to game. Opener may bid 3NT with some strength in the opponent's suit. Otherwise, the partnership will probably be better off in a contract of 5♣, or even 6♣.

♠ 7 6 5
♥ K J 9 3
♦ A 6 2
♣ 10 9 5

Double. This is a penalty double of the opponent's overcall. Since partner has a balanced hand with 15 to 17 HCP, you can probably get a sufficient penalty to compensate for any contract your side might make.

♠ A J 8 3
♥ 4 3
♦ K Q 10 6
♣ 8 6 3

Bid 3♥. The cuebid of the opponent's suit replaces Stayman. Opener will bid 3♠ with a four-card or longer suit, and you can raise to game. With fewer than four spades, opener will rebid 3NT, which should be the best spot for your side.

♠ K 7 5
♥ J 3
♦ Q 10 9 7 5 2
♣ J 5

Bid 2NT. Using the methods described so far, there's no way to show an invitational-strength hand with a long diamond suit after an opponent's interference bid. A bid of 3♦ would be forcing, committing the partnership to the game level. 2NT is a reasonable compromise.

Standard Methods when LHO Interferes

The situation is different if an opponent interferes following a conventional response. Bids carry the same meaning as they would with no interference. The opponent's bid may present other options. You are West, and the auction starts this way:

WEST	NORTH	EAST	SOUTH
1NT	Pass	2♣	2♥
?			

♠ A Q 8 3
♥ J 5
♦ K 9 6 2
♣ A Q 5

Bid 2♠. South's overcall doesn't prevent you from showing your four-card major suit.

♠ A J 2
♥ Q 6
♦ A 10 6 3
♣ K Q 8 3

Pass. If South had passed, you would have responded 2♦ to show no four-card major suit. After the overcall, you're no longer obligated to bid. Pass and leave the decision to partner.

♠ J 10
♥ K J 10 8
♦ A K 8 2
♣ A 9 5

Double. You were intending to respond 2♥ to partner's Stayman inquiry. It looks as though South has chosen the wrong time to wander into the auction. Your double suggests to partner that you would like to defend for penalty.

SUMMARY

The Stayman Convention

After an opening bid of 1NT, a response of 2♣ may be used as the Stayman convention, asking opener to show a four-card or longer major suit. Opener rebids as follows:

- 2♦ shows no four-card or longer major suit.
- 2♥ shows a four-card or longer heart suit. Opener may have four spades.
- 2♠ shows a four-card or longer spade suit and denies four hearts.

Responder's Rebids

With an Invitational Hand and 8 or 9 Points

- 2NT if opener responds in the "wrong" major.
- 2NT if opener denies a four-card major by rebidding 2♦.
- 2♥ or 2♠ with a five-card or longer suit, when opener rebids 2♦.
- 3♥ or 3♠, a raise of opener's major to the three level. This bid is invitational. Opener will pass with a minimum and bid game with a maximum.

With a Game-Forcing Hand and 10 or More Points

- Jump to 3♥ or 3♠, forcing, to show a five-card suit and to ask opener to choose between 3NT and four of the major suit.
- 3NT when opener denies a four-card major.
- A jump to game is a sign-off bid.†

† Except when responder bids 3NT after opener, holding four hearts and four spades, rebids 2♥. Opener then rebids 4♠.

Handling Interference over 1NT

- If the opening notrump bid is doubled, responder's bids retain their conventional meaning.

- If there is an overcall directly over the notrump bid, the standard approach is to treat all of responder's bids, except a cuebid of the opponent's suit, as natural bids.

- A cuebid of the opponent's suit replaces Stayman and asks opener for a four-card major suit.

Exercise One — Using the Stayman Convention

Your partner opens the bidding 1NT. What do you respond with each of the following hands?

1) ♠ K Q 5 4
　 ♥ A 9 8
　 ♦ 3 2
　 ♣ J 9 8 4

2) ♠ K 5 3 2
　 ♥ 9 4 3
　 ♦ 9 7 6 5
　 ♣ Q 2

3) ♠ 4
　 ♥ A J 9 4 3
　 ♦ K 3 2
　 ♣ 10 8 4 3

_____

_____

_____

4) ♠ J 9 8 4
　 ♥ J 9 8 4
　 ♦ A K
　 ♣ 8 6 2

5) ♠ 9 5 4
　 ♥ J 9
　 ♦ A 5 3
　 ♣ K Q 9 7 6

6) ♠ A K 8 7 6
　 ♥ 6 4
　 ♦ A 5 4
　 ♣ 9 6 5

_____

_____

_____

Exercise Two — Responding to the Stayman Convention

You open the bidding 1NT and partner responds 2♣, the Stayman convention. What do you rebid with the following hands?

1) ♠ A K 4 3
　 ♥ 9 8 5 3
　 ♦ A Q
　 ♣ K J 10

2) ♠ K Q 9
　 ♥ A J 4
　 ♦ J 5 4 3
　 ♣ A Q 8

3) ♠ 8 4 3 2
　 ♥ A K Q
　 ♦ K 10 9
　 ♣ K Q 8

_____

_____

_____

Exercise One *Answers* – Using the Stayman Convention

1) 2♣   — looking for a Golden Fit in spades.

2) Pass — not enough points to use Stayman.

3) 2♣   — looking for a Golden Fit in hearts.

4) 2♣   — looking for a Golden Fit in either major.

5) 3NT — no interest in game in a major suit.

6) 3♠   — asking partner to choose between 4♠ and 3NT.

Exercise Two *Answers* — Responding to the Stayman Convention

1) 2♥   — with both majors, bid hearts first.

2) 2♦   — no four-card major.

3) 2♠   — showing a four-card spade suit.

Exercise Three — Responder's Rebid after Using Stayman

Your partner opens 1NT and you respond 2♣, the Stayman convention. Opener rebids 2♥. What do you rebid with each of the following hands?

1) ♠ K 9 3 2
   ♥ A Q 4 3
   ♦ Q 8 4
   ♣ 8 6

2) ♠ A K 9 5
   ♥ 9 5
   ♦ J 9 5 4
   ♣ A 9 4

3) ♠ K J 4 3
   ♥ 8 5 4
   ♦ A 8 4 3
   ♣ 6 3

4) ♠ Q 9
   ♥ K J 7 3
   ♦ Q 8 4 3
   ♣ 10 9 8

5) ♠ A J 9 5 4
   ♥ 10 7 6
   ♦ K 9 3
   ♣ 8 4

6) ♠ K Q 7 4 2
   ♥ Q 9 8 7
   ♦ A 3
   ♣ 8 5

Exercise Four — More Rebids by Responder

After a 1NT opening bid by partner and a Stayman inquiry by you, opener rebids 2♦. What do you rebid?

1) ♠ 8 3 2
   ♥ A Q 8 5
   ♦ K 10 8 3
   ♣ 9 4

2) ♠ K Q 10 8 4
   ♥ 6 5 4
   ♦ 9 8
   ♣ K 5 4

3) ♠ A K 4 3
   ♥ Q J 9 2
   ♦ J 8
   ♣ 5 4 3

Exercise Five — Finishing the Bidding Conversation

You open 1NT, responder bids the Stayman convention and you reply 2♦. Responder now rebids 2♥. What do you do now?

1) ♠ A K 4
   ♥ K 10 8
   ♦ A Q 10
   ♣ J 10 9 8

2) ♠ K 10 5
   ♥ K J
   ♦ A Q J 6
   ♣ J 10 9 8

3) ♠ A Q J
   ♥ 10 6
   ♦ K Q J 10
   ♣ A 10 8 5

Exercise Three *Answers* — Responder's Rebid after Using Stayman

1) 4♥ — enough points to bid game.

2) 3NT — opener has the "wrong" major, but there are enough points for game.

3) 2NT — invite opener to bid game with a maximum hand, since opener has the "wrong" major.

4) 3♥ — invitational raise with 9 total points.

5) 2♠ — showing a five-card suit and an invitational hand.

6) 4♥ — enough points to bid game.

Exercise Four *Answers* — More Rebids by Responder

1) 2NT — invitational.

2) 2♠ — showing a five-card suit and an invitational hand.

3) 3NT — enough points for game and no Golden Fit.

Exercise Five *Answers* — Finishing the Bidding Conversation

1) 4♥ — Responder's bid is invitational, asking you to bid game with three-card support and a maximum hand.

2) 2NT — shows a minimum hand and no heart support.

3) 3NT — shows a maximum hand and no heart support.

Exercise Six — Handling Interference

Partner opens 1NT, and the opponent on your right overcalls 2♦. What do you bid with each of the following hands?

1) ♠ 10 2
   ♥ J 6 3
   ♦ 6 5 3
   ♣ Q 9 8 4 3

   ———————

2) ♠ K Q 8 7 5
   ♥ 8 4
   ♦ Q 9 3 2
   ♣ 7 5

   ———————

3) ♠ 3
   ♥ A Q J 6 5
   ♦ K 10 8 5
   ♣ J 8 2

   ———————

4) ♠ Q 10 8 6 5 2
   ♥ A 10 3
   ♦ 7 6
   ♣ K 2

   ———————

5) ♠ Q J 9 6
   ♥ A 10 8 5
   ♦ 6 3
   ♣ A 7 4

   ———————

6) ♠ 8 7 3
   ♥ A 4
   ♦ K J 9 2
   ♣ 10 9 7 6

   ———————

Exercise Six *Answers* — Handling Interference

1) Pass — Nothing to say.

2) 2♠ — This shows a mildly invitational hand with a five-card suit; with less, you would pass.

3) 3♥ — A jump in a new suit is forcing.

4) 4♠ — With 9 HCPs plus 2 for the six-card suit, there's enough for game.

5) 3♦ — The cuebid takes the place of the Stayman convention.

6) Double — Looks like your opponent has walked into trouble.

STAYMAN HANDS

Exercise Seven — Showing an Invitational Five-Card Major by
Responder

(#9, Deal 1 — Dealer, North)

The Bidding

North passes. With a balanced hand and 16 HCP, what is East's opening bid?

South passes, and West considers what to do. Does the partnership belong in game or in partscore? Does West know whether there is a Golden Fit in the heart suit? How can West find out?

North passes. What is East's reply to Stayman?

Dealer:	♠ Q J 10 5
North	♥ 4 3 2
	♦ 4
	♣ J 8 4 3 2

```
          ♠ A 4            ♠ K 9 8
          ♥ Q J 10 9 6     ♥ A K 8
          ♦ J 7 6 2        ♦ A Q 10 9 3
          ♣ 6 5            ♣ 9 7
                  ♠ 7 6 3 2
                  ♥ 7 5
                  ♦ K 8 5
                  ♣ A K Q 10
```

South passes. What should West rebid now? North passes. What should East bid now?

What will the final contract be? Who is the declarer?

The Play

Which player makes the opening lead?

What will the opening lead be?

How many losers can declarer afford? How many losers does declarer have? Are there any potential problems based upon which lead North chooses?

Exercise Seven *Answers* — Showing an Invitational Five-Card Major by Responder

The Bidding

- East opens 1NT.
- West is not sure.
- Not yet.
- Bid 2♣, Stayman, and then bid hearts. This would show an invitational hand with a five-card heart suit.
- 2♦.
- 2♥.
- East recognizes an invitational bid by West with a hand containing a five-card heart suit. East should bid 4♥ with a maximum notrump.
- 4♥.
- West.

The Play

- North.
- North has a great lead in the ♠Q, however, North may elect to lead the singleton diamond.
- Three.
- Two clubs plus the ♦K if the finesse loses.
- If North chooses the singleton diamond lead, West must not take the finesse or West will lose a diamond, two diamond ruffs and two clubs for down two. If West rises with the ♦A, West can safely pull trumps and lose the ♦K later, along with two clubs to make the contract.

Exercise Eight — Getting to the Right Contract
(#9, Deal 2 — Dealer, East)

The Bidding

East is the dealer and passes. With a balanced 16 HCP hand, what is South's opening bid?

West passes. North has 10 HCP. Does the partnership belong in game or partscore? Does North know if there is a Golden Fit in a major suit? What should North do to find out?

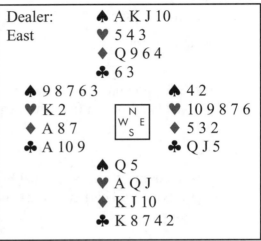

```
Dealer:        ♠ A K J 10
East           ♥ 5 4 3
               ♦ Q 9 6 4
               ♣ 6 3
    ♠ 9 8 7 6 3           ♠ 4 2
    ♥ K 2          N      ♥ 10 9 8 7 6
    ♦ A 8 7      W   E    ♦ 5 3 2
    ♣ A 10 9       S      ♣ Q J 5
               ♠ Q 5
               ♥ A Q J
               ♦ K J 10
               ♣ K 8 7 4 2
```

East passes. What should South's rebid be? What will North do?

What will the final contract be? Who will be the declarer?

The Play

Which player makes the opening lead? What will the opening lead be? Why would West make this lead?

How many sure tricks does South have? What should declarer do to make the extra tricks?

Exercise Eight *Answers* — Getting to the Right Contract

The Bidding

- 1NT.
- Game.
- No.
- Bid 2♣, Stayman.
- 2♦, since South does not have a four-card major.
- Bid 3NT.
- The final contract is 3NT.
- South is declarer.

The Play

- West.
- ♠9.
- Not only is the ♠9 the top of a sequence, but West has enough entries to hope to set up a spade trick.
- Five tricks: four spade tricks and one heart trick.
- Timing is important on this deal. South should win the first spade trick in hand and immediately play diamonds to establish three tricks in that suit. Declarer should take the heart finesse from the dummy. If declarer wins the spade trick in the dummy and takes the heart finesse before knocking out the ♦A, West can prevent South (declarer) from reaching the dummy to cash a good diamond. In order to do this, West would win the heart finesse, play another spade and not play the ♦A until the third round.

Exercise Nine — With an Invitational Hand

(#9, Deal 3 — Dealer, South)

The Bidding

South is the dealer. What should South do? What should West do?

What about North? East passes. What should South do? Does South know if the partnership belongs in game or partscore?

What will North rebid? The partnership has found a Golden Fit in spades. Does this change South's hand?

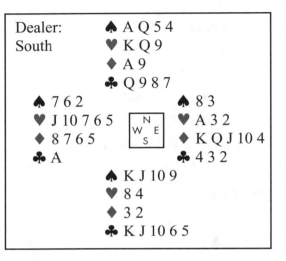

```
Dealer:        ♠ A Q 5 4
South          ♥ K Q 9
               ♦ A 9
               ♣ Q 9 8 7
   ♠ 7 6 2              ♠ 8 3
   ♥ J 10 7 6 5         ♥ A 3 2
   ♦ 8 7 6 5      N     ♦ K Q J 10 4
   ♣ A         W   E    ♣ 4 3 2
                  S
               ♠ K J 10 9
               ♥ 8 4
               ♦ 3 2
               ♣ K J 10 6 5
```

What is the value of South's hand? What should South bid?

What is the final contract? What should North do? Who is the declarer?

The Play

Who is on lead? What should East lead?

How many losers can North afford? How many losers does North have? How can North get rid of a loser? Can North afford to pull trumps? What should North do after pulling trumps? Will this hand make 3NT?

Exercise Nine *Answers* — With an Invitational Hand

The Bidding

- Pass.
- Pass.
- Bid 1NT.
- With 8 HCP plus 1 point for the length in clubs, South should bid 2♣, Stayman, to find out if North has a four-card spade suit.
- Not yet. South has an invitational hand before North's answer to the Stayman inquiry.
- 2♠.
- Yes, South will be the dummy in a spade contract, so South can count dummy points.
- 8 HCP plus 2 dummy points — 1 for each doubleton — giving a total of 10 points.
- 4♠.
- 4♠.
- Pass.
- North.

The Play

- East.
- ♦K, top of a sequence.
- Three.
- Four losers — two hearts, one diamond and one club.
- Ruff a heart in the dummy or establish the club suit on which to pitch a heart loser.
- Yes.
- Establish the club suit.
- No, the defenders can win four diamonds, one club and one heart for down two.

Exercise Ten — Uncovering a Golden Fit

(#9, Deal 4 — Dealer, West)

The Bidding

West is the dealer, but who will open the bidding? What would the opening bid be? South passes. Does West know if the partnership belongs in game or partscore? How can West find out if East has four spades?

With both four-card majors, what would East reply? What would West rebid?

Dealer:	♠ 4 3
West	♥ 7 5
	♦ K 9 8 7 6
	♣ 9 8 5 3

♠ K J 10 8		♠ A Q 9 7
♥ A 6	N W E S	♥ K 8 4 3
♦ 5 3 2		♦ A 10
♣ Q 7 4 2		♣ K J 6

	♠ 6 5 2
	♥ Q J 10 9 2
	♦ Q J 4
	♣ A 10

What should East do?

What should West do? What is the final contract? Who is the declarer?

The Play

Which player makes the opening lead? What will the opening lead be?

How many losers can declarer afford? How many does declarer have? How should declarer get rid of a loser?

If you did not use Stayman, you would end up in 3NT. Would a contract of 3NT be successful?

Exercise Ten *Answers* — Uncovering a Golden Fit

The Bidding

- East.
- 1NT.
- Game.
- Bid 2♣, Stayman.
- 2♥.
- 3NT.
- Since West showed enough points for game, but bid game via the Stayman convention, West is promising a four-card major. Since West doesn't have four hearts, West must have four spades. East should confidently bid 4♠ knowing this is the proper strain for the final contract.
- Pass.
- 4♠.
- East.

The Play

- South.
- ♥Q, top of the sequence, is the typical lead. Knowing that East has four hearts, however, South may elect to lead a spade.
- Three.
- Four — two hearts, one diamond and one club.
- East can ruff two heart losers in the dummy even if South leads a trump.
- In a contract of 3NT, against the ♥Q lead, the contract will probably be successful with four spades, two hearts, one diamond and two clubs. However, against the ♦Q lead, should South find it, 3NT will not make.

Exercise Eleven — Discovering the Right Final Contract

(#9, Deal 5 – Dealer, North)

The Bidding

North is the dealer. With a balanced hand, what is North's opening bid?

East passes, and South considers what the final contract should be. Holding 11HCP, there is enough for game – but which game? Does South start with Stayman?

How should North respond to South's bid? Why? How will the bidding go from

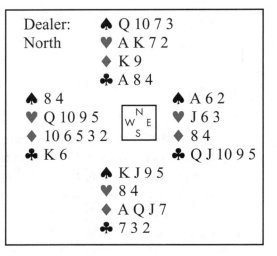

Dealer: ♠ Q 10 7 3
North ♥ A K 7 2
♦ K 9
♣ A 8 4

♠ 8 4   ♠ A 6 2
♥ Q 10 9 5   ♥ J 6 3
♦ 10 6 5 3 2   ♦ 8 4
♣ K 6   ♣ Q J 10 9 5

♠ K J 9 5
♥ 8 4
♦ A Q J 7
♣ 7 3 2

there? What will be the final contract? Which player is declarer?

The Play

Which player makes the opening lead?

What will the opening lead be?

How many losers does declarer have, and how many can declarer afford?

How will declarer play the hand?

Is there a chance for declarer to make an extra trick?

How might the defense accidentally help declarer make an extra trick?

Exercise Eleven *Answers* – Discovering the Right Final Contract

The Bidding

- North opens 1NT.
- South should use Stayman and bid 2♣ to look for a Golden Fit in spades.
- North has both major suits but will bid hearts first (2♥).
- South has enough points for game but no interest in hearts. South will respond 3NT. North, holding both majors, will correct to 4♠.
- North is the declarer.

The Play

- East is on lead.
- With the knowledge that South's 2♣ response was a conventional bid, East elects to lead the ♣Q, top of a sequence.
- North can afford three losers and can see one loser in spades, two in hearts and two in clubs. The heart losers can be ruffed in dummy or discarded on South's extra diamond winners after drawing trumps.
- North can afford to win the ♣A and lead spades, planning to drive out the ♠A and then draw the rest of the trumps. Following this line of play, North should lose at most one spade trick and two club tricks.
- North may want to try for an overtrick, after the opening club lead, by discarding a club loser on one of dummy's extra diamond winners before letting the defenders in with the ♠A. On the actual deal, East ruffs the third round of diamonds as North discards a club. North will still make the contract, since there will be only one club loser left to go with the spade loser.
- When East leads the ♣Q, West must play the ♣K. The lead of the ♣Q shows a sequence, and West can make this play with full confidence. If West doesn't play the ♣K, when East gets in the lead with the ♠A and continues playing clubs, the suit will be blocked. West will win the ♣K and won't be able to continue the suit. Declarer will make an extra trick.

Exercise Twelve – Using Stayman with Interference

(#9, Deal 6 – Dealer, East)

The Bidding

East is the dealer. After two passes to West, what should West open with a balanced hand and 16 HCP?

North has an interesting hand — a strong spade suit and 12 HCP. Is that enough to come into the bidding?

East has 10 HCP and knows that the partnership has enough points for game. Assuming North made an overcall, what should East bid? Can East use Stayman to look for a Golden Fit in hearts following an overcall?

How will the auction proceed? What will be the final contract? Who will be the declarer?

```
Dealer:        ♠ K Q J 7 5 2
East           ♥ 7 3
               ♦ A Q 6
               ♣ 9 4
     ♠ A 8 4            ♠ 6 3
     ♥ A Q 8 5    N     ♥ K 10 6 4
     ♦ K 8 2   W   E    ♦ J 7 5 3
     ♣ K 10 5     S     ♣ A Q 8
               ♠ 10 9
               ♥ J 9 2
               ♦ 10 9 4
               ♣ J 7 6 3 2
```

The Play

Which player makes the opening lead?

What will the opening lead be?

How many losers can declarer afford? How many losers does declarer have?

What is the main challenge of the hand? Can the defenders defeat the contract?

Exercise Twelve *Answers* – Using Stayman with Interference

The Bidding

- West has an excellent 1NT opening bid.
- North should enter the auction. Holding a good six-card suit, North should overcall 2♠. It is unlikely the opponents will double the overcall for penalty. Even if 2♠ is doubled and defeated, the penalty is likely to be less than the value of East–West's potential contract.
- With 10 HCP, East has the strength to take the partnership to the game level and wants to investigate whether there is an eight-card heart fit. After the overcall, 2♣ is no longer available as the Stayman convention. In this situation, a cuebid of the opponent's suit replaces Stayman. It is forcing and commits the partnership to game. East bids 3♠.
- Opener has the other major and shows it by bidding 4♥, the final contract.
- West is the declarer.

The Play

- North is the opening leader.
- North selects the ♠K, top of a sequence.
- Declarer can afford three losers and has some work to do. Declarer needs the defender's hearts to break 3–2 to avoid a trump loser. In addition, there are two spade losers and three possible diamond losers.
- Declarer's challenge is to hold the diamond losers to two. One spade loser can be ruffed in dummy. If the hearts break, one spade is ruffed in dummy and declarer loses only two diamonds. The contract will make.
- The defenders can't defeat 4♥ if declarer plays correctly. Declarer should win the ♠A and draw trumps. Next declarer should tackle the diamond suit by leading toward one of the honors. Declarer might start by leading a low diamond from dummy toward the ♦K, hoping South holds the ♦A. When the ♦K loses to North's ♦A, declarer still has a chance. Later, declarer can lead a low diamond toward dummy's ♦J, hoping that North holds the ♦Q. The second finesse works.

Exercise Thirteen – Looking for a Better Contract

(#9, Deal 7 – Dealer, South)

The Bidding

South is the dealer. Holding 15 HCP and a balanced hand, what should South bid?

West passes, and North considers what the final contract should be. With only 5 high-card points, North does not have the usual strength required for the Stayman convention. What should North bid?

What does the opening bidder respond?

```
Dealer:        ♠ J 9 4 3
South          ♥ K 9 6 2
               ♦ J 8 5 3 2
               ♣ —
   ♠ K 8              ♠ Q 10 6 2
   ♥ 8 5 4      N     ♥ A 7 3
   ♦ A 10 9   W   E   ♦ 7 4
   ♣ Q J 9 6 2  S     ♣ A 10 7 5
               ♠ A 7 5
               ♥ Q J 10
               ♦ K Q 6
               ♣ K 8 4 3
```

What is the final contract? Who is the declarer?

The Play

Which player makes the opening lead? What will the opening lead be?

How many losers can declarer afford? How many losers does declarer have?

Are there any potential problems for declarer?

What's the best line of play for declarer?

Will declarer make the contract?

Exercise Thirteen *Answers* – Looking for a Better Contract

The Bidding

- South has an ideal 1NT opening bid with 15 HCP.
- North does not have an invitational hand of 8 or 9 points, the usual requirement for using Stayman — but is void in clubs. North should bid 2♣, Stayman, because it is a relatively safe call.
- South doesn't have a four-card major and would rebid 2♦.
- North would pass any response by South and expect that contract to play better than 1NT.
- The final contract is 2♦, and South is the declarer.

The Play

- West is on lead and would probably lead the ♣Q, top of a broken sequence.
- Declarer (South) can afford five losers in order to make the 2♦ contract. Since the dummy (North) has the most trumps, declarer should count losers from the viewpoint of the dummy. North's hand has three spade losers, one heart loser and one diamond loser (if the diamonds divide 3–2).
- Declarer should be careful not to run out of trumps before developing enough tricks to make the contract. If declarer ruffs the first club lead in dummy and then starts to draw trumps, West may win the A♦ and lead another club. If declarer ruffs this trick, declarer can't afford to draw the remaining trumps and then give up a heart trick.
- On the lead of the ♣Q, declarer should discard a spade loser from dummy rather than ruff the trick. East will win the ♣A, but now declarer is in command. South's ♣K is a winner and can be used to discard another spade loser from dummy. Remember, the defenders can't force declarer to use dummy's trumps right away.
- Assuming that declarer discards a spade from dummy on the opening lead, South, when regaining the lead, can drive out the ♦A, draw trumps and then drive out the ♥A. South should finish with an overtrick, losing one spade — having discarded two spade losers on the clubs — one heart, one diamond and one club.

Exercise Fourteen — More Interference

(#9, Deal 8 – Dealer, West)

The Bidding

West is the dealer and must pass. North has a nice hand, but it is not quite worth an opening bid. North also must pass. With 16 HCP and a balanced hand, what will East do?

How will West respond?

What will North do?

How will East handle North's interference?

What will West rebid?

What will be the final contract?

Who will be the declarer?

```
Dealer:      ♠ 6 5 2
West         ♥ K Q J 10 6
             ♦ A 8 4 3
             ♣ 8
   ♠ J 10 7 4          ♠ A K 9 8
   ♥ 5          N      ♥ 3 2
   ♦ 7 6 5 2  W   E    ♦ K Q J 10
   ♣ A Q J 2    S      ♣ K 10 9
             ♠ Q 3
             ♥ A 9 8 7 4
             ♦ 9
             ♣ 7 6 5 4 3
```

The Play

Who will make the opening lead?

What will the lead be?

How many tricks can East afford to lose?

Will East make the contract?

Can South make a different lead that might lead to declarer's going down in this contract?

Exercise Fourteen *Answers* — More Interference

The Bidding

- East will open the bidding with 1NT.
- West will bid 2♣, Stayman.
- North will enter the bidding with 2♥.
- East will rebid 2♠, showing the four-card suit.
- West's hand now revalues to 11 total points, and West will rebid 4♠.
- The final contract is 4♠.
- East will be the declarer.

The Play

- South will make the opening lead.
- The lead will probably be the ♥A.
- East can afford to lose three tricks.
- East should not have a problem against the ♥A lead. East should lose the ♥A, the ♦A and probably a spade when East takes the finesse.
- South can make a number of interesting leads in addition to the ♥A. South can lead the singleton diamond, but that will not set the contract (unless South then underleads the ♥A) — it will just ensure that South will get a trump trick. The lead that might get declarer in trouble is the ♣7. If declarer wins this trick and then takes the spade finesse, South will win the ♠Q and then return a club for North to ruff. North can cash the ♦A and lead another diamond, which South will ruff. South then leads another club, which North can ruff. Since North–South are also due a heart trick, that totals six tricks for the defense! East can stymie this attack by winning the club lead, cashing the ♠A and ♠K and not taking the finesse.

APPENDIX

Scoring

Strong Opening Bids

Slam Bidding

Preemptive Opening Bids

Balancing

Glossary of Terms

SCORING

Bridge can be scored in several different ways. All methods follow the same basic scheme. Points and bonuses are awarded for bidding and making contracts and for defeating contracts, but there are minor differences. We will discuss the two most common forms of scoring — duplicate-bridge style and rubber-bridge style.

Duplicate Scoring

In duplicate scoring, each deal is scored independently. The score is a combination of the trick score for bidding and making the contract and appropriate bonuses. The size of the bonus is affected by vulnerability. On each deal, each side has been arbitrarily designated as either nonvulnerable or vulnerable. You know at the start of each deal whether or not your side is vulnerable.

Trick Score

Notrump	40 points for the first trick
	30 points per additional tricks
Hearts or spades	30 points per trick
Clubs or diamonds	20 points per trick
Doubled contract	Twice the undoubled trick score
Redoubled contract	Four times the undoubled trick score

Bonus Points	**Nonvulnerable**	**Vulnerable**
Partscore	50 points	50 points
Game	300 points	500 points
Small Slam	500 points	750 points
Grand Slam	1000 points	1500 points
Making a doubled contract	50 points	50 points
Making a redoubled contract	100 points	100 points

Overtricks	**Nonvulnerable**	**Vulnerable**
Undoubled	Trick score	Trick score
Doubled	100 per overtrick	200 per overtrick
Redoubled	200 per overtrick	400 per overtrick

Penalties (Undertricks)	**Nonvulnerable**	**Vulnerable**
Undoubled	50 per undertrick	100 per undertrick
Doubled	100 for first undertrick	200 for first undertrick
	200 per next two undertricks	300 per additional undertricks
	300 per additional undertricks	
Redoubled	200 for first undertrick	400 for first undertrick
	400 per next two undertricks	600 per additional undertricks
	600 per additional undertricks	

All bonuses are added to the trick score. For example, if you bid and make a slam, you also get the game bonus. Here are some examples:

2♥ contract, nonvulnerable, declarer takes nine tricks:

Trick score (30 x 2)	60
Partscore bonus	50
Overtrick bonus	30
Total score	140

4♠ contract, vulnerable, declarer takes 10 tricks:

Trick score (30 x 4)	120
Game bonus	_500_
Total score	620

6♦ contract, nonvulnerable, declarer takes 12 tricks:

Trick score (20 x 6)	120
Game bonus	300
Slam bonus	_500_
Total score	920

2NT contract, doubled, vulnerable, declarer takes nine tricks:

Trick score ([40+30] x 2)	140
Game bonus	500
Doubled bonus	50
Doubled overtrick bonus	_200_
Total score	890

Rubber-Bridge Scoring

In rubber bridge, points are recorded on a scoresheet divided into four parts by a vertical line and a horizontal line. The vertical line divides the sheet into a column for your points (WE) and the opponents' points (THEY). The horizontal line, called the line, is there so that scores for contracts bid and made can be put below the line and scores for bonuses, overtricks and penalties can be put above the line.

A rubber is made up of a series of deals which progress until one side bids and makes two games. No bonus is awarded when a partscore or game contract is made. Instead, a bonus is awarded to the side that wins the rubber. A partnership wins a game by scoring 100 points or more from the trick scores recorded below the line. These trick scores can be earned in a single deal or by accumulating them from several partscore contracts. When one side wins a game, a horizontal line is drawn under the trick scores of both sides, and a new game is started. Scores from previous partscores are not counted toward the next game.

When the rubber starts, both sides are nonvulnerable. When a side wins a game, that side becomes vulnerable for the rest of the rubber. The vulnerability affects the scores for bonuses, doubled and redoubled overtricks and penalties as in tournament (duplicate) scoring.

Bonuses for making overtricks, undertricks, slams and doubled contracts are the same as for tournament scoring. The bonus for winning the rubber replaces the bonus for making game or partscore in duplicate scoring. The bonus is 700 if the rubber is won by a margin of two games to none and 500 if the rubber is won by a margin of two games to one.

If only one side has a partscore in an unfinished rubber, that side receives a bonus of 100 points. If only one side has a game in an unfinished rubber, that side receives a bonus of 300 points.

A special bonus is awarded in rubber-bridge scoring if one player holds four of the top five cards in the trump suit (100 points for honors), all five of the top trump cards (150 points for honors) or the four aces in notrump (150 points for honors). To score honor points, all of the required honors must be contained in one hand.

At the end of the rubber, the scores are totaled for both sides. The winner is the side with the higher total. If you are playing a series of rubbers, the difference in scores at the end of each rubber is rounded to the nearest 100 points and is carried forward for each partnership or player to the next rubber.

Here is a sample score sheet:

	WE	THEY	
		150	(f)
(g)	500	30	(f)
(g)	750	500	(d)
(a)	50	60	(c)
			THE LINE
(b)	120		
(e)	90	60	(c)
		40	(f)
(g)	180		
(h)	1690	840	(h)
	–840		
	850		

(a)   The opponents bid 3NT and take only eight tricks (down one).

(b)   Your side bids 4♥ and takes 10 tricks (game).

(c)   The opponents bid 2♠ and take 10 tricks (two overtricks).

(d)   Your side bids 2♦. The opponents double, and you take six tricks (down two vulnerable tricks).

(e)   Your side bids 3♠ and takes nine tricks.

(f)   The opponents bid 1NT and take eight tricks (one overtrick). Declarer holds all four aces (150 points for honors). Their trick score of 40 below the line is added to their previous partscore (c) to make a game.

(g)   Your side bids 6♥ and takes 12 tricks (small slam). You get a slam bonus and also win your second game, winning the rubber.

(h)   Your side scored 1690 points, and the opponents scored 840. You win the rubber by 850. In carrying the score forward, 850 is rounded to plus 900 for you and your partner (minus 900 for your opponents).

STRONG OPENING BIDS

You have learned what to do with most hands as the opening bidder when you have between 13 to 21 total points. Let's discuss what happens when you are lucky enough to be dealt more than 21 total points.

First, you should recognize that you should not open the bidding at the one level. This would mislead your partner into thinking you had a weaker hand. Consequently, you could miss game or slam since the partnership would not be able to place the contract at the correct level. We use two different opening bids to describe very strong hands:

1. A 3NT opening bid promises between 25–27 HCP and a balanced hand.

2. A 2♣ opening bid is used for all other hands with 22 or more total points.

Balanced Hands

The first of these bids is very logical. We know that 25 total points are usually sufficient to make 3NT (or 4♠ or 4♥). Therefore, an opening 3NT bid states that you have enough points on your own to make 3NT, even if partner does not have any points at all.

Now we know that:

1. A 1NT opening bid promises between 15–17 HCP and a balanced hand.

2. A 3NT opening bid promises between 25–27 HCP and a balanced hand.

What about a 2NT opening bid?

A 2NT opening bid promises 20 or 21 HCP and a balanced hand.

It seems logical that the 2NT opening bid is about halfway between 1NT and 3NT. Notice that the range of a 2NT opening is only 2 HCP while the 1NT and 3NT openings both have 3 HCP ranges.

If your partner opens 2NT, you are the captain. You decide the level and the strain. You must determine if the partnership has 25 or more total points in order to decide to bid game. Don't forget you can use

Stayman (3♣ in this case) as well. You may even have enough points to bid slam.

If your partner opens 3NT, you are already in game. You need to decide on the proper strain and to determine if there is a possibility of slam.

What do we do with 22, 23 or other balanced point-count hands? This is a good opportunity to look at our entire notrump bidding structure when the notrump hand opens the bidding:

1. With a balanced 13–15 HCP, open one of a suit and make a non-jump rebid in notrump.

2. With a balanced 15–17 HCP, open 1NT.

3. With a balanced 18–19 HCP, open one of a suit and make a jump rebid in notrump.

4. With a balanced 20–21 HCP, open 2NT.

5. With a balanced 22–24 HCP, open 2♣ and make a non-jump rebid in notrump (2NT).

6. With a balanced 25–27 HCP, open 3NT.

7. With a balanced 28–30 HCP, open 2♣ and make a jump rebid in notrump (3NT).

8. With a balanced 31–32 HCP, open 2♣ and make a double jump rebid in notrump (4NT).

9. In the unlikely event you have 33 or more HCP, open 2♣, but do not let the bidding stop below slam. With 33 HCP, you have slam in your own hand without any help from partner.

Unbalanced Hands

The second bid to describe a strong opening hand may sound a little strange. All strong hands that don't qualify for notrump are opened with 2♣.

Look at this example.

♠ A K Q J 10 5 4   This hand contains 24 total points (21 HCP plus
♥ A K   3 long-suit points for the seven-card spade suit).
♦ A 5 4   We open this hand 2♣, saying nothing about our
♣ 7   wonderful spades for the moment.

The one thing that we must be assured of is that partner will not pass our 2♣ bid. This bid is an example of an artificial forcing bid. Simply stated, it means the bid says nothing about the suit named, clubs in this instance, and partner is forced to bid — no matter how weak partner's hand is, partner cannot pass.

When responding to a 2♣ opening bid with fewer than 8 total points, always respond 2♦. This bid is another example of an artificial bid — it's what responder bids when there is no other suitable call. All other responses to a 2♣ opening bid are natural bids promising at least 8 total points, and they force the bidding to at least a game contract.

Again, the basic consideration is the proper level and strain for the final contract — whether partscore, game or slam.

A thorough, in-depth discussion of strong opening bids and responses is covered in the *Play of the Hand in the 21st Century* text.

SUMMARY OF STRONG OPENING BIDS

Balanced Hands

20–21 HCP balanced hands, open 2 NT.

25–27 HCP balanced hands, open 3 NT.

Unbalanced Hands

22 or more total points, unbalanced hands, open 2♣.

SLAM BIDDING

The discussion in the text covering "What level?" concentrates on the choice between partscore and game, since this is the major decision the captain must make. A large bonus, however, is awarded in the scoring for bidding and making a slam contract. With considerable extra strength, the partnership should consider bidding a slam.

What Level?

Decisions as to whether a partnership has enough combined strength to bid a slam can be based on the points in the combined hands. With 33 or more combined points, the partnership generally has enough strength for a small slam. With 37 or more points, the partnership should have enough strength for a grand slam.

What Strain?

At the game level, the partnership usually plays in 3NT, 4♥ or 4♠. At the slam level, the number of tricks required is the same for every strain — 12 for a small slam and 13 for a grand slam. Slam can be played in any Golden Fit or notrump. Note, however, that a contract played in a Golden Fit often produces one more trick than one played in notrump.

Bidding a Slam

There are conventional calls (*e.g.,* Blackwood, Gerber, cuebids) that are sometimes useful when you are thinking of bidding a slam. They are, however, beyond the scope of this text. To keep things simple, jump to a small slam in a Golden Fit or notrump if you know the partnership has 33 or more points. Jump to a grand slam if you know the partnership has 37 or more points. For example, suppose your partner opens the bidding with 1NT.

♠ A Q 7   With 18 HCP, you know there is enough strength for
♥ K Q 5   slam, since opener has at least 15 HCP. When there
♦ K 9 3 2   is no known Golden Fit, jump directly to 6NT.
♣ K J 5

♠ A 3 2   With 16 HCP plus 2 points for the six-card diamond
♥ 4   suit, there is enough for a slam contract. Opener must
♦ A K J 7 5 2   have at least two diamonds. Jump to 6 ♦.
♣ A 7 4

If you know there is enough combined strength for slam but are
not sure of the strain, make a forcing bid to get a further description of
partner's hand, and then make your decision.

Inviting Slam

Sometimes you know the strain in which you want to play but are not
certain whether there is enough combined strength for slam. In this case,
you can invite partner to bid a slam by bidding one level beyond game.
Partner can bid again with additional values; partner can pass with a minimum hand. For example, suppose your partner opens the bidding 1NT.

♠ K J 10   Partner has shown 15 to 17 HCP. With your 17 HCP,
♥ J 9 8   you know there are at least 32 combined points in
♦ A K 3   the hand. There could be 33 or 34 points. Invite
♣ K Q 6 2   slam by bidding one level beyond game, 4NT. With
                           a minimum hand (15 HCP), partner will pass. With
a maximum hand (16 or 17 HCP), partner will accept the invitation and
bid 6NT.

♠ A   You have 16 points — 14 HCP plus 2 points for the
♥ K Q J 8 6 3   six-card heart suit. You know there is a Golden Fit
♦ A 9 5   in hearts. Invite slam by jumping one level beyond
♣ 10 8 6   game, 5 ♥.

There are more sophisticated methods for bidding and inviting slams
but they are beyond the scope of this text.

Summary of Slam Bidding

When considering a slam, use the following guidelines:

- 33 or more points: Bid a small slam in a Golden Fit or in notrump.

- 37 or more points: Bid a grand slam in a Golden Fit or in notrump.

When you are not sure there is enough combined strength for slam, you can invite slam by bidding one level beyond game.

PREEMPTIVE OPENING BIDS

Opening suit bids (other than the strong 2♣ opening) are used at the two level or higher to show hands that are too weak to open the bidding at the one level (*i.e.*, fewer than 13 total points) and have a long suit. The length of the suit determines the level at which you open the bidding. These types of bids are called preemptive opening bids or preempts.

The Theory behind Preempts

Why start the bidding at a high level when you don't have an opening hand? The advantage of a preemptive opening bid is that it takes up a lot of room on the Bidding Scale, and it makes it difficult for the other partnership to exchange information.

For example, if you were planning to open the bidding 1♦ and the opponent in front of you opened the bidding with 3♥, you would be faced with a difficult problem. How do you show partner that you have an opening bid when the auction is already at the three level? A preemptive bid may cause the opponents to reach a contract in the wrong strain, end up too high or too low or be unable to get into the auction at all.

Of course, there is the possibility that a preemptive opening bid may make it difficult for your partner to bid effectively. There is also a danger that you may be doubled by the opponents and defeated badly! You can minimize the risk and maximize the potential gain by only making a preemptive opening bid with the appropriate type of hand.

Requirements for Preemptive Opening Bids

- A two-level opening preempt (2♦, 2♥ or 2♠), also known as a weak two, promises a strong six-card suit and fewer than 13 total points.

- A three-level opening preempt promises a strong seven-card suit and fewer than 13 total points.

- A four-level opening preempt promises a strong eight-card suit and fewer than 13 total points.

Note that all of our preemptive openings must be based on a strong suit. The definition of a strong suit in this system is one that contains two of the top three cards (the ace, king and queen). The advantage of having a good long suit is that it is more difficult for the opponents to double the contract for penalty.

Responding to a Preempt

When partner opens the bidding with a preempt at the two or three level, you have a good description of partner's hand — a long suit with a weak hand. Responding to a preempt is more about counting tricks than counting points.

With a very strong hand, you may bid game in partner's suit or in notrump, or you may bid a long suit of your own (forcing if below the game level).

Competing against a Preempt

If an opponent opens the bidding with a preempt, you still can make use of the overcall and the takeout double to compete. Since you are starting the auction at a higher level, you need to have a stronger hand if you decide to enter the auction. For example, suppose the opponent on your right opens the bidding with 3♦.

♠ A K J 7 5 3   With a good six-card suit and 16 total points,
♥ A 9 2   overcall 3♠.
♦ 8 2
♣ Q 3

♠ K J 6 2
♥ A Q 5 3
♦ 3
♣ A J 8 2

With support for the unbid suits, 15 HCP and 3 dummy points for the singleton, make a takeout double.

♠ Q J 7
♥ K 9 6 3
♦ Q 8 2
♣ A J 5

Even though you have enough points to open the bidding, you do not have enough to start the bidding at the three level. Pass

---

Summary of Preempts

A preemptive opening bid shows:

    A strong six-card suit at the two level.

    A strong seven-card suit at the three level.

    A strong eight-card suit at the four level.

    Fewer than 13 total points.

If partner opens with a preempt, pass unless you have a strong hand. If the opponents open with a preempt, you may use the overcall and the takeout double to compete.

A thorough, in-depth discussion of preempts and responses can be found in the *Play of the Hand in the 21st Century* text.

BALANCING

It is beyond the scope of this text to examine all of the possibilities that may arise in competitive situations. You will learn from experience, however, that you sometimes have to bid in situations where you do not have quite enough strength for the bid you make.

When the Opponents Compete

Suppose your partner opens 1 ♥, and you have the following hand:

♠ 8 3
♥ A 10 9 4
♦ 8 6 5
♣ A 8 3 2

With 8 HCP plus 1 point for the doubleton spade, you raise to 2 ♥. Now, suppose the opponent on your left bids 2 ♠, and your partner and the opponent on your right both pass. You have a typical competitive choice. Should you pass and let the opponents play the contract or should you bid again to try to buy the contract? With a nearly maximum raise and four-card support for opener's suit, you probably should compete to 3♥. Maybe you will make that contract; maybe your bid will push the opponents to 3♠, which you might defeat. Even if you go down, the penalty may be less than the value of the opponents' partscore contract. If you had a weaker hand or wanted to defend with spades as the trump suit, you would pass. Partner will not assume that your 3♥ bid suddenly shows a strong hand. You already limited your hand to the 6 to 9 total point range with your response of 2♥. You are just showing a desire to compete to the three level.

The situation is more awkward if it is your partner who bids 3♥. If the opponents had not interfered, this would show a medium hand of 16 to 18 points, inviting you to bid game if you are near the top of your range. However, partner may be stretching a little, unwilling to let the opponents play in 2♠. Should you bid on to 4♥? This is one of the things that makes the game interesting. As your experience grows, you will find yourself better able to judge what to do in such situations.

When the Auction May Stop

Suppose you have the following hand:

♠ K J 8 4
♥ 9 2
♦ A 6 3
♣ Q 10 6 3

The opponent on your left opens 1♥, and your partner and the opponent on your right both pass. You do not have quite enough for a classic takeout double, but if you pass, the opponents will play in a contract of 1♥. Looking at your hand, it seems likely they can make that contract. It might be better if your side played a partscore in your best trump suit. It is also possible that if you bid, you may push the opponents to a contract they can't make. In such a situation, it is usually best to be slightly aggressive and make a takeout double with less than normal strength. The opponent on your left has at most 21 total points and probably fewer. The opponent on your right has fewer than 6 points. Partner must have some of the missing points, so it should be safe to compete. Since partner passed over the opening bid, it is unlikely partner will have enough strength to get your side too high by jumping to a game contract.

Experience will help you decide when to bid and when not to bid in such situations. For now, you should just be aware of the possibility of balancing in this situation.

When You Passed Originally and Had a Chance to Open the Bidding

There is one situation where you can always bid on less than normal strength without misleading your partner. If you passed originally, when you had a chance to open the bidding, you can't have a hand worth 13 or more total points. Look at this hand:

♠ J 3
♥ A J 10 9 7
♦ K 8 3 2
♣ 6 4

You are the dealer and pass, since you don't have 13 total points. However, suppose the bidding now proceeds 1♣ on your left, pass from partner, 1♠ on your right. You may overcall 2♥. Even though you are entering the auction at the two level, partner will not expect you to have a better hand because you passed earlier.

Many similar situations arise in competitive auctions where you have limited your strength earlier and enter the auction at a later point. Both you and your partner will have to be on your toes to recognize such situations.

GLOSSARY OF TERMS

Advancer — Partner of an overcaller or takeout doubler.

American Contract Bridge League — The main authority and governing body for organized bridge activities and promotion in the United States, Canada, Mexico and Bermuda. It is usually referred to as the ACBL and is a not-for-profit organization.

Auction — A series of bids and calls which determine the final contract.

Balanced (hand) — A hand with no voids, no singletons and no more than one doubleton. There are three balanced hand patterns: 4–3–3–3; 5–3–3–2; 4–4–3–2. The numbers refer to the number of cards in a suit.

Bid — A commitment to take at least the number (plus six) of tricks named in the specific strain.

Bidding — The various bids and calls that make up the auction.

Bidding Message — The information given by a bid: either forcing, invitational or sign-off.

Bidding Scale — The order in which bids may be made.

Blackwood Convention — A convention invented by Easley Blackwood of Indianapolis in 1933 which enjoys worldwide popularity. It is used when players are on their way to bidding a slam and one player wants to know the number of aces held by partner. The details are beyond the scope of this book and are discussed in *More Commonly Used Conventions in the 21st Century*.

Bonus — Points scored for making a partscore, a game, a slam or for defeating the opponents' contract.

Book — The first six tricks won by the declaring side.

Break — The distribution of the outstanding cards in a suit.

Call — Any bid, double, redouble or pass.

Captain — The partner who knows more about the combined hands and is responsible for directing the partnership to its final contract. Usually the responder is the captain.

Chicago — A form of rubber bridge where a rubber consists of only four deals and vulnerability is predetermined for each deal.

Club Series — The original title of this book, the first in *The ACBL Bridge Series*.

Combined (hands) — The cards making up both hands belonging to one partnership.

Contract — The final bid in the auction that commits declarer's side to take at least the number (plus six) of tricks named in the selected strain.

Convention — A bid (or call) that conveys a meaning other than that which would normally be attributed to it.

Convention Card — A document which contains all of the partnership's agreements and is available for perusal by the opponents during the auction and the play.

Cuebid — The bid of a suit first mentioned by the opponents.

Deal — This term covers the following actions: the even distribution among four players of the fifty-two cards in a pack; the privilege of distributing the cards; the act of dealing; the cards themselves after they have been dealt.

Dealer — The player who distributes the cards. The dealer has the first opportunity to open the bidding.

Declarer — The player who first bid the strain of the final contract. The player who will try to fulfill the final contract by playing the cards for the partnership.

Defeat — To prevent the declarer from making the contract.

Defense — The side that did not win the contract.

Describer — The opening bidder.

Diamond Series — The original title of the second book in *The ACBL Bridge Series* called *Play of the Hand in the 21st Century*. It reviews bidding, presents the play and introduces defense.

Discarding — The playing of a card, other than a trump card, of a suit different from the suit led.

Distribution — The number of cards held in each suit by a particular player or by a partnership. The number of cards held in a particular suit by a partnership.

Distribution Points — In hand valuation, points that take the shape of the hand into consideration.

Double — A call that (literally) increases the scoring value of tricks (penalty double). A takeout double is conventional and asks partner to bid the best suit in the hand with a preference for the majors.

Doubleton — A holding of two cards in a suit.

Drawing Trumps — The playing of trumps until there are none in the opponents' hands.

Dummy — Declarer's partner. The hand that is placed face up on the table after the opening lead.

Dummy Points — In hand valuation, points used when planning to support partner's suit. A void is assigned 5 points, a singleton 3 points and a doubleton 1 point.

Duplicate Bridge — The form of bridge in which the same deal is played more than once.

Entry — A card that provides a means of winning a trick in a particular hand.

Finesse — An attempt to win a trick with a card that does not rank as high as one held by the opponents.

Five-card Major System — A method of bidding which requires the opening bidder to have at least five cards in a major to open the bidding with that suit and is the basis for this text.

Follow Suit — Play a card in the suit that is led.

Forcing (bid) — A bid that requires partner to bid again.

Game — A total trick score of 100 points or more.

Game Contracts — 3NT; 4♥; 4♠; 5♣; 5♦.

Game Raise — A raise to one of the five game contracts: 3NT; 4♥; 4♠; 5♣; or 5♦.

Gerber Convention — A convention invented by John Gerber of Houston, Texas in 1938. Like the Blackwood convention, it is used by players on their way to bidding a slam to find out the number of aces, and sometimes kings, held by partner.

Going Down — Being defeated in a contract.

Golden Fit — At least eight cards in the same suit between your hand and your partner's hand.

Golden Game(s) — 3NT, 4♥ and 4♠.

Grand Slam — A contract to take all 13 tricks.

Hand — The cards held by one of the players; the position at the table (e.g., second hand).

Hand Valuation — The number of total points, adding both high-card points (ace=4, king=3, queen=2, jack=1) and distribution points (1 point for each card in a suit over four) or dummy points.

HCP — The abbreviation for high-card points.

Heart Series — The original name of the third book in *The ACBL Bridge Series* called *Defense in the 21st Century*, which focuses on defending and reviews bidding and play.

High-card Points (HCP) — The value of the high cards in a hand: ace=4; king=3; queen=2; jack=1.

Higher-ranking (suit) — A suit higher on the Bidding Scale. Spades is the highest ranking suit; clubs is the lowest ranking suit.

Honor (card) — One of the five top cards in a suit — an ace, a king, a queen, a jack or a ten.

Honors —Special bonuses in rubber-bridge scoring.

Invitational (bid) — A bid that invites partner to bid again.

Jump Raise — A bid in partner's named suit which jumps one level of the bidding. If you jump two levels, it is a double jump.

Jump Shift — A bid in a new suit at a level one higher than necessary.

Lead(ing) — The first card played to a trick.

Left-hand Opponent — The player on your left, often abbreviated LHO.

Length Points (distribution points or long suit points) — The value of long suits in a hand: five-card suit=1; six-card suit=2; seven-card suit=3; eight-card suit=4.

Level — The number of tricks a player contracts to take when making a bid. It includes an assumed six tricks (book).

Limit Raise — The raise of a one-level opening bid to the three level. It shows a hand with about 10 or 11 total points and support for opener's suit.

Loser — A card in a player's hand that could lose a trick to the opponents.

Lower-ranking (suit) — A suit lower on the Bidding Scale. The lowest ranking suit is clubs.

Major Suits — Hearts and spades.

Make — To take enough tricks to fulfill the contract.

Minor Suits — Clubs and diamonds.

Nonvulnerable — State of the scoring before a side's first game is scored (rubber bridge) or as predetermined in duplicate and Chicago.

Notrump — A contract without a trump suit. The highest card played in the suit led wins the trick.

Notrump Series — The original name for the fifth book in *The ACBL Bridge Series* called *More Commonly Used Conventions in the 21st Century*.

Offense — The partnership that made the last bid in the auction and declares the contract.

Opener's Rebid — The second bid by opener.

Opening Bidder — The player who makes the first bid in the auction.

Opening Lead — The card led to the first trick by the player on declarer's left.

Overcall — A bid made after an opponent has opened the bidding.

Overtrick — A trick won by declarer's side in excess of the contract.

Partnership — The two players seated opposite each other at the table.

Partscore — A contract with a trick score worth less than 100 points.

Pass — A call indicating that a player does not want to bid at that turn.

Penalty — The bonus awarded to the defending side for defeating a contract.

Penalty Double — A double with the intention of increasing the penalty bonus for defeating the opponents' contract.

Plan — The four steps declarer goes through before deciding how to play a contract. They are: (1) *Pause to consider your objective;* (2) *Look at your winners and losers;* (3) *Analyze your alternatives;* (4) *Now put it all together.*

Play (of the cards) — The part of a deal following the auction during which the declarer tries to make the contract and the defenders try to defeat the contract.

Point Count — The high-card valuation introduced by Bryant McCampbell in 1915 and publicized by Milton Work and Charles Goren: ace=4, king=3; queen=2; jack=1.

Preemptive (bid) — A bid made to interfere with the opponents' auction. It usually is made with a long suit and a weak hand.

Promotion — The increase in the trick-taking potential of a card as the higher-ranking cards are played.

Raise — To support partner's suit by bidding that suit at a higher level.

Rank (of cards) — The ace is highest, followed by the king, the queen, the jack, the ten ... down to the two.

Rebid — A second bid by any player.

Responder — The partner of the opening bidder.

Responder's Rebid — Responder's second bid.

Reverse — Any rebid in a suit higher ranking than the original one.

Right-hand Opponent — The player on your right, often abbreviated RHO.

Rubber Bridge — The form of bridge in which a deal is not played more than once. The unit in scoring is a rubber, which denotes the winning of two games by one side.

Ruff(ing) — To play a trump on a trick when you are void in the suit led.

Set — To defeat the contract.

Shuffling — Mixing the cards.

Sign-off — A bid that asks partner to pass.

Singleton — A holding of one card in a suit.

Small Slam — A contract to take 12 tricks.

Spade Series — The original name for the fourth book in *The ACBL Bridge Series* called *Duplicate*. The *Spade Series* text was rewritten to focus on conventions and is called *Commonly Used Conventions in the 21st Century*.

Split — The distribution of the outstanding cards in a suit.

Stayman Convention — A convention invented by George Rapée and publicized in an article written by Sam Stayman. An artificial response of 2♣ to an opening bid of 1NT asks opener to bid a four-card major suit if opener has one (or both). Also an artificial response of 3♣ to an opening bid of 2NT asks opener to bid a four-card major if opener has one (or both).

Strain — The suit or notrump specified in a bid.

Strong Raise (forcing jump raise) — An old-fashioned raise of a one-level opening bid to the three level. It shows a hand with 13 or more points and support for opener's suit.

Strong 2♣ — The traditional use of an opening two-bid in a suit to show a hand which can virtually guarantee game or even slam.

Suits — The four groups of cards in the pack each having a characteristic symbol: clubs; diamonds; hearts; spades.

Support — The number of cards held in a suit that partner has bid.

Sure Trick — A trick that can be taken without giving up the lead to the opponents.

Takeout Double — A double of an opposing bid that asks partner to bid.

Touching — Cards that are adjacent in rank (*e.g.*, the queen and the jack).

Treatment — An approach to bidding or a special way of handling certain hands that is beyond the scope of a basic bridge course.

Trick — The unit of play consisting of four cards, one contributed by each player in clockwise rotation, which starts with the player on lead.

Trick Score — The points scored for contracts bid and made, not including overtricks.

Trump (suit) — The suit named in the contract.

Unbalanced (hand) — A hand containing a void, a singleton or more than one doubleton.

Valuation — The method of determining the value of a particular hand during the auction. Usually a combination of values for high cards held and length.

Void — The absence of cards in a specific suit.

Vulnerable — The condition of the scoring that affects the size of the bonus for making or defeating the contract. Bonuses and penalties are higher if the declarer is vulnerable.

Weak Two-Bid — The use of an opening bid of two in a suit other than clubs as preemptive. Classically, this bid describes a hand with fewer than 13 total points and with a strong, six-card suit, two of the top three honors.

ARE YOU A MEMBER?

The American Contract Bridge League (ACBL) is dedicated to the playing, teaching and promotion of contract bridge.

The membership of 160,000 includes a wide range of players — from the thousands who are just learning the joy of bridge to the most proficient players in North America. The ACBL has long been the center of North American bridge activity. The organization is looking forward to celebrating its 75th Anniversary in 2012. ACBL invites you to join in the excitement of organized bridge play.

ACBL offers sanctioned games at local clubs, tournaments, on cruise ships and on the Internet! The ACBL is a service-oriented membership organization offering considerable benefits to its members, including reduced playing fees at tournaments!

If you are not a member of the ACBL, join today to take advantage of the reduced rates for first-time members and to receive our outstanding bridge magazine — *The Bridge Bulletin*! You will receive an ACBL player number, and any masterpoints (the measure of achievement for all bridge players) you win at ACBL clubs and tournaments will be automatically recorded to your account!

You can enjoy the fun, friendship and competition of bridge with an ACBL membership. Join today by visiting our web site **www.acbl.org**. ACBL is a Great Deal!

American Contract Bridge League
6575 Windchase Drive
Horn Lake, MS 38637-1523
www.acbl.org